JOHN BAILEY'S
FISHING
ENCYCLOPEDIA

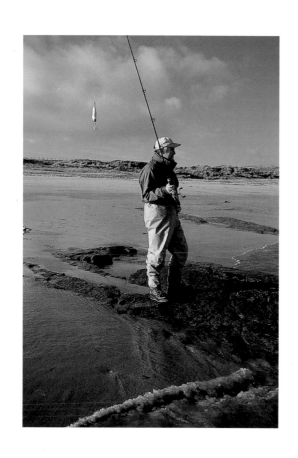

JOHN BAILEY'S
FISHING
ENCYCLOPEDIA

NEW HOLLAND

First published in 2007 by New Holland Publishers (UK) Ltd
London • Cape Town • Sydney • Auckland

www.newhollandpublishers.com
Garfield House, 86–88 Edgware Road, London, W2 2EA, UK
80 McKenzie Street, Cape Town 8001, South Africa
14 Aquatic Drive, Frenchs Forest, NSW 2086, Australia
218 Lake Road, Northcote, Auckland, New Zealand

10 9 8 7 6 5 4 3 2 1

ISBN 978 1 84537 254 5

Publishing Manager: Jo Hemmings
Senior Editor: Steffanie Brown
Designer: Alan Marshall
Copy Editor: Ian Whitelaw
Indexer: Christine Bernstein
Production: Joan Woodroffe

Reproduction by Pica Digital Pte Ltd, Singapore
Printed and bound by Tien Wah Press Pte Ltd, Singapore

Cover and Preliminary Pages
Front cover: (top) John Bailey plays a creek wild brown trout; (bottom) A brown trout makes its move.
Back cover: (top left) Howard Croston and Juan del Carmen discuss bass flies; (top right) A selection of lures for predator fish; (bottom left) A beautiful grayling caught in the height of summer; (bottom right) Ian Miller and Neil Stephens fly fish for pike.
Front flap: Shirley Deterding holds a fly-caught trophy.
Back flap: John Bailey holds a fine barbel.
Half-title page: Sea fishing from the shore.
Title page: Fishing for barbel in mid-summer; (opposite) Fishing the bonefish flats.
page 5: (top left) Bait fishing a Spanish river; (top right) Exploring an English lowland river; (bottom left) Tackling big Russian carp; (bottom right) large-mouth bass.
Page 6: (bottom left) An autumn salmon river awaits; (bottom right) River floats.
Page 7: (top right) Andy Murray on the Spey; (bottom left) Black bass leaps for freedom: (bottom right) Complete concentration

Author Acknowledgements
Firstly, I would very much like to thank everybody at Hardy and at Greys, the great tackle makers from the north of England for all their help. Particular thanks go to Howard Croston, John Wolstenholme, Andy Murray, Ian McCormack, Andy Sowerby, Tony Anderson and Ian McGreary. Very many thanks indeed for your modelling, use of photographs and your wise words.

I would like to thank many other professionals in the game, including Juan Del Carmen, Nick Hart, Rebecca Thorpe, Pete Staggs, Mitch Smith, Lee Collins, Ken Whelan, Nick Zoll and especially, John Horsey for his excellent piece on pike fly fishing. I would also like to thank many friends who have been a constant source of inspiration and encouragement – thank you to Ian Miller, Neil Stephens, Tim Ellis, Al Whitelaw, Nick Gould, Simon Channing, Richard Hewitt, John Gilman, James Ellis, Phil Humm, Jim Tyree, Ian Whitelaw and Dan Goff.

Can I also thank Rob Olsen and Andy Steer for their illustrative work and their encouragement.

I would also like to thank Mike Atherton and Ian Botham – both cricket stars, captains and excellent anglers and sportsmen. Cheers.

Can I thank Arni from Iceland for all his generosity and high spirits out in India where mention must go to Subhan, Anthony, Bola and above all, Saad.

As ever, I'd like to thank Shirley Deterding for her support and friendship and, especially, my great Dane, Johnny Jensen. Though we don't travel as much together, and that includes the three of us, you're always there in my heart.

Special thanks also to the team that put this book together – Jo Hemmings, Steffanie Brown, Naomi Waters, and Alan Marshall at New Holland; and above all, to Carol, for her painstaking and patient dealings with this particularly disorganized author.

Contents

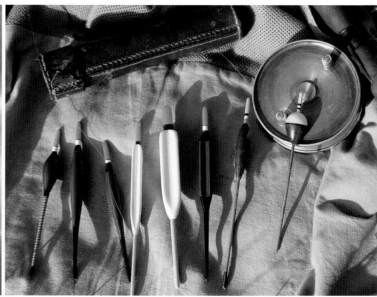

Introduction

A part of my year is spent guiding in many different countries of the world. I enjoy this for many reasons – meeting new people, fishing new waters, facing new challenges and helping to fulfil dreams, to name but a few. Above all, as an angling writer and photographer, guiding helps me understand the types of problems that most anglers face. As an angling writer it is easy to become cocooned, shut off from the people you are writing for. As a guide, this is impossible. You must constantly be tuned in to your clients' shortcomings and needs.

▼ *Decision time*
Howard Croston and John Wolstenholme are on a black bass water and the question of the best fly to use is in their minds. Do they go for poppers on the surface, stream flies or nymphs deep down?

▶ *A question of timing*
Mike Atherton, one-time England cricket captain, loads rod and arrows a long line out across a Scottish salmon river. His guide can only watch and admire.

The Better Angler

Of the 200 or so anglers that I fish with each year, I would say that a handful are good or very good and a smaller handful bad or very bad; the vast majority are fair to reasonable. It concerns me when they worry about this and think they should be better. Most hold down busy, successful positions in society. They simply don't have the time to become experts – after all, being a brain surgeon is more important than being able to catch a bass! But what these reasonable anglers can – and often do – achieve is to improve. They learn new methods, take fresh approaches and enjoy their fishing much more as a result. One of my deepest hopes with this book is that it will make you a better, more rounded and ultimately more satisfied angler.

So what makes an angler stand out? A good angler has a oneness with the water before him. He can read and interpret waters that are strange to him. This comes partly from experience but there's more to it. A good angler loves the water as a companion, its secrets becoming less and less hidden until one day they are almost totally unveiled.

Skills and Talents

Equally, good anglers share special access to the ways of fish. In defiance of all logic, they have an uncanny ability to interpret how fish behave. All aspects of a fish's life and feeding merge to become the most sophisticated of jigsaw puzzles, and only good anglers seem to have all the pieces.

There are also the physical gifts that most good anglers share. Obviously, there's the question of eyesight: whether you're watching a tiny float or a small gnat at dusk, it's a great help to be able to see! Strength, too, can be useful especially when trying to haul a conger up from a hidden wreck. Toughness and endurance are also important. If cold and hunger get to you and all you can think about are a meal and a hot bath, then you simply won't fish as well as you could!

◀ *Indian gold*

This quite staggering Indian mahseer was taken by Chris Parkinson down in the south of this wonderful country. After a long fight, the fish is quite exhausted and has to be tethered onto a rope for some time until it is strong enough to swim away without harm.

Effortless Control

The good angler has other, less obvious attributes – for example, lack of a level head has lost many a big fish. Though tense, the great angler is rational throughout hooking, playing and landing. If a fish breaks free, it will not be through human error.

It has been rightly said that a great fisher has a good pair of hands. Watch him cast delicately and control the reel, float and fly with the deftness of a maestro – so elegant and so deceptively simple. When the fish runs, see how he anticipates its moves and works the rod with the necessary guile and force. Control is effortless and unconsciously beautiful.

Good anglers exhibit an indefinable grace when wading or casting and are comfortable in all situations. Nothing is hurried yet somehow everything gets done.

Dedication

No angler ever becomes good without loving his art. Frost, snow, gale and wind are as much a part of water life as the lazy days of the mayfly. A good angler is dedicated to a point that bewilders the average person – time, effort, cost and hardship are part of the game. True pleasure is a serious business. Through it all the angler sees enchantment and excitement, knowing he wouldn't want to be anywhere else.

Learning the Skills

If you want to be a good angler, you must know how to do it properly. To be a good, all-rounder, capable of catching fish in salt or freshwater, still or running water, on fly, bait or lure, you need a wide range of skills. Here, you will find those skills laid before you.

I hasten to add that I myself am not an expert in all these skills. Okay, I'm proficient in most, but at times I've had to admit I'm not good enough. Fortunately, I have legions of fishing friends and some are truly expert in the areas where I palpably am not. So I offer many, many thanks to the experts who have helped me to make this book into what I believe is one of the most secure fishing foundations you'll come across.

A Companion Book

It's been a delight to put this book together and I've thoroughly enjoyed all my days out on the water, watching and learning from the maestros. I hope that all the excitement and pleasure of angling are conveyed to you, the reader. I'd like this book to open up the world of fishing to you. If you're prepared to learn and experiment, then you will ultimately succeed in reaching that enviable status of the good angler.

Enjoy the book, enjoy your fishing and enjoy the progress that you make.

▼ *All at sea*

Now Howard Croston is pursuing sea bass, this time off the Spanish coast. Good fish come close inshore, just a few yards out in the surf.

Chapter One
The Basic Skills

Make no mistake, angling is a sport, not a hobby. Moreover, it's a sport that demands the utmost in physical and mental skills. Sport fishing is, then, a very apt term, and the accomplished sports fisherman will have a deep knowledge of the fish, the waters, the tackle and the methods available. He or she will develop scores of skills as the years pass, and the experience bank will build up until a real and satisfying level of expertise is reached.

Learning The Basics

There is no more diverse sport in the world than that of angling. With most sports – football, for example – it doesn't matter whether you're a professional player or you just like to kick a ball around in the park. The rules are the same: you are essentially trying to score goals, or keep them out. The same holds true for baseball, basketball, cricket, and most other sports that you care to name – except fishing.

100 Sports in One

An angler on a wild, winter coast hurling heavy leads way out into angry seas could not be fishing more differently from the man stalking a delicately rising trout on a crystal river. There's just no comparison between what the two fishermen are doing. Similarly, twitching a popper back along the surface for a black bass is a totally different sport to casting 100 yards plus for a carp or wreck fishing for conger eels.

Shared Skills

This variation in species, waters and techniques is one of the joys of angling, and there will never be anybody who is totally expert in every aspect of the sport. There is always more to learn and more to try. That said, there are basic skills that are common to every angler, whatever he or she is doing. For example, you've just got to make sure that the knots that you use don't pull apart under pressure. Equally, you've got to be able to read the water in front of you, and it doesn't matter if it's the Atlantic shoreline or a tiny upland river. Wherever you are fishing, you have to know which features will hold fish and where you are likely to find them. When you catch a fish, whether it's a cod, a carp, a catfish or a Chinook salmon, you

▼ Let's get physical
An angler and his guide out on the flats of the Bahamas. They've walked for miles through shin-deep water and soft, clinging sand. The temperature has been baking, the sun relentless. It might look beautiful and the fishing is certainly thrilling, but it is actually a really gruelling sport.

must know how to play that fish successfully, land it and then deal with it as humanely as possible once it is yours.

Shared Courtesy

Another thing we should all have in common, wherever we fish, is courtesy towards other fishermen. Even fishing somewhere as large as the sea, you still don't cast over or near another angler's bait. You should always give a fellow angler room and never crowd his or her space. Give advice if requested or if it is obviously needed.

Essential Qualities

There are some basic skills that you can't really begin to describe, but it's good to look out for them and begin to recognize them. I've been very lucky over the years that I've fished to have accompanied some really great anglers, and the factor that unites them all is, for want of a better word, comfort. Perhaps this is the most essential, fundamental skill of them all: to be comfortable in whatever branch of angling you are enjoying. Your approach to any fishing situation

should be unhurried, relaxed, inconspicuous and confident. Take time to work out a strategy and then have the confidence to stick with it and see it through.

Physically, the really excellent angler will always (or as often as possible) be in control. You won't find many really experienced fly anglers wrapped up in their lines like a Christmas parcel and you won't find many expert lure fishermen falling off rocks or spending all their time snagged up in trees.

Practical Philosophy

In large part, the basic skills can be taught from a book, but they can only really be effected through actual practice on the water. The more you practise, the greater your experience and the better everything will become. Even techniques that once seemed all but impossible soon become easy. Little by little, frustrations get ironed away and the basic skills become more like a stepping stone to your fishing than a millstone around your neck. An important basic skill, therefore, is to accept the problems that you are bound to face with a good spirit.

▼ *All the skills*
These three photographs say it all. Look, on the left, at the balance and co-ordination that Mike Atherton, the one-time cricket captain, shows as he punches out a salmon line. And then, in the middle, there's the focus and accuracy of Juan Del Carmen's casting as he approaches a wild fish in a crystal stream. On the right, there's big Mitch Smith, a world-champion carp angler, showing the cerebral side of fishing: how to construct a rig that will outwit even the most cautious carp.

Don't Spook The Fish

Second only to the section on water safety, this is the most important of all the fishing skills. Scare the fish, and everything else you read in this book is absolutely academic. A scared fish will rarely, if ever, feed – no matter how good your bait, tackle or tactics – so don't shoot yourself in the foot before you've made a single cast.

▶ **Learning young**
These kids have learnt to keep a low-profile when approaching clear-water fish. And this is just the time to learn: when you're young, lessons are hard learnt and tend to stick in the memory.

The First Approach
It's dawn and you're at the riverbank. Look hard in the dew or, if you're after grayling or pike in the winter, at the frost. Are there any footprints heading along the bank? If so, tread resolutely in the opposite direction. You're not being anti-social, but the probability is that if you're not the first on the river, someone else has already blown your chances clean away.

The Noise Factor
Whatever you do, bear in mind that sound is intensified by a factor of about five under water, so watch your footsteps. Don't tread heavily, and don't hurry to the waterside. Be controlled and patient, and keep the disturbance down. If you can, choose a grass or mud bank rather than gravel, on which it is almost impossible to tread quietly.

It's the same with your voice. Speak in quiet tones or not at all. Remember that fish are especially sensitive to sound in shallow water, or when lying in the surface layers.

Visibility
Consider what you wear. The colour and texture of your clothing do matter. Think drab and soft. A hat is good for shielding the flash thrown when the sun strikes a pale face – or a shiny pate.

Walk upriver so that you are approaching fish from behind, and think about how you walk. Be aware of your shadow, and know

▼ **The human heron**
Here I've dressed myself as inconspicuously as possible. Even though I'm wading, I move my feet with extreme caution, trying not to send out any noise or, just as bad, ripples. I'm so close to the fish, I hardly dare breathe.

that it lengthens as the sun sinks. Don't point at a fish, as this abrupt gesture will always spook it. Be particularly careful to avoid scaring small fish in the margins, or they will flee and trigger off a chain reaction of fear. Don't be proud – realize that if the water is clear and shallow it's best to creep and crawl and make yourself as tiny as a mouse.

On the Fly

If you're fly fishing, make the first cast count. If you've got a guide, listen to him. Watch the lie and take your time until you've worked out a strategy. Remember that the more casts you put over any piece of water, the further your chances fall. Don't false cast more than you have to. Learn to cast lying on your back, from a crouching position or even on your stomach. Learn to roll cast and spiral cast so that trees are no problem. Cast slowly and methodically, and avoid jerky movements. Think about your silhouette all the time. Remember that you must strive for distance only when you've spooked the fish, and the more you strive, the more you will spook them. Don't become a human windmill.

Aim to cast one foot above the water so your line and fly fall lightly. On thin, clear water you'll need to cast a long leader if you're to avoid lining a fish. Put a fly line over a wild trout and you've said goodbye to it. Dull your leader down to avoid glint in bright conditions; rub it in dirt or clay if necessary. When you're spinning or fly fishing on a still-water, don't be impetuous. Put a few casts down each margin before exploring the water. If you don't, you'll scare any close-in fish, so try to catch that one first.

Use everything that happens around you to your advantage. Learn to cast when there's a natural disturbance that will help mask your own unnatural intrusion upon the fish. For instance, fish close to a feeding swan – but not so close that you could run the risk of hooking it. If you see drinking cattle, get close to them and flick a fly imme-diately downstream. Use a floating weed to break up the silhouette of your fly line or to mask a float.

The Subtle Float

The considerations that apply to fly fishing are largely true for bait fishing, too. This is why holding back a float is so important when you're trotting for grayling or roach: this way, the first thing the fish sees is the bait and not the shot that, as often as not, will rap it on the nose. Floating weed or other debris will help to mask a float and avoid spooking wary fish.

Think up your own tricks. For example, in crystal clear water a carp could be afraid of a commercially made float. Providing you don't have to cast far, a discarded goose feather will cause it no concern. If you're grayling fishing in clear winter water, chances are that a strike indicator could alarm a wily shoal. Take it off and tie on a piece of twig or a sliver of reed. If wading is allowed, go a fair way upriver and kick up the bottom – the slight discoloration will increase your chances five-fold.

Feather your spool on the cast if you are bait or lure fishing, so that your tackle lands on the water with as little disturbance as possible. Remember that accuracy is more important than distance.

Know When to Stop

Don't overcook a lie if you're fly fishing or a swim if you're bait fishing. Catch a fish and move on. This is good for the fish because you're not overstressing them and, as a result, it becomes good for the fishing. Play fair by the river and it will play fair by you.

▲ *Gently does it*
A very big carp approaches a piece of floating bread. The fish is feeling most vulnerable as it nears the surface. A bird overhead will cause it to bolt, but so too will the flash of a rod or an out of place footfall.

▼ *Eye to eye*
Richard gets close to his quarry so he can see the exact moment his fly is sipped in. He's approaching from downstream, so he's behind the fish, knowing they won't see him.

Fish Watching

Learn to watch fish. It's an art that will stand you in great stead. Discover their patrol routes, feeding grounds and body language. You will find yourself entering into a fascinating and unique world and, of course, you'll improve your results as well.

What You Need

Polarizing glasses are one of the great boons of the modern age. Glare on the water's surface is minimized or obliterated, and suddenly the fish and the underwater contours become magically apparent. Good glasses give you a true gift of sight, so choose them carefully. Scratch-resistant lenses, tough but light frames and comfortable nose pads are all essential items. Wrap-round lenses also give enhanced glare protection. Grey and copper-coloured lenses are great for medium to bright conditions, while silver flash mirror lenses are best for bright weather. Amber lenses are best in medium to low light conditions. Think carefully about which colour will suit the bulk of your fishing, unless you want to invest in several pairs.

Binoculars are also an essential tool for getting in close. Focus in tight to the fish and you'll be able to see the insects they are eating or what it is exactly about your end rig that is turning them away.

Chest waders are invaluable. In clear, bright water you can get out and stand close to fish that are nowhere near as spooky around you as when you are on the bankside. A canoe, too, can be a very useful means of getting you close to where the action is taking place.

And then there is what nature can give you. The cover that vegetation, banks and rocks can provide is invaluable. This is a stalking game in which camouflage plays a vital part. Look out, too, for climbable trees or handy bridges that offer you the opportunity to get up above the waters and look down on them with maximum vision. Sunlight is, of course, a great boon, opening up the water to your polarized gaze.

Where to Look

On still waters, the key areas for fish spotting are shallow bays, reedy margins, the fringes of islands, shallow plateaux or the broad backs of trailing gravel bars. Look out, too, for feeder streams and water sheltered by overhanging branches. In a river, check out the backwaters, weir pools, confluences and clear, bright water over sand and gravel.

Look for fish around sunken vegetation: underwater cabbages, ranunculus weed or lily pads. Check out submerged branches and fallen masonry. Remember that fish are concentrated in places where they feel safe from predators, sunlight and strong currents.

When to Look

Get up around dawn and you probably stand the best chance of seeing cyprinids and predators feeding. Look out for strings of

▼ Gotcha!

Gerry has spotted a fish and is pointing it out to cricketing hero, Ian Botham. It might just be a gleam that has caught Gerry's eye, or the flick of a tail, or even a glimpse of white as the fish's mouth opens. In part, it's experience, almost a sixth sense calling out 'fish!' to him.

bubbles on a calm surface, and for brown water where fish are feeding in the mud. Dusk, too, is great for many species, especially on still waters, where there are often big hatches of insects as the light fades.

For general fish watching, a clear, bright, calm day is the best. Good amounts of sunshine illuminate the water and the lack of breeze cuts down on ripple and glare. You can lose yourself in fish watching, so beware of dehydration and sunburn. Cover up well and take plenty of water on board.

How to Look

First of all, have patience and take your time. This is not a job to be rushed. The fish can see you more easily than you can see them, so make sure all your actions are calm, controlled and, above all, slow.

So how do you actually, physically watch for fish? Look at a piece of water in soft focus for just as long as it takes. Let yourself fall into something like a trance and then, if there's a fish around, it will move and something about that movement will attract your eye. Something will stand out from the rhythm of the river, to which you have adjusted. Perhaps it will be just the flash of a shifting flank or the waft of a drifting tail, but something will make an impression and then immediately your gaze transforms into intense focus. Let your eyes really bore into the water where you've seen the telltale sign. Then do nothing at all until you've established exactly where the fish is lying and the extent of its feeding range. Fish are like ghosts. They drift in and out of the shadows and depths, and you've got to expand your own consciousness to encompass their fluidity. Fish watching is an art and a pleasure in itself: it's a skill you'll be proud to master.

▶ ▲ *What the water tells us*

The top and bottom photographs show us the importance of good Polaroid glasses, taking your time and really examining the water in front of you. And there are always clues. Look at the middle photograph. The fish is almost invisible against the background of silver sand. But you can see its dark eye, a trigger for any predator.

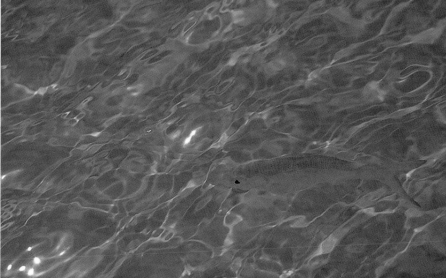

The Fisherman Naturalist

Two of the great skills of fishing are to be able to read the water and the immediate aquatic environment, and to interpret what is going on around you. The angler with these skills reaps an enormous benefit: if you're conversant with plants and water-weed, birds, aquatic mammals, insects and all the other many forms of life that go to make up the world's waterways, then you simply draw more pleasure out of the fishing experience.

▲ Getting down to basics
It always pays to spend some time on a new water, especially wading the shallows and turning over stones looking for samples of life beneath. This way, you will be able to gauge how rich or poor a river is and what the majority of food items are. It's a very handy exercise indeed for the fly fisherman, and also for the bait fisherman wanting to use naturals.

Practical Benefit

The second motivation behind learning the skills of an aquatic naturalist are more prosaic: the more you understand about how waters work, the better you will be at predicting where fish live, how they behave, how and on what they feed and how best to catch them. The very best anglers of all don't just catch fish out of some sort of intellectual vacuum: the finest catchers of fish are always observing what is going on around them and interpreting the signs.

A skill like this is supremely visual, so let's look at the following sets of photographs and see what, if anything, can be learnt from them.

▲ Pool of promise
This pool is an ideal place to look. It is emptying out and becoming shallower all the while. There are plenty of boulders and large and small stones to look under.

◄ The fertility of summer
Here you'll notice that the water is comparatively shallow and clear, and once again runs over a bed of clean stones. The ranks of ranunculus weed, too, will be full of life, so this is an area of the river where insect populations will be at their highest. It's not surprising that the slightly deeper water upstream is highly favoured by many big fish.

▼ ▶ Companions on the riverbank

If you can get as close to bears, otters, water voles, foxes and lizards as this, then there is absolutely nothing wrong with your stalking skills. Seeing wonderful creatures like these should make any fishing expedition worthwhile, whether successful with the rod or not. Keep in mind the fact that ninety per cent of anglers fail before they make their very first cast simply because of their approach. If you can fool the fox and the otter, then you can certainly fool the fish.

◀ Up from the sea

If your approach is that of the heron, you will see a lot in shallow water – spawning sea lampreys in this case, which are especially interesting. Coming up many European and American rivers after spending most of their adult life out in the oceans, they team up with their sexual partners and excavate holes in the river bed by moving stones and rocks using their limpet-like mouths. The eggs are then laid, fertilized and covered up again with smaller stones. As the adults drift helplessly back to the sea, dying on their way downstream, the baby lampreys begin to hatch out. This fascinating life cycle is of interest to the fish catcher. As the baby sea lampreys emerge, they are hugely attractive to big shoals of hungry salmonids, especially trout, and also to cyprinids such as barbel and chub.

▲ *The feathered fisherman*

Bird life can not only be enjoyed by fishermen; it can also tell you a great deal about where fish might be lying. Cormorants and other fish-eating birds obviously aren't going to be hunting in pools where there are no fish! Keep your eye on them and they will draw you to some of the best swims on the river.

▲ *Bird clues*

A swan and its cygnets present a gorgeous river scene as they progress upstream. However, as they feed they dislodge huge amounts of insects that have been hiding in the tresses of weed. Fish know this, and will often follow swans hoping for easy tidbits.

▲ *Fast food*

Watch where ducks and other diving birds repeatedly work. The chances are that the bottom will be rich with foodstuffs that attract more than birds alone.

◀ *Running the river*

These are definitely spawners. Great numbers of trout are swimming up the streams of New Zealand's south island as the spawning season approaches. You wouldn't want to fish for these even if they showed any interest in your fly. Let them pass and allow them to do what nature intended.

◀ *On the Gravels*

Here's an interesting one. Are these chub on the gravels to spawn, or have they already spawned and are they now cleaning themselves, hungry and quite possible to catch? In fact, it's the latter. The fish spawned just a few yards upstream four or five days ago, and now they are regaining their strength and feeding hard, often on the eggs they've just laid and fertilized.

▲ Feeding frenzy

This, for all the world, looks like a huge congregation of spawning fish – but it's not! This is one of those rare occurrences when fish of all species gather together to exploit a particularly generous and often unexpected food source. In this case, flies are coming to the surface ready to hatch and take to the air. For some reason, they're concentrated in one tiny part of the river, and fish from all over the pool have been attracted. First a couple of fish appeared and began to feed, then more and more, until all the fish within half a mile have picked up on the excitement.

▲ Seeking the shade

Watch what's going on on the bankside. The animals around can frequently help your cause. You may see a group of cows gathered under a tree in the margins of a lake, and it's easy not to give the scene a second glance. Wrong. As these cows wade and snort and splash and drink, they are colouring up the water and digging deep into the mud, releasing all manner of insect life. Fish know that cattle drinking like this spell a food bonanza and will come close inshore to make the most of the feast.

▲ An unusual food source

This is an interesting shot of fruit bats taken in India. The Indian guides know that whenever bats or monkeys take shelter in large numbers in trees that overhang the river, the fish are bound to congregate beneath. The reason is simple: the creatures in the branches above drop all manner of foodstuff into the water, providing the easiest of pickings for the fish. Even the monkey's digested meal is favoured by many species. It might not appear very pleasant to you or me, but the serious angler knows that it is full of nutrients upon which the fish thrive.

▲ The digger

A sea angler digs for bait, but he's very careful to give this colony of nesting terns a wide berth, and to not encroach upon the fenced-off area.

▶ The saddest sight of all

Always be on the lookout for any signs of water pollution. This is particularly likely after heavy rain, when streams can overflow and push all manner of toxic substances into water courses. A poisoned fish is just about the saddest sight any of us can see.

The Psychology Of Fishing

I'm well aware that mind-set isn't a skill in the physical sense, and it's a little out of the ordinary run of things, but that doesn't make a scrap of difference to its importance. Believe me, as a guide I have seen hundreds of days ruined for fishermen who have simply failed to see the big picture, and have made themselves miserable over matters of very little consequence indeed.

The Right Attitude

Whether you enjoy the day or not is purely a matter off attitude. Frankly, it's quite stupid to ruin the best days of your life worrying about something as inconsequential as catching a fish! I mean it. To make matters worse, the more desperately you want to catch fish, the harder it becomes. You put pressure on yourself that stops you from fishing to your ultimate potential. I can't think how many times I've seen people hound themselves into demoralizing failure.

There's another aspect to this, too. It's often the fish you don't catch that you remember; and the worst trip; and the foulest weather. It might seem bad at the time but, providing you live through it, I'll guarantee you will look back on the tough times and they will be amazingly vivid in your mind for ever, so don't discount any experience, however unpleasant it might seem at the time.

Obsession

Try to avoid all the dangers that come with obsessional fishing, and there are plenty of them. I know – I've been there. Believe it or not, I actually used to feel guilty if I wasn't out there on the bank, day and night, thrashing the water. I can barely believe it now, but 20 or 30 years ago the obsession was startlingly real.

If I lost a good fish I'd be suicidal, and there'd be no comforting me. I couldn't get my head around the fact you can't lose what you've never had. A simple failed hook-hold was somehow life kicking me in the teeth.

Talk about making your own life a misery for yourself!

Weights and records and personal bests meant everything to me. A pike would be worth nothing if it came in even a fraction of an ounce under twenty pounds, and somehow a magical creature if it flickered above that weight. I was absolutely blind to the beauty of what I was seeing, totally enslaved to what I now realize were false values.

Monarch of the River

I've fished with many people over the years who've wanted to be king – or queen – of the river at the end of each and every day's fishing. It's impossible. Remember that however good and skilful an angler is, there's still a massive element of chance. Fishing is a wheel of fortune, and luck may be with you for a while before settling on your partners. That's the way it should be, although not everyone sees it like that. I've had clients sulk for days because they're not catching the biggest fish. Greed and jealousy has oozed from every pore, and their surly reaction to the success of others has soured the atmosphere. There's been competition for the supposed best places, groups of fishermen have become fragmented, and there's been no semblance of the brotherhood and generosity that fishing should be all about.

This type of mental set is one that I absolutely abhor, and I fight it tooth and nail if I suspect its presence in one of my camps. I'm always on the lookout for a potential would-be king of the river, and I'm ready to remind him that if he celebrates the success of others then they will celebrate with him when his turn comes, as it surely will.

Being There

The philosophy that I try to put across, and which I've now followed for 20 years, is simply 'being there'. You see, it doesn't matter who catches the fish, whether it's you, Don, Tom or whomever. It's the fact that you are there, that you're in a wonderful place with good company and you've had the massive good fortune to see a wonderful fish caught.

Take on board that it is seeing the fish that's important, and not necessarily being the captor of it. In fact, in absolute, honest truth I can say that I would much, much prefer my clients and my friends to catch fish before I do. I'll do anything to make sure they have the best places, the best baits and the best chances.

Believe me, it's a relief when this philosophy takes hold of you. Just the desire to be there removes a colossal burden of expectation from your shoulders. King of the River? The thought never enters your head.

Fair to the Fish

Once you've embraced this laidback

▲ *The fellowship of the angle*

Nick and Rebecca are both instructors in the world-famous Hardy and Greys' Academy. One of the skills taught there is that fishing is to be enjoyed.

▼ *A team effort*

A big, beautiful mahseer falls to Nick's rod, but his friends gather round him, equal partners in the triumph.

▶ **Tales from the riverbank**

Sebastian works hard, and he knows that even a bad day on the river is better than the best of days in the office. Especially when there's a fish running hard upriver.

▼ **Friends worldwide: campfire tales**

Batsokh lives on the borders of Mongolia and Siberia, and is like a brother to me. He has, over countless years, shown me where the fish are, and has provided me with shelter, support and many delicious meals of cooked trout.

approach, you begin to find that you are becoming much fairer to the fish and this, I think, is of major importance. Once you stop being fish hungry, everything begins to fall into place. For example, you won't use any of the dubious tactics or baits to catch a fish. Catching a fish is no longer the be all and end all of your existence, and you know there's no point pulling stunts to catch one. You also no longer have to subject each and every fish to the indignity of being weighed. Weights actually become less and less important to you. A fish is simply a beautiful creature, and you admire it for a second or two before slipping it back into the water. What are weights apart from artificial standards that we impose on wonderful living creatures? Of course, if a fish is particularly special to you, then weigh it carefully and kindly. There can be no problem with this but, hopefully, you will soon find that weights become less important as your fishing career progresses.

Make no mistake, fish don't like being caught. If you're on a shoal of feeding fish it's all too easy to fall into a type of frenzy. This is your red letter day and you've got to catch them all! Of course I can appreciate that, but you've got to realize that this approach does a shoal of fish serious harm and subjects them to noticeable stress.

Once you start being fair to the fish you will recognize a situation like this, perhaps catch a couple and then you'll move on to look for others. This way, shoals are not traumatized, stretches of river remain relatively unpressured and you'll be treating the river and its inhabitants with total respect. You'll be happier and, importantly, so will the fish.

Friendship

When you reach this psychological state, you begin to discover what true fishing friendships are all about. You'll meet up with similar characters who would do anything for you, for their other friends, the fish and the environment. There's no jealousy in these friendships, no hoarding of secrets. Everything they possess is out there to be shared. You'll begin to enjoy total, implicit trust. You'll rejoice to see these people on the river and not inwardly curse because you fear they'll be on the best lies. Everything will become more relaxed. There'll be no rush for the best places, no thrashing of the water to catch the most fish. You'll be just as happy to brew up, have a cup of tea and discuss the meaning of fishing and of life.

Odds are that soon you'll enjoy rod sharing. There's no more civilized way of fishing than this. One rod and two or three friends, walking the river, watching fish, discussing challenges and working out solutions, taking it in turns to wield the rod or issue instructions, loads of leg-pulling and lots of genuine congratulations. Each fish is a shared fish, and the pleasure you are taking from your sport is enhanced as a result.

Smell the Roses

Fishing is the most wonderful sport. It's a vast kaleidoscope of skills, and it can be practised virtually anywhere on the planet in wonderful places for wonderful species. Perhaps only mountaineers see nature as clearly as anglers do. Learn to appreciate sunrises, sunsets, storms and the endless play of light on the water. Learn the names of the waterfowl. Recognize water plants. Develop your interest in aquatic insects. Take binoculars with you so you can look at birds and wildlife. Push yourself to fish different places and catch different species. You'll meet new people, eat different food and learn fascinating customs. Be disciplined with yourself and try out all the skills mentioned in this book. It's not just about becoming a better angler; it's about savouring new ways of fishing. You'll find very often that you don't actually have to catch a fish using a particular method in order to gain huge satisfaction from practising it. Take the Spey cast, for example. I've seen anglers fish hour upon hour on rivers without a single salmon being present, but they've been Spey casting and they've loved it, and the day has been a joy. Remember, even a bad a day on the river beats a good day in the office. The wise angler learns to appreciate all the gifts of his or her sport.

▲ *Pass the vodka*
A typical late-night scene in a fishing hut that could be anywhere in the world. Befriend your guide and you will have a friend for life.

▼ *Lending a hand*
Here I am guiding, hopefully bringing pleasure to a young friend who is just about to land a very serious fish indeed.

Water Safety

This is possibly the most important skill-set in this book. Water safety may not directly help you to catch fish, but at least you'll still be alive to keep trying. Remember, we're not fish, and water is potentially a lethal element for us. You will be trying to get close to the water, on it if you're boating, and even in it if you're wading, and you may well be on your own. In these circumstances, things can get dangerous.

Learn to Swim

No matter what kind of fishing you enjoy, you should learn how to swim and, especially, learn how to be proficient on your back. As a bank angler, if you should fall in, your best bet by far is to float down river on your back, shouting for help, gradually paddling yourself in towards a safe landing place. Don't panic. Keep your head (preferably above water!): it is panic that drowns most people. The human body is buoyant, especially with layers of clothing trapping extra air. It's important to keep your mouth shut should you unexpectedly hit the water's surface. Keep cool, don't swim against the current, don't wave your arms about, keep your mouth closed and you will survive.

▼ **The danger beneath**
This river looks wonderful at dawn, smoking as the sun begins to rise. But the currents are actually treacherous. The water is deep and cold. However picture-perfect the river might seem, make sure you don't mess with it.

Be wary of steep banks after rain, especially if there isn't much in the way of long grass or shrubbery. If you must fish in such places, a rope tied to yourself and a tree is a good idea. Be wary of undercut banks, which can collapse with heavy rain and swollen rivers, and be especially vigilant after dark. Whether you are bank fishing or wading, always make sure that your boots have an excellent grip and that they aren't worn smooth.

Wading

When you are wading, with chest waders in particular, there's a great temptation to push into ever-deeper water. Take care. Never wade in water that makes you uneasy, that is

too deep and too fast for your safety, or that doesn't offer good visibility – you could easily step off a safe ledge into a deep hole. Be wary of wading in, or soon after, heavy rain – a river can suddenly rise, colour up and put you in danger. Just two extra inches of water can result in a tremendous increase of pressure – enough to throw you off balance. Check you are not below any kind of water flow control system, such as a sluice. There are locations where water can suddenly rise by a matter of feet! Never wade between steep, impenetrable banks, only where there is easy access to and from the water.

Always wear a personal flotation device when wading. Choose products that are certified to turn you over and keep your head out of the water, even if you are unconscious. Choose a lifejacket that automatically inflates within a few seconds of water immersion, and don't forget that most safety devices require annual servicing to ensure total reliability.

Don't neglect the use of a wading staff, preferably on a staff retractor that pulls the wading staff to your side when it's not in use. A wading staff really does act as a third leg and is of massive support in quick currents, as well as being useful to check the river bed in front of you.

Boats on Freshwater

Never go out in a boat that doesn't have a bailer, a spare oar and rowlocks. Even if you have an engine, don't forget the oars. Make sure the engine is reliable and that you have enough fuel. Always check weather forecasts and don't go out if there's any possibility of approaching storms.

Take care when stepping into a boat and always put your feet on the floorboards as near the middle as you possibly can. Always fish sitting down in a boat and don't stand up unexpectedly. If you need a pee, use the bailer bucket rather than risking standing up, and never succumb to the temptation to have a quick swim unless the boat is firmly anchored in shallow water.

If your companion falls overboard, don't throw him a rope without first tying a bowline in it. The loop must be big enough for the man in the water to get his head and shoulders through it so that it can hold him underneath his armpits.

▲ *Safety first*
When deep-wading or wading amongst slippery rocks, never get into a position that frightens you. A wading stick is always a sensible precaution.

▲ **Neighbourhood watch**

When fishing with a partner in a boat, always be aware of where he or she is and what he or she is doing. Watch how you cast. Keep the boat balanced. Look out for rocks and other potential hazards.

▼ **Heading to sea**

Howard is heading out to the open sea. There's a stiff wind and a strong tide running, and he and the crew will be constantly aware of any changing conditions.

Be particularly careful when you want to up-anchor in a strong current. The current can swamp a boat if your weight is transferred forward too quickly. Take care and make every move a cautious one.

If your boat does capsize, keep your mouth shut when you hit the water. If the wind is blowing you towards the shore then it pays to cling to the upturned boat or to oars. If the wind is blowing you away from the shore and there is no help in sight, you might decide to swim for it if the shoreline is close. Even if the shore is close, don't be tempted to take clothes off to make swimming easier – cold is going to be one of your major problems. If you tire, turn on your back but keep your arms and legs moving so you're still making progress. When you reach the shore, get on your feet quickly and move about to avoid paralyzing cold setting in.

Boats at Sea

If you're a novice boat-owner, join your local club for some expert advice and tuition. Never go out on your own until you have complete confidence in your abilities.

If your engine dies, drop anchor and stabilize the situation. Make sure that you have sufficient anchor chain and rope to hold bottom. Keep calm. A breakdown is a mind-numbing experience, but gather your composure as quickly as possible and set about asking for help.

Don't rely on a mobile phone for talking to lifeboats or rescue helicopters. You need a properly installed VHF to get you through to the emergency services or neighbouring boats, and your boat should be properly fitted with the right radio equipment. Listen to the regular weather bulletins put out by your local coastguard every few hours. If there's a sudden change in the weather, head for shore. Don't be afraid to admit that you've got a problem. As soon as you sense danger, make that call. Act swiftly and don't let a crisis develop. Charts are useful, and always have a compass with you. Always try to give the coastguard your exact position in a crisis.

You might have to wait for help, so always take lifejackets, warm clothing, food, water and flasks along with you. Make sure that you have flares on board, particularly at night. Always tell somebody where you are going. If you change your plans, phone through the information. No matter how good the fishing is, don't leave it too late to return to port, as this can be very worrying for those on shore.

Familiarize yourself with your boat and its engine. Make sure you carry spares and know how to use them. It's also a good idea to have alternative means of propulsion. Stick an old outboard engine, for example, somewhere down in the boat's hold. Even a pair of oars can make a difference. Make sure everyone on your boat – you included – is wearing a lifejacket. Drinking alcohol is unacceptable out at sea, especially if you are the skipper. Keep a clear head at all times and make sure anybody fishing with you does the same.

Carbon and Electricity

Nearly all modern rods are composed of carbon fibre, which makes them excellent at conducting electricity! You should thus be very careful in storms, and be especially wary of any overhead power lines. Keep in mind that a rod doesn't even have to touch a live wire for it to kill you – high-voltage electricity can arc across several feet. Don't cast over a power line as this, too, can cause a shock, particularly when using a lead-core fly line.

A Sharp Reminder

Always wear polarizing glasses to protect your eyes and a hat to shield those vulnerable ears from high speed hooks, especially when fly fishing, but even when bait fishing or spinning. Be particularly careful when fly casting in a cross wind – a tube fly thudding into the back of your skull is a most unpleasant experience as I, from painful memory, can tell you.

If you do manage to hook yourself, then there are obvious advantages in having a barbless hook. If the hook is not barbless, however, and you are anywhere within reach of civilization, get yourself to a doctor or a hospital rather than doing a botched first-aid job on the bank. In a worst-case scenario, nip the eye off and push the hook out point first – it hurts less that way! And make sure that you're completely up to date with your anti-tetanus jabs.

▲ *Care of fish and angler*
Big Bob's glasses protect his eyes from artificial flies and enable him to watch this lovely BC Steelhead as she slips away.

▼ *A bit risky*
I'm not happy with myself in this shot. The light has fallen yet I've removed my Polaroid glasses. And I'm standing up in the boat – I was sure of my balance here, but never do this in choppy water.

Glossary Of Knots

It is essential for every angler to know how to tie a selection of knots. Knots are used to secure the line to the reel and to join a hook or lure to the line. Although there are thousands of different knots, the basic knots illustrated below will be sufficient for most angling purposes.

Half blood knot

The half blood knot is commonly used for joining hook to line. This type of knot, when tied in nylon line, will not come undone.

Step 1

Thread the free end of the line through the eye of the hook.

Step 2

Pass the free end underneath the line and bring it back over the line to form a loop.

Step 3

Continue to loop the free end over the line (as step 2) until you have approximately four turns.

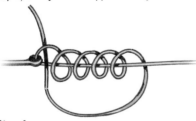

Step 4

Pass the loose end between the eye of the hook and the first loop.

Step 5

Pull on the loose end to tighten the knot. Trim off the end.

Double overhand loop

Also known as the surgeon's loop, this knot can be used to create a loop at the end of a fly line, to which a looped leader can be attached.

Step 1

To begin, double the end of the line back against itself.

Step 2

Next, tie an overhand knot in the doubled line.

Step 3

The doubled end should then be tucked through the loop again.

Step 4

To finish, pull the knot as tight as possible and trim off the end.

Blood bight

This knot has similar properties to the double overhand loop. If the end of the knot is not trimmed, several loops can be created to attach, for example, mackerel flies.

Step 1

Fold the end of the line back against itself (this is known as a bight).

Step 2

Cross the the doubled end once around the line.

Step 3

Pass the looped end of the line back through the turn.

Step 4

Pull the knot tight. Trim off the end of the line to finish.

Water knot

This knot is also known as the surgeon's knot. The water knot is used to join two lines together, for example attaching a lighter hook length to the mainline. The bulk of the knot will stop a sliding bead, and can be useful when ledgering.

Step 1

Put the ends of the two lines alongside each other so that they overlap by about 6in (15cm).

Step 2

Take hold of the two lines and make a wide loop.

Step 3

Pass the ends of the line through the loop four times. Be sure to hold the two lines together.

Step 4

Pull the lines tightly so that the loop makes a knot. Trim the two ends.

Blood knot

The blood knot is also used to join two lines together. As in the water knot, begin by overlapping the ends of the two lines.

Step 1

Take one end and twist it four times round the other line. Then pass it between the two lines.

Step 2

Repeat with the other free end. Make sure that the first stage does not come undone.

Step 3

Wet the knot to lubricate it, then pull it tight. Trim off the two ends.

Needle knot

The needle knot shown here can be used to tie monofilament to a fly line.

Step 1

Push a needle through the end of the fly line, Heat the needle until the line begins to bend.

Step 2

When cool, remove the needle. Thread the mono through the fly line and five times around it. Bring the end back and hold it against the line.

Step 3

Now take the large loop and bring it several times around the fly line, trapping the mono.

Step 4

Pull on alternate ends of the mono to tighten. When the knot is firm, pull the mono tight.

A BRAID LOOP

Although some fly lines are fitted with braided lines for attaching a leader, it is a simple task to form your own from braided mono.

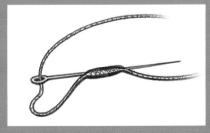

Step 1

Push a large-eyed needle into the braid. Thead the braid through the eye.

Step 2

Push the needle through the braid until the loose end emerges. A matchstick will keep the loop from closing.

Step 3

Adjust the loop until it is the size you require. Cut the loose end until it lies flush, and seal using waterproof super glue.

Fly Recognition

As a fly angler, it's absolutely imperative that you recognize at least the four main groups of insects and food types that make up the bulk of the fish's diet. These are the items from the fish's menu that you are going to try to imitate, so recognition becomes a core skill.

▶ *Prehistoric!*

Big nymphs like this will turn into dragonflies of one type or another. They are aggressive and eat a whole range of aquatic food items. However, they are prey as much as predator, and will often feed under the cover of darkness.

▶ *An easy meal*

A mayfly has reached the end of its lifecycle and has collapsed to die on the surface of the river. It has drifted into the still water on the edge of a river eddy, where it will very possibly become an easy meal for a big, lazy trout.

▶ *Daddies*

Daddy long-legs, or crane-flies, come into their own in the late summer, when there's a good breeze blowing them off the land and onto the water. Trout and black bass in particular come to the feast.

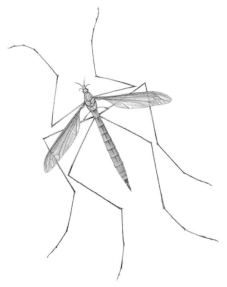

Up-Winged

Firstly, there are the up-winged flies, notably the olives and the mayflies (*Ephemeroptera*). These are recognizable by their tall, graceful, sail-like wings and their long, delicate tails. They begin life as a nymph and can spend years living in the sand and gravel of the riverbed. They then hatch into a dun, and then transform again into the spinner, the completed insect. It is now that mating takes place before the females return to the water to lay their eggs and die. All these life phases can be imitated by the fly tier and used by the angler.

Roof-Winged

The next most important family are the roof-winged flies (*Trichoptera*). These fold their wings across their bodies in the form of a roof. The most common of the family are the sedges. Their life cycle goes through the different stages of egg to larva to pupa and finally, adult.

Flat-Winged

The flat-winged flies (*Diptera*) are also important. This family includes hundreds of species, from tiny midges to the relatively goliath daddy-long-legs. However, all share some common features: six legs, a pair of short wings and a well-segmented body. The most common aquatic members of this family are the chironamids, often referred to as buzzers or, in Ireland, duck flies. The buzzer begins its life as a bloodworm before transforming into a pupa and finally hatching out to become the adult midge.

... and the Rest!

Other food items include crustaceans,

A slow rise, where you see the head, then the back, the dorsal fin and the tail, suggests a trout feeding on buzzers and dead insects in the surface film. Try fishing just subsurface and move your fly very slowly indeed, even letting it hang immobile for a minute at a time.

Sometimes you will simply see a boil on the surface with no sign of the fish itself. This is a trout taking food, often an ascending nymph, a few inches beneath the surface. Cover a disturbance like this with a quick sinking nymph or a buzzer weighted to get a couple of feet from the surface in quick time.

Audible Hints

Sometimes you will hear rises as well as seeing them. In calm conditions especially, listen for a sip, a suck or a full-blooded slurp! These noises are made by trout consuming buzzers or spinners very close to the surface, often in the surface film itself. Try a dry fly or a buzzer pattern when this activity is taking place.

On other occasions, rises can be seen far off as explosive splashes. These often indicate trout hurrying after a big meal that they don't want to lose – for example, a mayfly on the point of lifting off into the air. Alternatively, these could be fish feeding on fry or even taking buzzers on their route to the surface if there's a big hatch on. Try a big dry fly, a small fish-resembling lure or a buzzer until you discover the key. If you don't immediately succeed in matching your imitation to what the trout are feeding on then you've simply got to try one pattern, intelligently chosen, after another until you get there. So, read the clues, watch for the signs and you will be on your way to becoming the ultimate nature detective.

◀ *Study the water*
Neil believes in getting as close to the water as possible, and watching exactly what is happening in the stream. He's looking at how the trout behave and noting what they are feeding upon.

▲ *A dangerous life*
Fish will eat almost everything that they come across in the water around them, including recently hatched baby newts .

▼ *Matching the hatch*
On many waters, the advent of the mayfly in early summer signals the most exciting and frenetic fishing of the season. All fish, but trout especially, gorge on these beautiful insects.

corixids, and the many terrestrial insects that alight on still and running waters. Common crustaceans include freshwater shrimps and snails. Corixids (*Corixidae*) are also known as waterboatmen, and they look like small beetles, living in shallow water and grabbing bubbles of air from the surface. Common land insects found during autopsies on trout include alder flies, black gnats, hawthorn flies, reed smuts, moths and flying ants. The fact is, fish will target virtually anything edible, and that includes wasps, grasshoppers, tadpoles, fry, fingerlings and even ladybirds.

The Rise as a Clue

It's worth noting that you don't have to see the insect to get a clue as to what a fish is feeding upon. Trout, especially, will give the game away by the manner of their rise.

Reading Rivers

Think of a river as your friend. Learn to live with it. Learn to love it. View your relationship with it with confidence. While still waters can be beautiful, mysterious, awe-inspiring or beguiling, it's moving water that really stirs the blood, and pretty well every serious fisherman I know would pick a river over a lake nine times out of ten.

Getting to Know the River

Rivers don't always give up all their secrets easily. You've got to learn to read them, to recognize the clues and the signs that they give away, so let's take a walk down an imaginary river and see what we can learn. Remember that we are looking at the major factors of river reading – the strength and the direction of the current, the depth, the amount of cover and the make-up of the riverbed.

There are certainly exceptions, but most species of fish like to hang where the current is neither too strong nor too slow, where there's enough water to make them feel secure and where they can find shelter from predators. Clean gravel or sand is also the bottom make-up that most species prefer, as this fertile structure harbours prolific stocks of food.

Moving Water

First we come to a weir, or maybe a mill pool. Where the water tumbles over the sill it's white and foaming, well oxygenated and bringing lots of food from upstream. Fish love it. They also love the fact that this churning water has, over the years, created a big, deep pool and possibly an even deeper central channel. There are likely to be large rocks, too, providing some shelter from the current and predators. As the pool steadies and shallows there is more good water, about six feet deep and pushing over a gravel bottom. Towards the end of the pool, the water shallows to perhaps four feet but again there is gravel and now there is more weed – ranunculus, which holds a lot of insects and is therefore hugely attractive to many fish species.

Food and Shelter

Walking on down the meadow we come to some fallen willow trees that have collapsed in a late winter storm. A raft of rubbish, dead weed, leaves and driftwood has built up around the branches, creating dark, still water beneath. Predators love areas like this, and so do fish species such as chub.

Moving on a further hundred yards we come to an old road bridge, probably constructed some two or three hundred years ago. It has a couple of arches and the river divides around a large, central buttress – a great place for fish. Over the decades the force of the water, where it has narrowed and deepened, has created a large pool downstream of the bridge, and it's full of food. Over the years, passers-by have thrown rocks into the pool, there's an old lorry

▼ Reading the features
You can read rivers like a book. They're just so full of character. Bridges, weirs, overhanging trees, rapids and bays can give hundreds of clues to where the fish are lying.

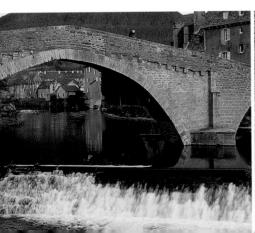

wheel, the remains of a cart – all objects that have settled into the river and now provide a haven for food stocks and for the fish that feed upon them. Of course, bridges are also the most perfect vantage points for anglers, giving them the height to peer into the depths beneath.

Twists and Turns

Now we are coming to a series of bends, and on a river a bend almost invariably means fish. Bends are attractive in winter and summer alike – in winter because the deeper pockets of water give protection from floods, and in summer because there is always depth on a bend however low the water level sinks. Food also tends to drop onto the bottom when the flow begins to decrease over the deeper part of the bend itself. Look out, too, for what anglers call the crease – that's where the current is separated from the slack water that all bends produce. You can see where the fast and slow water meet because there is a very visible dividing line there. Fish like to move backwards and forwards along this crease, slipping into the faster water to feed and then back into the slower water to rest and digest.

Shade and Structure

Way downstream, we can see that the river enters a thick, unkempt wood, and both predators and prey fish love stretches of water overhung by trees and bushes. Areas like this offer security from overhead attack, shelter from the sun and added food sources in the shape of terrestrial insects falling into the water from the leaves and branches.

I happen to know that in the shade of this wood there lie the remains of an old stone

1 THE RAPIDS
Fish of all species move into the rapids to feed, especially at night or when oxygen levels are low.

2 THE POINT
A place like this gives an angler tremendous access to the river.

3 INTO THE DISTANCE
It's always exciting to see what's round that next bend. Trees, in particular, always harbour fish.

boat jetty that disintegrated half a century ago. The rocks are now strewn along fifty yards of the riverbed and have attracted a lot of fish. Once again, the rocks provide a haven for all manner of invertebrate life, and fish are attracted to the honey pot. You see, fish are exactly like us: all they really want from their home is comfort and security and a well-stocked kitchen. They don't like places that make them feel at risk and exposed, where the water is too open and shallow and where there aren't enough food stocks. Of course, until fish talk, we'll never know exactly why one piece of water is so attractive and another is shunned, and you will occasionally find swims that look exactly right in every way but that hardly ever hold anything. Experience counts for a lot, but you will always meet up with surprises.

▼ *The power of water*
Rivers run ceaselessly, their currents pushing stones and gravel hither and thither as they run. Yet many fish can more than hold their own in even the fastest flowing water.

Reading Stillwaters

Stillwaters aren't, at first sight, quite as easy to decipher as rivers. Large stillwaters, in particular, can be especially daunting, and yet the signs are nevertheless there if you keep a cool head, keep watching for them and keep trying to interpret them.

▲ Lunar landscape
This reservoir may look barren, but you can bet the fish don't find it that way. Turn over any of the stones lying in the margins and you will find endless types of invertebrate life. Black bass in particular love the margins.

Depth and Shade

Let's kick off with dams. The dam wall of a reservoir or estate lake is always a good starting point for locating fish. The depth is attractive to them and there are nearly always insects sheltering amongst the brickwork. Added attractions like water towers only increase the drawing power of these places.

Next, never ignore weed, reed beds or lily beds. Smaller prey fish will never stray far from the refuge of cover, and this is exactly what vegetation gives them. Where there are prey fish you will find predators, too, and larger, non-predatorial fish like to browse amongst vegetation, reaping the benefits of plentiful food items. Lily pads, in particular, have magnetic qualities for fish, especially carp and tench, which love to graze on insects that inhabit the undersides of the pads and the stems that lead down to the bottom silt. Watch for the subtlest move-ments as the fish pass beneath and rock the stems. Reed beds are another major attraction, bulrushes probably being the most sought after because they like to grow on a hard, clean, gravely bottom – just the sort of place in which tench, for example, prefer to feed.

Islands are another key feature in any stillwater complex. They are particularly attractive when they are overhung by trees or lined by heavy reed growth. Islands are a prime location when there's no way onto them from the main fishing banks. When they are quiet and distant, they offer complete sanctuary, and fish are always looking to escape from noise and irritation.

Water Supplies

Inflows and feeder streams are always real hotspots on stillwaters of any size or type. Fish tend to congregate where water enters, hoping to profit from food being washed from

1 COVES
Fish of all species love to investigate coves and inlets on the lake shore.

2 POINTS
Areas like this catch the winds, which in turn blow food towards the fish and are highly attractive.

3 INTO THE WOODS
Many terrestrial insects fall off the branches of trees and end up in the water. The fish know this.

4 THE OPEN WATER
The middle of a lake might seem featureless, but you'll find some of the biggest fish here.

the fields around. This activity is particularly pronounced during periods of heavy rain, when lobworms are washed from the land. The incoming stream might also help colour up the lake and make fish feed with extra confidence. Always look for clouded water – another sure sign that fish are feeding.

Springs frequently bubble up to the surface of lakes and pools. These can be very attractive to fish in hot weather conditions, when the water gets stale and begins to lack oxygen. Springs are usually cool and they bring hot summer temperatures down to more acceptable levels. Trout especially are attracted to springs.

Focus on Features

Look carefully at the bottom contours of your stillwater. As an example, deep central channels often run down the middle of estate lakes. These are frequently the old stream beds that were dammed hundreds of years ago to make the lake in the first place. Fish will often congregate in this deeper water for the security and rich feeding that it offers. Look for plateaux, gullies and drop-offs close to your bank – especially if these are lined with reeds or overhanging trees. A stillwater may look like a large and feature-less saucer, but in nearly all cases if you lift the veil and look under the surface there will be all sorts of clues to fish location. Look also for any man-made structures. Boat houses, for example, attract large perch shoals. The perch like to rub themselves against the submerged timbers and they enjoy the shade from bright sunlight. Piers and jetties are equally attractive, and fish will also congregate under temporary 'constructions' such as a moored boat. Perch, again, like to rub their bodies against anchor ropes.

Keep Looking

Never settle at the first swim on any new stillwater, but walk as much of the lake's circumference as you can, watching carefully for any telltale signs; binoculars can be helpful. What are you looking for? As I've mentioned, clouded water, which is generally a

sign of feeding fish. I've also talked about twitching reed stems and lily pads – they don't have to move much to indicate the presence of a very big fish indeed. Watch for clusters of bubbles hitting the surface: these may be just marsh gas, but more likely they're being produced by fish feeding on the bottom. Look carefully at the water and see if you can spot any flat areas in patches of rippled water. These are caused by fish moving heavily just under the surface. Look, too, for fish physically breaking the surface: slow, steady porpoise rolls often indicate fish taking hatching midges just subsurface.

Pay close attention to the wind direction. Many, if not most, types of freshwater species tend to follow the wind, gradually moving towards the bank that it is hitting. In Europe, we are generally faced with westerly winds and this tends to mean that the eastern shores are a good place to start.

▲ *At peace with the world*

There's little doubt that fish know how to enjoy themselves. Carp, especially, adore the warmth of the summer sun and will always be found wallowing in shallow, weedy areas where they feel safe and can enjoy the day.

▼ *Strength in numbers*

Small silver fish like these rudd invariably swim in shoals. A group of fish, darting here and there, flashing and then scattering, can confuse a predator.

Fly Casting

Casting a fly is an art, but it's actually fairly easy to master even though it looks quite complex. Much like riding a bicycle, good fly casting is all about technique, timing and balance. And furthermore, contrary to what many people think, good casting isn't particularly about physical strength; indeed, some of the best casters are women, children and slightly built men.

The roll cast and the overhead cast are the two basic casts in any fly fisherman's armoury. They both have to be mastered before you can really fish with any proficiency. The double haul cast is the best tool for the angler on large stillwaters, while the single spey and the double spey are primarily casts to be used with double-handed rods intended for salmon or steelhead, or for fishing on large rivers where distance casting is necessary.

▲ *Fearless casting*
Fergus casts fearlessly into the brisk Hebridean breeze. Perfect control, perfect focus, perfect technique.

The Basic Roll Cast

The roll cast straightens an untidy line before you move into an overhead cast. It's also a very important cast in its own right, especially on small rivers or when there's no room to back cast because of tree cover. You can also use it for safety, especially in a boat when the weather is very windy. It's also the ideal cast to lift a sunken line out of the water.

2 When you get the rod to about 11 o'clock you should pause. You'll have a lot of line off the water and the rest will be slowly moving towards you.

3 Now sweep the rod smoothly back in a wide arc, round and up until your thumb is level with your right ear (or left ear, if you are left-handed), and the rod is pointing back to 2 o'clock. Pause again. The loop of line should have formed behind the rod looking much like a perfect 'D'.

4 Now it's time for the hit. Drive your thumb forward in a flicking movement as if you were swatting a fly on the wall just in front of you. Aim straight at the target and stop the rod sharply at 10 o'clock.

5 You'll find this movement should flick the line off the water and push it through the air towards the target, landing straight and true.

1 Start with the rod tip touching the water and then lift slowly but smoothly.

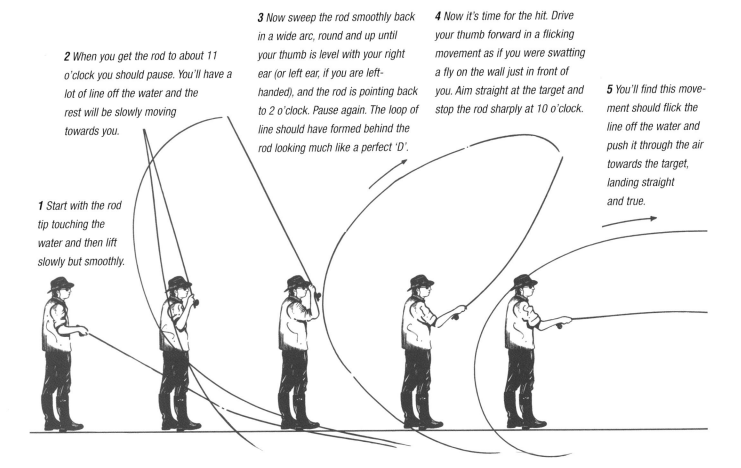

The Overhead Cast

This is the main cast in the fly fisher's armoury, and you must learn it before going on to other techniques. It's simple – there are only three basic movements – the lift, the back cast and the forward cast. So don't be intimidated.

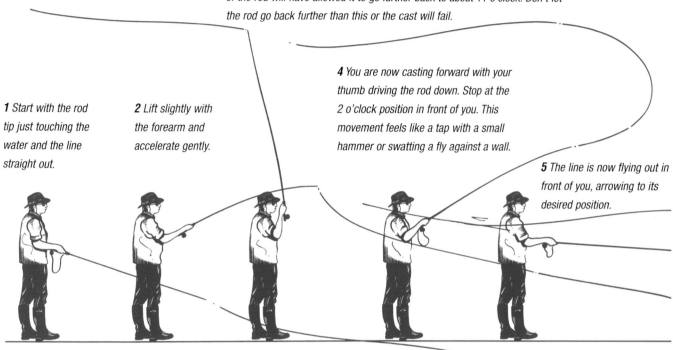

3 *Your thumb should now be level with your right eye (or left eye if you are left-handed), with the rod pointing at about the 12 o'clock position. The inertia of the rod will have allowed it to go further back to about 11 o'clock. Don't let the rod go back further than this or the cast will fail.*

4 *You are now casting forward with your thumb driving the rod down. Stop at the 2 o'clock position in front of you. This movement feels like a tap with a small hammer or swatting a fly against a wall.*

1 *Start with the rod tip just touching the water and the line straight out.*

2 *Lift slightly with the forearm and accelerate gently.*

5 *The line is now flying out in front of you, arrowing to its desired position.*

◀ *A river master*

Don's casting is immaculate. He has the fish in his sights and knows exactly where to drop the line and place a fly. And look how still he is – there are no telltale ripples from his legs as he pushes the line out.

The Double Haul

The double and single haul casts are primarily to get distance, especially on stillwaters. They can also be used to increase the line speed and to combat wind.

1 Hauling is basically a technique where the non-casting hand tugs at the spare line being held between the butt ring and the reel.

2 This method increases the inertia and, therefore, the loading of the rod spring on the forward or back cast, or both.

3 The result is that every-thing works harder and faster, and it's possible to shoot extra yards of line that can prove to be critical.

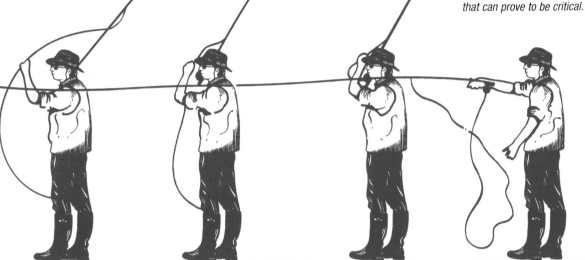

The Single Spey

The single and double spey casts are used on lazy rivers fished with double-handed rods. If there is an upstream wind, the single spey cast is used because the fly and the loop in the line are swept upstream before hitting out to the target.

3 Turn right with your upper hand and sweep away and out. Your right thumb comes round to the side of your shoulder and up to a position level with your ear. You will now have the 'D' loop formed behind the rod, facing the target.

4 Punch the rod smartly forward before stopping sharply at 10 o'clock in front of you. This flicks the loop of line out across and above the water. This is a wrist and forearm flick, not a shoulder heave.

1 Stand square onto the target. Leave the rod pointing down-stream with the tip of the rod at the water.

2 Raise the rod by bend-ing your upper forearm at the elbow slightly towards the near bank. Think of 10 o'clock on your rod clock.

SAFETY CONSIDERATIONS

1 You will already have picked up throughout this book that I'm a firm believer in anglers wearing polarizing glasses at all times, because you can see so much more through the surface of the water. This is especially important when fly casting, as you want to target your fish as accurately as possible. These glasses also help you to see the riverbed when wading, and may prevent you stepping into a deep hole!

2 The eye protection that glasses offer is vital. Remember that you have a hooked artificial fly travelling round your head and body all day long, frequently at great speeds. There is a real possibility that a gust of wind could blow it directly at your face. I've seen people with hooks in their noses and ears, and I've had one in my scalp. That's bad enough, but the thought of a hook in the eye... wear those glasses!

3 To avoid hooking yourself, always check wind speed and direction. Be very wary of a wind that is blowing the fly line actually toward you. If you're right-handed, this obviously means a wind coming from the right. Try to avoid such a situation, especially when you're a beginner.

4 Once again, as in nearly all forms of fishing, use a barbless hook or flatten the barb when you're fly fishing. Should anything go wrong, a barbless hook slips out with relatively little pain or fuss.

5 Always check above and behind you for any power lines. Remember how easily electricity is conducted through carbon.

6 When fly fishing, always be aware of anybody moving behind you along the bank. Never risk that quick cast before they arrive – you may have your timing wrong.

7 When changing position, always look behind you to see if there is any problematic foliage...or livestock. I've actually seen a bullock get hooked in the ear!

8 If you're wading on a river or stillwater, it's often tempting to go out just a bit further to reach rising fish. Do so carefully, always making sure you're within your depth. It's also sensible to bring a wading stick for balance and depth testing. Be extra careful if there is a rapid current.

The Double Spey

If there is a downstream wind, you'll need the double spey cast, where the fly and the loop in the line are kept downstream before hitting out to the target.

1 With the rod across your stomach and your right hand uppermost, your hands will not be crossed.

2 Tow some line upstream, lifting the rod tip until your hands are crossed over like they were for the single spey. Leave the fly still downstream of you.

Lift as you did for the single spey, up to 10 o'clock and slightly in towards the nearside bank.

3 Sweep the rod around and back downstream, lifting back up until your hand is level with your right ear (or left ear if you are left-handed). The line will peel back and round and form the 'D 'loop.

4 Hit the loop out, as in the single spey. All these actions are done to a rhythm and not rushed or flustered.

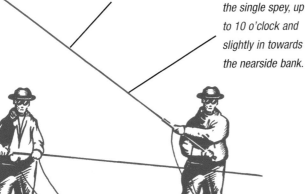

The Snake Roll Cast

Andy Sowerby is an expert caster and a leading member of the Hardy and Greys' team, perhaps Britain's premier tackle company. Andy is in the lucky position of fishing in the north of England and having access to some of the great salmon rivers of the Scottish borders. Here he discusses his snake roll cast technique for deep water. This cast is particularly useful if there's a downstream wind, especially if you are deep wading.

'Casting a double-handed rod in deep water has its own limitations,' Andy says. 'To overcome these, you need to make some small modifications to your casting technique. Deep wading presents many problems, and

1 *'When starting the cast, I like to hold the rod away from my body.'*

2 *'The cast begins by drawing the fly line in a slow, progressive movement.'*

3 *'As I'm drawing the rod back, I slightly lift it very quickly – just 2 to 3 inches. This creates a small "bump" that runs down the fly line from the tip of the rod. This lifts the line in a quiet, relaxed manner so it leaves the water with minimal disturbance. In the photograph you can actually see the "bump" running down towards the water, lifting the line as it goes. The rod has stopped at the 11 o'clock position, with my upper arm held at eye level.'*

6 *'I lift and draw the line with my upper hand higher than normal to compensate for the depth I'm wading at. This allows the line to run out behind me smoothly. I'm also allowing the line to key itself on the water no further than a rod length away from me. This acts as an anchor and creates the "D" loop every caster is trying to form.'*

7 *'That "D" loop is nicely illustrated here. A smooth push of the upper arm combined with a quick pull in of the lower arm towards the chest stops the tip of the rod high. This flexes the rod, storing up and then releasing its power.'*

the snake roll cast is one of the easiest ways of putting out a fly line in this situation.

'My personal tips? Well, a net is a nuisance but it's better than dragging a fish up dry gravel and then releasing it. Often I net fish without moving into shallow water, as I find it is quicker and less stressful to net in waist-deep water. Notice how I always use a weighted stick with a rubber button attached. If you're not sure of the bottom, it is better to stay dry and comfortable. Finally, grease your reel regularly. As you can see in the photograph, my reels spend a great deal of their lives in the water, and it's surprising how quickly a reel loses its grease when immersed for long periods.'

4 *'Now the rod is pushed forward with the upper hand and pulled in with the lower hand. This creates a roll cast following the same angle that the line has been drawn up from.'*

5 *'I now want to face the target area rather than the area from which I have originally drawn my line so I turn my body from the hips to change my angle of view.'*

8 *'With this power I can punch the line out over the water with minimal disturbance towards the target position. The fly turns over, settles and commences its swing round in the current.*

9 *'The cast is complete and the fly is fishing. Notice how I hold the tip up and follow the line round, watching the loop down to the water. I hold 1 inch of line in my hand and allow this to go when I feel a fish take. I then lift the rod and tighten up into the fish.'*

Casting A Multiplier

If you're going to be serious about catching big fish, then at some stage in your career you're going to have to learn to master a multiplier reel. Why? Well, in the first place, a multiplier will almost certainly hold a greater length of heavy line than any fixed spool reel. So if you're after fish that can run off 250 yards of 30-pound line, you're certainly looking at a multiplier. Secondly, the clutch on a multiplier is generally stronger than that of any fixed spool reel. This means that you can put enormous pressure on a big fish in a fast current without the reel locking up or even exploding. And thirdly, multipliers are built for the most rugged fishing situations imaginable. If you're embarking on a real white-knuckle adventure, a multiplier of reputable make is unlikely to let you down.

▲ *Armed to the teeth*
An investigation of any rod stand in any Indian camp will show that multipliers are the 'must have' reel.

Cast Mastery

Playing fish on multipliers isn't particularly difficult. Of course, before setting out after big fish you should take as many hours as you need to familiarize yourself with the reel. That said, you can learn how to use the clutch and drag system blindfolded, but it's actually the casting that causes most people problems. Either they can't cast far enough, or the bait just whistles out and causes over-

runs. There's nothing worse than spending half a day fiddling around with birds' nests, those great tangles of line that bring your reel to a total standstill.

To demonstrate, we're going to India to look at the techniques of two master multiplier fishermen. On the subcontinent, fishing with multipliers is second nature and, as you can see, the guides there are brought up with them from childhood.

▶ *Casting for gold*
Anthony has been my guide in India for more years than either of us cares to count. I nicknamed him 'The Fox', simply because he is the most cunning guy I've ever fished with. Here you see him cradling one of the biggest mahseer we caught together – an absolute lunker.

▶ *The start of the cast. The bait is a ball of ragi paste and there's a spiral Indian lead some two feet above it. Before the cast, Anthony likes to compose himself, look at his bait and look out over the water to where he is going to cast it. This is also the moment to check the tension of the reel. If he takes his finger off the spool now, the weight of the bait and lead should just slowly take off line. If line gushes out, the tension is too slack. If the spool doesn't give any line, then loosen it bit by bit until it does.*

◀ *Ready to go. The rod is at about 45 degrees behind the caster with the bait some four feet beneath the rod tip. He holds that position for a few seconds to ensure his own personal balance, and to check that the reel is free and the cast is ready to go.*

▶ *The cast winds up. Great force is put into the cast through the shoulders and down the forearms. At the 12 o'clock postion (when the rod is directly overhead), Anthony will take his thumb off the spool and allow the line to follow the bait out on its course over the river.*

▲ *Once the bait is on its way, Anthony watches its course, hawk-like, with his thumb on the spool ready to feather the cast as the bait drops towards the water.*

▶ *As soon as the bait hits the water Anthony's thumb will stop the spool completely to avoid overrun. This is a critical moment because if the spool keeps revolving once the bait has hit the water, there will be line everywhere! Notice how relaxed Anthony is at this stage in the cast.*

▲ Subhan has been a guide with me for well over 20 years and he's probably the most famous name on the subcontinent in his line of work. Mola is one of his sons, and he's learning the trade of river guiding from the master. Mola is showing every sign of being just as good.

▲ Unlike the situation in which Anthony was casting, Mola is fishing a much narrower stretch of river, where accuracy is far more important. The cast is only going to go about 40 yards, but it has to be pinpointed behind a rock.

◀ Like Anthony, Mola keeps perfectly still before the cast. The bait, again, is about four feet beneath the rod trip, but look how Mola is looking fixedly at the point in the river he wants to reach.

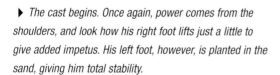

▶ The cast begins. Once again, power comes from the shoulders, and look how his right foot lifts just a little to give added impetus. His left foot, however, is planted in the sand, giving him total stability.

▲ At the 12 o'clock point, Mola's thumb comes off the spool and the line is free to run out. He still has his gaze fixed firmly on the bait's entry point.

▲ ▶ The bait is well on its way and the rod is moving down towards its final angle. Still Mola is watching the bait in flight, and his thumb is just above the reel's madly spinning spool, ready to clamp down as soon as the bait hits the water…

▶ …which it is doing exactly now. The cast has come to an end and you can see Mola still watching those very last stages. His thumb is now clamped down on the spool and he's about to turn the handle to re-engage the reel. Fishing can now begin.

AN INCOMPARABLE MAHSEER FISHERMAN

Subhan is one of the greatest Indian mahseer guides in history. His understanding of the river and the fish is second to none, and he has a serious list of big fish to his credit. However, it's in the fight that Subhan really proves his worth. He has endless tricks to beguile fish out of snags, and he'll even dive to free a fish if it's wound the line around underwater rocks or sunken trees.

Bite Detection

Not every fish drags the rod from your hand when it takes the bait. Takes to fly especially, but bait and lure as well, can be infinitely gentle, and therefore easily missed. This can be because the fish are educated and are wary of our bait, our tackle or our approach, but sometimes fish are merely curious and not particularly hungry, and they simply pick up a bait to sample it rather than wanting to eat it. Sometimes fish are feeding ravenously on tiny, plentiful food items, and if your bait is one of these they will simply sip it in and carry on eating without giving any real indication of a bite whatsoever.

▲ *Getting close*
Here you see me fishing a European river in the height of summer. This is a great spot – trees overhanging and quick, well-oxygenated water. I'm taking care to get as close to the fish as possible so I can actually see a take on the line or visually in the water.

▼ *The thrill of the chase*
In the photograph on the left, a large carp is on the point of taking a surface bait. Now is the time to still your beating heart! In the right-hand photograph, Andy Murray is on the verge of tempting a big surface-feeding tarpon into taking his fly. One of the more exciting moments in fishing.

Missed Takes
The long and the short of it is that if you're not catching fish, perhaps you're getting the bites and not knowing about them. Years ago, a friend of mine ran a large, crystal clear commercial trout fishery. He spent all day watching the anglers on his water and he came to form many considered opinions about their abilities. One of the most certain of these was that ninety-five per cent of takes from those trout were missed and generally not even registered!

Eye Witness
The best and simplest way of knowing if you have a bite or not is to actually see the fish take your offering. If the water you're fishing is clear, reasonably shallow and you're not fishing at too vast a distance, then devote a great deal of care and time to engineering a situation where you can actually see what is going on. If you're fly fishing or lure fishing, you might decide to target a single fish or a group of fish and try them with offering after

offering until you get them to accept. You might have to try several different patterns and as many different types of retrieve, but the chances are that in the end a fish will make a mistake – and you'll see it! If you're bait fishing, then you might consider putting out some free offerings in a zone of water where visibility is good. Wait until fish move in and start feeding, and then carefully introduce your hook bait. Watch it closely because as fish begin to feed heavily they can stir up the bottom and cloud that visibility. Watching fish at close quarters take bait, fly or lure is infinitely thrilling, so be careful not to strike prematurely. It's all too easy to pull a bait from a fish's mouth in the excitement of the situation when the adrenalin is really pumping.

Circumstantial Evidence
Of course, actually seeing the fish take your offering is not always as simple as you'd think. In an ideal world you would see the fish approach, open its mouth, take the bait

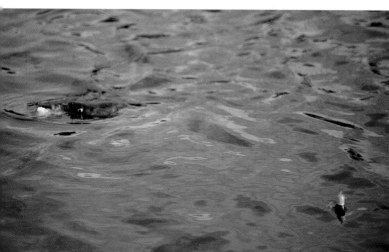

and whoosh, you're playing it, but it's not always like that. Say you're fishing a tiny fly five feet down in quickly moving water for a big grayling. You can just about make out the fish and you just about know where your fly is, but you're never going to watch it disappear. Instead, you have to gauge where your fly is and watch the body language of the fish. For example, if the grayling suddenly moves six inches right, left, up or down then it's a safe assumption it is intercepting something in the current – and that something might be your fly.

If you're trout fishing in a similar situation you will often see just a gleam of white as the trout opens its mouth. Again, something is being sipped from the current and it could be your fly. Sometimes the mere flash of a fish turning in the current to take a bait can be enough, or you might see a fish suddenly drop backwards as it reaches for something sweeping past it. So, you see, a real skill is emerging here. You've got to learn how to see the fish and also how to interpret its body language.

Distant Clues

If you can't actually see the fish or the bait, then you've got to learn to identify the take itself, and by that I mean the moment a bait, a lure or a fly has been consumed. Again, in theory, this should be easy: a float should dive under, a rod tip should wrench round or line should fly off the spool. In the real world, takes can frequently be infinitesimal. A line may merely tighten, or fall momentarily slack, or merely hesitate for a millisecond in the current. A float can just tremble and then remain still again. Even when you're lure fish-

ing, don't always expect huge crash-bang-wallop takes. Sometimes you might just feel the smallest peck on the lure or a slight drag as though it is pulling through weed. The important thing is to learn to use your eyes and recognize anything, any clue at all, that indicates something out of the ordinary is happening at the business end of your line.

Staying Connected

If you need to work on what your eyes are telling you, so too must you improve your sense of touch. You'll soon be reading about touch legering (see page 160), which is all about tactile fishing, but there's more to it. Let's suppose you are nymph fishing on a large reservoir, inching an artificial fly back close to the bottom. A trout can suck in that fly and blow it out again in a fraction of a second, and all you'll feel is the most delicate of touches – and probably not even that if there is any bow or slack in the line between you and the fish.

One of the most exciting examples of this in my fishing life is out in India, hunting the mighty mahseer. These fish can easily grow to over a 100 pounds in weight, and they live in the most volcanic of churning waters, and yet, despite their size, they can still pick up a piece of paste or a dead fish so gently you can barely believe it is happening. You simply feel the line tighten for perhaps two seconds and then drop back slack again. There's no pull really, certainly not a tug, but just a gentle feeling that something is alive out there. So, just as you must learn to use your eyes, you must begin to trust your fingers and develop your understanding of the messages that they are sending to your brain.

▲ *A Spanish maestro*
Raffa is edging his plastic lizard imitation along the rocky bottom of a Spanish reservoir. He can feel a big bass taking an interest. Now he's trying to excite its curiosity and stimulate its hunger.

▼ *Two approaches*
Sometimes it pays to be relaxed, take your time and to let events take their course. At other moments, however, you've got to be more proactive – become the hungry hunter.

Fighting The Fish

▼ Piling on the side strain

A big fish is running strongly for a snag, and if you're not going to lose it, instant action is called for. Clamp down on the reel and throw the rod down to the side in a decisive effort to turn the fish's head and manoeuvre it from danger.

Make no mistake, fighting a big fish, especially in a current, is a true skill in itself, and consistent success is largely a matter of experience. A successful outcome to the battle is essential both for your sake and for the fish's. The chances are that you've put time, effort, thought and money into this hook-up and you don't want to mess things up now. As for the fish, you owe it big-time to land it, remove the hook and release it with the minimum of fuss and trauma. For these reasons, take the fight seriously, in fact more seriously than any other aspect of your fishing. Here are some basic considerations.

Check Your Tackle

Make sure your tackle and knots are all up to the job in hand. Don't be tempted to fish too light in any situation. You might hoodwink a fish more easily with light line, but what's the point if you're not going to land it? Check and recheck all knots. Double check your hook for sharpness, and be particularly wary of a curled-over hook point. Check your line frequently for any signs of wear or abrasion. If you hook a big fish and the fight is a tough one then it pays to change your line altogether. Make sure your spool has enough line on it or, if you are fly fishing, that you have adequate backing.

Think Ahead

Always have a plan of action if you're about to strike into a big fish in challenging circumstances. Think what the fish might do when it's first hooked and think of a strategy to counter this. Make a strong mental note of any potentially lethal snags and have a clear idea in your mind of where you're eventually going to land your fish.

Consider your fighting technique. Don't let a fish work up pace, because it will be far more difficult to stop. The key is to be bold in the first stages of a fight and impose your will quickly on the situation. Try to pull the fish off balance. Once hooked, swing it away from weed and submerged branches.

Make sure the clutch on your reel is set at exactly the right tension. Ideally, it should

KEEPING UP THE PRESSURE
This shot shows a fantastic reel hard at work. Notice the big drag adjuster knob on the right-hand side of the reel that's sensitive and very easy to use. Also, see how large the arbor (or spool) of the reel is. This loads the line in large coils so that it has less memory as it is cast through the rings of the rod. You can also load line back on it more easily during a fight as a fish begins to tire.

yield line under a pressure that is just beneath the breaking strain of the line. You don't want to give line too easily, because you want to wear the fish out quickly, but be wary of a screwed-down clutch that won't yield line at all and causes it to break. Ensure the balance is right before the hook-up.

Steer the Fish

Side strain is an important technique in fighting fish. The concept involves moving the rod either right or left, parallel to the water's surface to pull a fish off a potentially dangerous course leading it into snags. Go on. Pile on the pressure. You'll be amazed how tough your gear is and it's far better to take control now than it is to let a fish get into a snag.

Pumping is one of the essential arts of playing a very big fish. Start with the rod tip close to the water's surface and then gently and steadily lift the rod almost to the vertical, pulling the fish up towards you through the water. Then lower the rod tip once again towards the water's surface: the tension on the line is released and you can reel in quickly and rhythmically before repeating the process again and again. Of course, there will be times when you have to pause because the fish powers away, but a steady pumping motion is by far the quickest way to land a big fish.

Big fish can frequently be walked away from a potential hazard, providing they are not alarmed. In the very early stages of a

▼ Easy does it
This stage of the fight is one of the most crucial ones. The fish is coming close, and the water is crystal clear. It still has energy enough to boil on the surface and a last, serious run could test a weak tippet critically. Notice how I'm crouching down so that the fish sees less of my profile.

▲ *Letting her run*
The intensity of the battle.
Look at how Ian is control-
ling the spool of the reel
with his fingers and how
much pressure he is putting
on the rod. Too many
anglers go too softly with a
hooked fish.

▼ *Beaten at last*
It's when you think the fish
is yours that things can go
wrong. Big carp (left) and
barbel (right), can still make
a final break for freedom.

fight a fish may not even realize it is hooked. Keep the rod high, maintain a gentle pressure and physically walk the fish away from a waterfall, rocks, sunken trees or any other potential snag. It's often possible to lead a fish many yards like this – even for a couple

HANDLINING
If a big fish buries itself in weed, then try hand-lining. Point the rod directly down the line towards the fish and tighten up as much as you can. Then grasp the line between the reel and the butt ring and pull backwards and forwards in a sawing motion. This can gradually work the fish loose and back into open water.

of minutes – until you've manoeuvred it into open, trouble-free water.

Landing and Unhooking
The fish is tiring and it's time to think about landing it. This is another crucial moment, with the possibility of a potentially damaging last run when the fish sees the net or you, the angler. Make sure your rod is held high and your clutch is properly set for this moment in the fight. If you are using a landing net, make sure it's a large one and that it's already in the water waiting for the fish to be drawn over it. Bring the fish to the net: if you chase a fish with the net you will only panic it into another run. If the fish is big, once it is in the net put down the rod and take hold of the net's frame with both hands. Then simply lift the fish into the shallow margins or onto an unhooking mat.

Ask yourself whether you always need a net, which can in extreme circumstances dislodge scales or even tear fins. If you are wading, for example, it's comparatively easy to draw a fish to you, hold it in the water and slip the hook out. It can be held for a second above the water's surface if a fellow angler wants to take your photograph.

Always ensure that you have adequate unhooking tools. Forceps will usually be enough, but if you're fishing for predators and using treble hooks you might need pliers for a more secure grip. Always have your forceps to hand, and make sure they are

BRAID OR MONOFILAMENT?

There's no doubt that modern braids offer huge advantages in terms of strength, limpness and load diameter. This makes them very useful alternatives in many fishing situations. However, if you are pursuing fish that fight deep and the water is full of rocks and snags, then treat braid with great caution. The problem is that if braid gets round a rock, severe pressure quickly frays it, leading to an inevitable break-off. Modern monofilament, by contrast, is much more abrasion resistant and should, therefore, be the choice in snaggy conditions.

long-nosed in case the hook is deep. Consider using either a barbless or a micro-barbed hook: these may not be adequate for all situations, but they are much easier to slip from the fish's mouth and, consequently, they inflict less damage.

▲ *Caring for the catch*
If at all possible, net your fish and unhook it in the water so you never need to bring it into the air at all.

▶ *Love your bass*
It's important to minimize the amount of time that bass have to spend outside of their natural environment. Admire your fish, then return it promptly to the water.

▼ *A helping hand*
Mitch is helping Ian land his first ever big carp. He's positioning the rod against Ian's forearms to provide a better grip and more leverage.

Expeditions At Home And Abroad

The majority of fishing sessions are probably only a few hours in length, but the highlight of anyone's fishing life is either the weekend expedition or, even more thrilling, a long trip abroad. Both call for specialized preparations.

▲ **The inner man**
When the excitement of fishing gets its grip on you, it's easy to overlook your diet. On gruelling trips especially, you need to eat well in order to replenish lost energy.

▼ **Tackle and bait**
Make sure you have all the tackle and bait you'll need before you set off on your expedition. Replacements can be elusive and expensive.

A Weekend by the Water

Even though you may be only a few miles from home, it still makes good sense to check everything out thoroughly before you set off, because the waterside can be a lonely place in the middle of the night if things are going against you. Weather forecasts are essential. You're planning to fish fairly close to home and you can go anytime, so it makes sense to choose favourable weather conditions. Even in summer, nights can be cold when it's pouring with rain or there's a strong wind. Thunderstorms can be particularly disruptive. Delay the trip if the weather is going to spoil things.

Ensure you have adequate shelter, bedding and clothing – that invariably cold period before dawn will catch you out otherwise. Don't allow yourself to become hungry or, worse, dehydrated. If you're not comfortable, you won't fish to your maximum ability

and you'll probably cut the whole trip short. Creature comforts are more than just a luxury – they're essential.

Check and double check all your tackle and bait. There is nothing more annoying than setting up for a two-day session only to find you've forgotten something crucial. That doesn't just mean the big stuff – crucial things can include less obvious necessities such as sun block, insect lotion and torches. Ensure your mobile phone is fully charged in case you need to make an emergency call.

The Big Foreign Trip

If you're going abroad – with all the investment of time, effort and funds that that involves – this may be the angling experience of your life, so get it right. Do your research meticulously. Make sure that you're going at absolutely the right time of the year for your chosen water and quarry. Getting this wrong can prove disastrous.

For your first serious expeditions, I would definitely recommend going with a professional outfitter who will provide the transport, accommodation, permissions, guides, boats and everything that the inexperienced person is likely to overlook. However, there are good and bad outfitters, so don't rush to the first one that pops up on the internet. Phone as many as you like, ask them all the same questions and compare their replies. Remember that the cheapest isn't necessarily the worst and nor is the most expensive always the best. Ask to be put in touch with people who have been on the trip in the past, and see what they have to say.

▶ **Into the unknown**

Rob stands here on the lip of paradise: miles and miles of river previously unfished, virgin water enough to excite even the most adventurous of anglers.

Fishing Tackle

Ensure you know the exact methods and gear that the trip will demand. To go with inadequate tackle makes no sense whatsoever. You're forking out a lot of money for the expedition in the first place, so don't ruin your chances by cutting corners. Remember that most of these trips will be way into the wilderness where there's little chance of stocking up on gear. Take more than you think you're going to need, especially line, hooks and flies, all of which can easily become trashed.

It's never more important to get your clothing right than on big trips abroad. If you're too hot, cold or wet for days on end, your pleasure will be completely ruined. The ultra-modern, lightweight materials are a breeze to wash, so you only need two sets of kit along with some socks and a supply of underwear. If the weather is going to be cold, pack a couple of sets of thermals to wear underneath. Make sure you've got a totally waterproof shell as well, and also something warm and snug for your head, from which most of your body heat escapes. If you're going somewhere really cold and need a sleeping bag, be sure to buy the best.

Be Prepared

It may be stating the obvious, but ensure your passport is well in date, that you have a visa if it's needed and that you receive all the necessary injections. Don't get neurotic about the latter, however: stick to what your doctor recommends and don't come out looking like a colander. Ensure your cards have plenty of credit available: you can never be absolutely sure what lies in store. Check that your travel insurance is up to date, covers the area you are travelling to and extends beyond your expected return date. Take more money with you than you think you're

CHECKLIST
- Loo paper – many airports in the developing world run precariously short!
- You can always do with strong tape to wrap round rod tubes or luggage, or to coil round a small torch so that you can hold it between your teeth.
- A small pair of sharp scissors can often cut through things a knife can't.
- A good, piercing whistle is a real boon in a tight spot when you need help.
- It's a good idea to have a dental check-up before leaving, but a small phial of clove oil could save you from many a sleepless night.
- Don't forget pens for children if you're visiting a less developed country – much better than sweets and probably more appreciated.
- It's not a bad idea to know at least a few words of the local language. Even just 'please' and 'thank you' said with a smile will put you in pole position!
- Never forget Deet or a similar insect repellent, a head net and perhaps even mosquito coils. Take your malaria tablets as instructed if you're going to an infected area. I've had malaria and it ain't funny!

going to need and hide it carefully in various pockets about your person. A good strong money belt strapped to the chest is a sensible investment if you're visiting any of the more dangerous parts of Africa, Asia or South America. And be sure to take plenty of small bills, because change isn't always readily given.

Hints and Tips for the Big Trip

Take care of yourself physically. Any accident or ill health can ruin things for others as well as yourself. Drink several pints of water everyday. Always go for mineral water – fizzy is best because you can tell if the top has been tampered with. In camp, make sure that the water is boiled, and add some flavoured vitamin-enriched powders to make the taste more acceptable. In most countries you should avoid ice in drinks like the plague (which it may be!). The same goes for ice-cream. Don't let your guard down when you get back to a city and a hotel: camp food is often plainer, simpler and more hygienically prepared than it is in the kitchens of a big city restaurant.

In tropical climes, make it a habit to shake your boots out each morning in case any creatures have set up shop, and don't go near scorpions, snakes or other nasties. If you do get ill or stung, don't panic, and be prepared to take local medication and advice.

Allow yourself plenty of time for transfers to airports: if it can go wrong, then it probably will. Because of this potential annoyance, work on your patience levels. You may find your patience tested at airports, at hotel check-ins, and in camps with guides who come from different cultures and have looser schedules and unfathomable – or so it may seem – timetables.

▲ *A jewel from the Caspian*
My great Danish friend, Johnny Jensen, cradles an enormous beluga sturgeon weighing well in excess of 250 pounds.

◀ *Time for tea*
A brewing Kelly-kettle makes for a great break from the intensity of fishing.

Try not to moan, however tough conditions become. You will only demoralize yourself and those around you. Look on the bright side and you will soon see the beauty around you. If you're homesick, don't be. You will be home soon enough, and by the time the bills are opened, the chores are sorted and your work has begun again, you'll no doubt be wondering why you ever longed for a return to your old humdrum routine.

When you come home, give your body some time to readjust. Your sleep patterns will be disrupted, so don't worry if you wake up at 4am every morning for a week – your body will recalibrate. Take care with food, though, and give your stomach a chance. Don't gorge on your favourite, rich meals for a while if all you've been used to for weeks is plain rice.

▲ *You naughty monkey*
Monkeys may seem fun, but they can wreak havoc in a camp. Make sure your tents are zipped up, and leave nothing outside that can be stolen.

▶ *Alone with his thoughts*
This is how every true angler likes to imagine himself: endless miles from the maddening crowd.

Night Fishing

To be a true, all-round angler you simply have to take on board the concept of night fishing. There are certain species that feed predominantly at night, most notably, perhaps, sea trout. Many other species are likewise more confident once dusk pulls in, especially on pressured waters.

The time of year also plays a big part. In the warm months particularly, daytime temperatures can be too high for fish to feed comfortably, and it's often only as temperatures begin to drop after nightfall that they begin to look for food. Even in winter, night fishing can be the most productive time for species such as roach, barbel or chub.

On the sea, too, the night is an important time, and there can be good winter fishing off the beach for cod and whiting or, in the summer, for bass and sea trout in the surf.

Be Prepared

Remember that, even in summer, temperatures at night can fall quickly, and it can become very cold, especially just before dawn. Make sure your clothing is adequate: you can always take clothes off but you can't put them on if you've left them at home.

Ensure that you have enough food with you, and especially a flask of soup or coffee. This can be comforting in the wee hours, and gives you a much needed energy boost.

You must also ensure you have an adequate light source. My preference is for a large, powerful torch for emergencies and a smaller, dimmer light for tying on hooks, baiting up and other chores that demand complete vision. But be disciplined with the use of torches. Use them as little as you can and learn to depend on your night vision.

Plan Ahead

For your first night trips, it's best to stick with waters that are familiar to you so that you have a good overall mental plan of the banks and the water features. Waters are very different at night, so any familiarity is a benefit. It's also a great help if your first trips are with a friend, especially one with night fishing experience. You'll find both the experience and the company reassuring. Furthermore, it's a good idea to choose nights for which good weather is forecast for your first trips. It also makes sense to begin your night fishing career when there will be a decent moon.

Visit the venue during the day and make mental notes of where you will be fishing after darkness. Check out the banks, steep drop-offs, fences, trees, snags – anything that could prove dangerous or hamper your fishing.

Bait Fishing

One of the major considerations with bait fishing is ensuring your bait is cast into the area in which you want it. Line up features on the opposite bank to get angles right. Trees or tall buildings stand out against the darkest night sky, and give you a target at which to aim.

▼ *As the night begins to settle*

The three anglers here, making the most of the falling light, all know full well that fish will soon be coming onto the feed. Both on the seas and on freshwaters the pattern is the same once temperatures and light values begin to fall.

Now that you've got your angles right, you need to get the correct distance, so cast to your chosen area in the daylight. Once you've positioned the bait exactly, either tape the spool or clip the line so that the required distance is guaranteed for every cast.

Make your life simpler by strapping white or reflective tape on items such as the landing net handle and the unhooking mat. In the heat of night action you don't want to be fumbling around, and turning on a torch can scare that big fish when it's close to the bank. Also, keep everything in its right place so you can find it fast when things get hectic.

Don't Neglect the Margins

In modern-day bait fishing there is an obsession with casting to the horizon. It's true that many big fish are caught at the 100-yards-plus range, but carp and tench also love to feed around the margins, especially at night, when they are often looking for leftovers deposited by daytime anglers. It's a good idea to take an unsliced, white loaf with you and, once darkness has fallen, scatter 20 to 30 small pieces around the margins.

Have a rod ready. Reel, rod, line and an unweighted large hook are all you need. Flick out a piece of crust into the general area of the disturbance and wait for the line to run out. Don't be in too much of a hurry to strike and, when you do, use a slow, controlled, steady lift. Anything wild or panicky can result in a break-off on a big fish close in.

Fly Fishing

Begin your nocturnal fly-fishing adventures on open water: trees will often ruin the cast. They also block out the light from the night sky and make everything darker still.

If you're wading, be very careful – for your safety's sake and for the good of your fishing. Wild fish are particularly sensitive to disturbances at night.

Don't be too ambitious to begin with – make your casts short and precise. Learn to use your ears, and this way you'll hear any rises and be able to pinpoint them. You'll also begin to gauge where your line and fly are lying in the water.

If you have the choice, cast towards the west for the first part of the night, especially if you're out on a boat. You'll find the afterglow of the sunset helps to silhouette the rise of a taking fish. If you're out very late, end the night by fishing towards the east to benefit from the first of the dawn light.

Sea Trout

Don't start too early on a sea-trout pool; wait until darkness has firmly settled. This way, you won't spook any jittery fish and you'll be casting to trout that are confident. Equally, don't give up too early in the night. There can be a dead period after midnight until around 1.30 or 2 o'clock in the morning. Things can be brisk again from then until dawn, when often the biggest fish come out. Sunrise also gives you a third bite of the cherry – the period that the great sea-trout fisherman Hugh Falkus used to call 'extra time'. You also stand the chance of an early morning salmon if you're prepared to delay your breakfast.

On a well-stocked sea-trout river, try to stick to a single pool all night long. There'll be fish coming in as the night progresses, and the less you move around the river, the fewer disturbances you create. Also, the more you fish a pool, the more you get to know it.

▼ **By lake, river and seashore**
Sea trout (middle photograph) almost always move once true darkness has fallen. Geiri (right-hand photograph) knows this only too well, and is making the best use of the short Arctic night. In the left-hand photograph, a fisherman waits for the carp to begin their feeding.

Care For The Fish

Good anglers love their fish and always want to do their best by them, and this is an important part of the sport. Angling is now very much in the public eye, and we are always being judged by how we behave and by how we treat our catch. Looking after our fish is a real skill in itself and is absolutely central to what we do. Think very carefully indeed about every aspect of fish welfare and you'll be well on your way to becoming a better and more compassionate angler.

▲ *A jewel of the seas*
Notice how carefully Juan is holding this juvenile sea bass. Bass can take up to twelve years to reach five pounds in weight. It is essential that any bass, particularly undersized specimens, are returned as quickly and carefully as possible.

▼ *Caring for the pike*
Pike look mean, but they're actually as vulnerable as any fish. When fishing for pike, use a barbless hook if possible, as these are much kinder to the fish.

Be Fair

Before you even put a bait in the water, just remind yourself that every element of your tackle must be up to the job in hand. A weak knot, frayed line or inadequate reel could result in a breakage and a hook left in a fish. Equally, are you absolutely sure that you stand a good chance of extracting a fish from the water where you are actually placing your fly, bait or lure? If the snags and potential hazards look just too serious, then give the fish a break and move on to an easier area. There's no point in hooking a fish that is bound to break you in seconds, and a hooked and tangled fish can easily remain tethered to a large underwater obstruction and literally starve to death.

Fish for the Table

During your angling career, at times you're very likely to want to eat your catch. After all, this is the most fundamental reason for fishing. The act of taking a fish as food for your family is a noble one – and an ethical one when compared with the abuses that are so common in the production of poultry and cattle. A quick, decisive blow to the back of a fish's head with a properly weighted and balanced priest means that death is absolutely instant and painless. Again, this compares well to the poor fishy souls dredged up by trawlers, left to virtually suffocate and then thrown into freezers, sometimes still alive.

Obviously you should not take rare fish, threatened fish or immature fish, and don't take more fish than you need at any particular moment. There's no sadder sight than a freezer jammed full with the frosted remnants of last season's catch.

1 Always try to unhook a pike in the water if you possibly can.

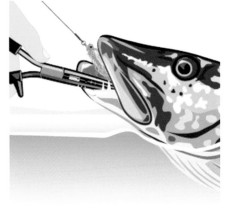

2 When removing the hook, ensure that you have long, strong pliers, so that your fingers stay away from any sharp teeth.

3 If possible, fish for pike using single hooks, as they're much more easily extracted than trebles.

Handling the Fish

So, let's say that the catch is to be returned. Whenever possible, unhook a fish in the water without taking it onto the bank. You will have a pair of forceps and you will be using a barbless or semi-barbed hook so that removal is instant and easy. This way the fish doesn't have to be touched or lifted out of its own environment – it is that emergence into the air that fish really don't like.

Unhooking fish in the water like this is easy if you are wading or if the banks are safe and the margins are shallow, but this is not always the case. If a fish needs to be netted, ensure that the net is large, that the mesh is soft and that the design of the mesh is modern and won't catch the sensitive rays of the fish's fins. Once a fish is lifted from the water, place it on something soft and damp – thick moist grass, a bed of water weeds or a purpose-built unhooking mat.

Don't let a fish flap around – sometimes a wet cloth over the eyes is a good way to calm it down. Handle the fish as little as possible, and always make sure that your hands are thoroughly wet, especially in hot conditions.

Weighing – if You Must

It is imperative that you get the fish back into the water as soon as you can do so. There are occasions, however, when you might want to weigh a fish. Perhaps it is a personal best, a fish that means something special to you. Perhaps it could be a record, either for the water or even nationally. Perhaps you are part of a scientific survey. All are acceptable reasons to weigh a fish, but make sure that you do it in a correct and caring fashion. Always weigh a fish in a wetted, soft sling that is big and strong enough for the fish in question. There is nothing more damaging than a large fish falling out of an undersized sling. Preset the scales before putting the fish into the sling so time out of the water is reduced. Try to do the job with close friends. More hands make for quicker work, and it's not a bad idea to rehearse the routine with a log or a stone so the operation with a fish will go as smoothly as possible.

A Photographic Record

Many of the same comments are applicable to photographing a fish. Have all your equipment ready to take a photo. Don't mess with flash guns and apertures with the fish out of the water – make sure all that is done beforehand. If you must hold the fish for a trophy shot, support it as completely as possible. Make sure that its stomach isn't distended or straining unnaturally. Put as little pressure as possible on the fish's bone structure. Bear in mind that all the fish's natural life is spent supported by water, and once it is out of its environment it loses this cushioning effect.

▲ *Easy does it*
Grayling are very difficult to unhook. They writhe when held, so, if possible, slip a barbless hook from their lips while they lie in the shallows.

▼ *The moment of truth*
A big fish is hoisted onto the scales. The fish is safely cradled in a big sack so that it can't fall out. It is wet and dark inside the sack, keeping trauma to a minimum.

▲ **Fair to the fish**
Held just above the weeds, only inches from its natural environment, this barbel poses for a quick photograph before being released.

▼ **Signs of health**
A vigorous aquatic environment is home to strong fish populations, plentiful weed, diverse insect life and, my own favourite, the newt.

My own favourite photographs are not trophy shots at all. I much prefer to lay fish in shallow water or on weeds and water flowers in the margins. The advantages of this approach are enormous: most obviously, the fish suffers much less harm this way and that's the important thing, but also the fish takes centre stage and it's the beauty of the catch that attracts the eye. There will also be other important 'props' in the picture that are all part of the story – the type of water weed or flowers, the fly or lure and general tackle used. What this creates is an overall picture of the day, and a photograph like this doesn't require my ugly mug in it to be truly complete!

Careful Release

Once a fish is ready to be returned, support it against the current in shallow water where the pace isn't too quick. Hold the fish there for as long as it takes for it to recover. In warm conditions, when a fish has fought hard, and especially if it's been weighed and photographed, this may take many minutes. Don't lose patience. You have inflicted this discomfort on the fish and it's up to you now to look after it to the best of your ability. Too many fish appear to have revived, only to

turn over once they are out of sight, often in deep, powerful water that they're not yet equipped to combat. Wait until you are absolutely sure the fish is ready before letting it swim away.

The Broader Picture

Care of fish is more than simply looking after something that's taken the offering on your hook. As anglers, it is up to us to watch the aquatic environment and protect it from pressure. On a simple level, removing litter, watching out for pollution and reporting any suspicious incidents to the relevant authorities are things we should all do. On a wider level, it's part of our duty to attend work parties, if we can, that replace gravel riffles, plant willows and generally benefit the whole of the aquatic environment. Remember that improving the water like this doesn't just help our own fishing, but it also helps all waterside wildlife. In the UK, for example, members of the Salmon and Trout Association, the Wild Trout Trust and the Anglers' Conservation Association all show concern and commitment for healthier water courses. Our care for fish shouldn't just stop with a day on the bankside.

Tackle Choices

Let's end this section with a few questions that we can ask ourselves. First of all, do we really need to use treble hooks when often singles will do? As we have seen, singles are much easier to remove from a predator's jaw and cause much less damage.

Secondly, are we waiting too long to strike, just to be sure of hooking the fish? Always strike as quickly as possible when using a bait, for the longer you delay, the more deeply a fish is likely to take it and the more potential damage will be involved in the unhooking process.

Thirdly, is our bait fishing rig totally safe for the fish? This is especially important when carp fishing with modern techniques. If the line breaks, is the hooked fish going to be left towing a large lead weight around the lake, or have we made sure that the weakest link is as close to the hook as possible?

Notice how I haven't even mentioned the use of keep nets in this particular section. While I accept they have a place in the match scene, for general angling I find them almost impossible to justify. I'll leave that one with you for now.

▲ *Back to the stream*
If there is one thing that fish don't like, it is being taken from the water to be weighed and photographed. Bringing a fish into the air only increases the stress of being captured.

▶ ▲ *Careful release*
Before you let a fish go in the current, make absolutely sure that it is strong enough to remain upright and cope with the flow. If it falls on its side, then it will be very vulnerable. If necessary, you will have to wade out, recapture it and hold it again until its strength returns.

▶ *Gaining strength*
Big Indian mahseer fight until they're exhausted. By putting them on a stringer, they can be tethered for an hour or so until their strength returns completely. Only then is it safe to slip them free.

Chapter Two

The Tackle

Many anglers place too much confidence in their tackle, thinking that all they have to do is buy the right rod and success will be guaranteed. Far from it. The skill is in choosing the right tackle for the job in hand. The focus of your attention should be the fish and your strategy, but the tackle is there to help you in your approach, and should be as effective as possible. So choose the best tackle you can afford, and then concentrate on applying your angling skills.

Tackle – An Introduction

Tens of thousands of years ago, our hunter-gatherer ancestors regarded fish simply as an aid to their survival. I don't know if you could call what they used then tackle: methods were crude but effective – rocks aimed at the skulls of salmon lying in ankle-deep water, spears, bows and arrows, primitive poisons, harpoons, dams to drain off water – any way would do. Around 15,000 years ago, the first crudely fashioned fish hooks began to appear, made from bone or flint. Then, a mere 2,000 years ago, rods and reels started to be used in areas of China and Macedonia. They were, however, a far cry from the light, beautiful and efficient gear that we demand today.

Pleasure Above Efficiency

In my journeys around some of the wilder parts of the planet I still frequently see tackle in use that would not have been out of place thousands of years ago. In many areas of the world, fish – and big fish at that – are still caught on hand lines made from wood and twine. I've seen many reels used that are no more than sticks with line wrapped round them. I've seen many different types of net employed and even cormorants trained to dive, catch fish and bring them back alive to their fishermen owners.

We, in the developed world, are fortunate. Few, if any, of us need to catch our fish to survive in an age when there is a supermarket on every corner. We fish for fun, as a sport only, and this is how tackle comes to play its central part. We demand more than simple efficiency. Today, the right tackle does not just do a satisfactory job but it makes that job satisfying. If you use nice gear, gear that is perfect for the fishing situation in hand, the pleasure of the whole experience is greatly enhanced. If you are always struggling with your tackle, then concentration is broken and there is no time to immerse yourself in the more important aspects of the sport. You know your tackle is right when it is so much a part of you that you are using it subconsciously, almost totally oblivious to its existence, treating it just like an extra limb.

Decisions, Decisions

How do you know how to choose the right gear? A first trip to a tackle shop can be a totally confusing experience. Today there are so many companies making so many different items of tackle that even an expert often has difficulty coming to the right decision.

Generally, there are three key questions that you need to consider. What types of water will you be fishing most? What species of fish will you generally be pursuing? And what methods will you want to use to catch them? Ideally, you need a tackle dealer that is welcoming, takes time with you and is generous with advice. It's also a good idea to go to a large tackle dealer: the chances are

▼ *A lure angler's selection*

There's a bit of everything here – a couple of plugs, a jerk bait, a mouse pattern and a couple of rubber fish. They're all exciting to use, and demand different techniques. The skill is knowing exactly what every lure in your box will do for you – how deep it will work, the violence of its action and the best way to work it on the retrieve.

that he deals with many different companies, won't be biased and won't be pushing you towards a brand or product that is not necessarily the right one for you.

Do Some Research

It pays to do your homework. Ask advice from fellow anglers on the bank. Look at each item of tackle and ask their views on it. While people might be coy about giving away their fishing secrets, most of them will want to brag about the gear that they are using.

Buy relevant fishing magazines. All of them contain reviews on the best gear to buy. These tend to be relatively unbiased and will point you in the right direction.

Go to tackle shows and country fairs. Here you will find many of the major companies on show. It's a perfect opportunity to talk with their representatives and gather their views. Gradually, you will become totally clear in your mind about what you need, and you won't get talked into buying what you don't want.

Quality and Choice

It's never a good idea to wildly exceed your budget, but in the case of fishing tackle, as with many things in life, you tend to get what you pay for. Don't cut too many corners or you will find yourself with tackle that is unpleasant to use and that could let you down at the crucial moment.

The good news is that fishing tackle now is almost always of a standard we could not have believed even 20 years ago. Rods are lighter and more positive than ever. Reels are smoother and have clutches that actually work. Line is thinner, stronger, more abrasion-resistant and with less memory. Fly lines float better, cast better and sink faster. Hooks are lighter and stronger. The choice of lures is infinitely broader and there's always something new to try. Even clothing has now progressed beyond all recognition: today, you can fish in the freezing cold and remain warm, in the pouring rain and stay dry or in the gruelling heat and keep your cool.

All in all, it's a great time to become an angler.

▲ *Give yourself options*
It doesn't matter if you're a float fisherman or a fly fisherman; don't restrict yourself to just a few flies or floats. To a degree, the more flies or floats you have in your box, the more likely you are to find the killing pattern on any given day.

▼ *Travelling light*
Rebecca knows the advantage of travelling light: it means she can be mobile throughout the day without becoming tired.

Fly Fishing Tackle

Of all the different types of fishing tackle, it's most important to get your fly gear correct. Above all, you're looking for balance. Your rod and reel should complement each other, and the line weight should make both work to perfection. Don't rush into making a decision when purchasing gear. Seek out advice and read product reviews.

▲ *Tackle galore*
Lovely fishing tackle is a joy to behold and to use. You won't need a battery of rods like this, but remember that different rods play different roles. Similarly, certain rod actions can make a huge difference in the distance you cast, and different lines on different reels will allow you to fish at a variety of depths.

▶ *Flies big and small*
This selection of poppers (left) and streamers (right) are perfect for big bold predators.

Choosing a Fly Rod

An old wag of a fishing writer once said that choosing a fly rod was much like choosing a wife – you hoped to stick with both for life. Although times have changed – both socially and piscatorially – a good fly rod is still a big investment and you should choose carefully.

Choose a reputable make, preferably from a company that offers a lifetime guarantee, because rods do have a habit of breaking, either in action or in a car door! Choose, also, a rod that is cosmetically pleasing: you'll be spending a long time together. Consider how the rod feels. Are you happy holding it? Does it seem light enough? Is it responsive enough? If at all possible, try the rod in action or on a casting pool if one is available, and do make sure the rod is the right length and weight for the job that you have in mind for it. There's no point in buying a light 3-weight outfit if you're going to spend your time fishing for sea trout!

The Four Major Rod Actions

Most rods, especially for trout fishing, come in four major actions:

• An ultra tip is an extremely fast action rod. By fast action, we mean that it will return very quickly to its original position. Rods like this are ideal for the more experienced caster and are excellent for distance casting, but they require power and precision timing and they are not the best bet for the relatively inexperienced.

• A tip action rod is still fast, still good for long distances, but just a little more forgiving of mistakes.

• A middle to tip action rod is more forgiving still and, while it can cope with distance casting, it's also happy at short to medium range. This rod is the ideal all-rounder, perfect also for the beginner.

• A middle to butt action rod is a slower action rod that recovers less quickly after it's been bent. The rod flexes closer to the butt

rather than to the tip. Rods like this are ideal for delicate presentation at shorter distances. This type of rod also encourages slower casting of a short line when you are targeting a rising fish… in other words, it's a really good river rod.

Choosing a Double-handed Rod

Coming fresh to the world of double-handed rods, there's probably a whole array of questions in your head. Which length? Which model? Do you even need to go double-handed at all? First, let's have a look at the question of length.

A 12-foot double-hander is ideal for smaller spate rivers. It will take an 8-weight line – exactly what you should be using for grilse, steelhead and heavier sea trout. A rod like this will give you good casting distance in tight, enclosed stretches of water and much more line control than a standard, single-handed 10-foot rod. You will find that you are mending the line better and you're fishing through deep pools much more efficiently. A 12-footer is also perfect for spey casting, so this makes the rod ideal for heavily-wooded banksides.

A 13-foot rod is the perfect light rod for larger rivers. For example, a 13-footer is ideal for summer salmon fishing. This is the rod for floating or intermediate lines in the 8- to 9-weight category, and you will find that you are able to turn over much larger flies with a 13-footer than you can on any single-handed rod. This is the perfect length for most Scandinavian and Icelandic rivers.

Fourteen-foot rods are for larger rivers still. They are excellent for throwing out even larger patterns of fly. Many people find the 14-footer the perfect all-rounder because it's a great compromise rod. It will tackle the largest of rivers, but is still light enough to use all day long. You can also handle both floating and sinking lines with ease.

The 15-foot, double-handed rod is the ultimate big river weapon. A 15-footer give you great advantages when you are wading deep, because the longer leverage can lift a far greater length of line. The 15-foot rod is an excellent all-season companion. It's perfect in spring and autumn when big flies are in use, generally on sinking lines. You'll find 15 feet gives you superb line control at distances.

Choosing a Fly Reel

It used to be said that a fly reel is nothing more than a reservoir for the backing and the fly line itself. That was partly true in the days when reel technology was less advanced

than it is today, but the angling world has moved on. For example, far more of the fish species that are targeted in the 21st century really pull and can shred line off reels, so if the reel's clutch mechanism isn't up to the job you're in deep trouble. There are many brands and models of reel on the market today, the vast majority of them of superb standard. They're not cheap, so it certainly pays to do your homework and buy the one, or ones, that are perfect for the tasks you have in mind.

A Reel for the Light Rod

Firstly, you have to choose a reel that matches your rod and is suited to the job in hand. If you're fishing small streams with a 3-, 4- or 5-weight rod, then you obviously need a reel of similar rating. It will be small and light, and it needn't have huge line capacity because you will probably be fishing for small fish that are only going to run a few yards. However, its clutch must be highly adjustable and

▲ *Lightening quick*
We all love grayling, one of the most delightful species of the northern hemisphere. However, they can be devastatingly difficult to catch on fly; they can intercept, suck in and eject a fly faster than you can blink. Connecting with grayling is one of the biggest skills a fisherman will ever have to face.

smooth as silk. It's probable that you will be using lightweight tippets in these situations and they must be protected. When line is taken off your reel there must be none of the jolts or jerks that can wreck the finest of points. There's no tolerance whatsoever when you use such light lines.

Capacity and Drag

You'll come across the word arbor used frequently in reel terminology. This word basically refers to the depth and width of the reel's spool. The deeper and broader the spool the greater the amount of backing that can be loaded up. The larger the spool, also, the less tightly the fly line is coiled. This tends to make for smoother casting, as kinking is less pronounced.

If you're fishing bigger waters with a heavier rod for bigger fish – say from 7- to 11-weight – the line capacity of your reel is going to be more important. So, too, will be the drag system. If a big fish is running fast you will need to adjust the tension of your clutch quickly, easily and effectively. Is the drag system, therefore, easy to operate, and will it operate successfully over and over, no matter how hard and frequently it is pushed?

When you're choosing, bear in mind that better quality reels tend to be more adaptable. For example, in its Gem reels, Hardy use Avcarb – a carbonfibre material used in the braking systems of Stealth Bombers and Formula One racing cars. Avcarb disperses heat very quickly indeed, and it hardly

expands or contracts in either ferocious heat or freezing cold, so it doesn't matter whether you've hooked a monster at the Pole or the Equator.

Personal Preferences

There are other considerations, too. You might want a reel that is not caged but has an exposed rim so that you can control a running fish with the palm of your hand. If you are going to share your reel with a partner or friends you might want a system that is easily changed from right to left hand wind. If you are fishing big stillwaters, where your approach can change many times during the course of a day, you might want a reel system that features a series of spare spools so you can kit yourself out with a variety of floating, intermediate and sinking lines.

Choosing Fly Lines

There are as many different types of line as there are rods and reels. Some fly lines are meant to float, others to hang just under the surface film, and others to sink at differing rates. For example, if you're trying to get a fly down as deep and as quickly as possible, perhaps in cold or very hot conditions, then you will go for a fast sinker. If you want to slowly explore the depths, then you will choose a slow sinker.

It's a good rule to choose the best fly lines that you can afford. Rods and reels are obviously important, but a top-quality fly line can make fly casting so much easier.

▼ **It's all about the action**

It doesn't matter if you're fishing a big river in Siberia or for black bass (right) – intense concentration is always called for.

Changing Tactics

Most stillwater fly fishermen around the world have a whole armoury of different lines stored away on separate spools that are interchangeable. This can be important: you could arrive at your stillwater early in the morning and find a flat calm with fish taking from the surface. You'd obviously rig up a floating line and either a dry fly or perhaps something fished in the film. The day clouds over, a wind begins to rise. There's nothing showing on the surface and you've got to go down deeper. This is where a sinking line is important. Or, let's say the day continues bright. The heat increases as the sun climbs, and the fish drop ever closer to the bottom. Now you've got to pursue them in the depths, so you'll need a fast sinker. The sun sinks, the wind dies and once again, as evening approaches, the fish are on the surface. Now you need that floater again.

Line Profile

The decision isn't just about weight and where the line fishes in the water; there are also different line profiles. The most traditional is a double taper, which has a significant belly and is thinner towards each end. This means it casts well and the line closest to the fish lands gently. The weight forward lines are intended for medium- to long-distance casting and once the tip and belly of the line are aerialized, the thin running line passes easily through the rod rings. Shooting heads consist of short lengths of fly line backed by fine braid that produces little resistance when flying through the rod rings. These are more advanced and designed for very long distance casting.

There are all sorts of very specialized lines. For example, Greys now produce the Wake Saver line. This is a full floating line with a short, clear, intermediate sink tip section merging into it. The sinking line eliminates leader wake on the slowest of retrieves and reduces the angle that the tippet makes with the fly. The high-visibility floating section helps detect subtle takes and the taper allows for good long range presentation. The Wake Saver is suitable for a whole variety of techniques, such as static nymphs, wet hoppers, loch-style drifting and fishing suspended buzzers.

Salmon Fly Lines

Be aware that many lines are far too long bellied to be cast in normal situations. Lines are made for angling, for the fly fisher out there wading the river, and not for the tournament caster on a platform.

When you are wading and spey casting, do bear in mind that the length of line belly you require is dependent on the conditions in which you are fishing. If you are fishing a small, tree-lined river, then a short-bellied line is needed to keep the 'D' of the cast relatively small and precise. However, when fishing on more open water, you can choose a mid-bellied line that throws a larger 'D', creating longer, unimpeded casts.

▼ *The travelling*
fly angler
Destination fishing now is a major part of the fly fishing scene. Multi-piece rods help hugely if you're considering air travel. Make sure your reels are well packed and protected against possible damage in the hold.

Similar considerations should be observed when you are wading. The deeper you go, the less line you can lift. Deep wading, therefore, calls for a short-bellied line. If you are wading shallow, a mid-bellied line can be fully utilized.

When fishing for salmon, the choice between floating and sinking lines is made with regard to water temperature and how deep the fish are lying. In running water, the current has an important bearing. If it is quick, fish will come up to a fly presented on a floating line but they might find the line is going round so fast that the fly is skating. If this happens, a sink-tip line or a full sinker can help prevent the line skating across a quick current.

Line Colour

The colour of fly lines has been a point of controversy for endless years. We will probably never know how fish actually see colour on the fly lines. It's perhaps best to take a logical approach. Choose fly lines that are designed to mirror nature – soft blues and greens tend to merge with the aquatic environment. However, the colour should be easy to pick out and watch without effort, because not all takes, even from large salmon, are overly dramatic.

With sinking lines, if you're fishing in the top layers of the river, choose clear lines to merge with water that is light and bright. If you're moving down between 2 and 6 feet, go for green coloured lines to reflect the water weeds that begin to appear at these depths. Drop between 6 and 10 feet, however, and it's a good idea to choose lines that are brown to merge in with the lack of light and increased sediment.

Don't ever forget to look after that fly line. Wash it regularly in warm, soapy water to clear grit and sand, which make casting difficult and can ruin your precious rod rings.

Backing

Your fly line will need to be attached to a long length of backing, both to fill the spool of the reel and also for safety if you have a big, fast-running fish. Ideally, you're looking for backing that offers low stretch, fine diameter and excellent strength. Look for a high-visibility colour such as pink, which allows you to keep track of a big fish in the water. Many modern backings are made from Gel Spun, which has an incredibly low diameter, giving you loads more backing on your spool.

Leaders

Your leader is very important, because this is the length of nylon that is attached to your fly, that dictates how your fly works and what the trout sees. One of the modern materials used is copolymer, and a copolymer tapered leader guarantees one of the best possible presentation methods. If the taper is finely tuned, you will achieve a perfect turnover of your flies, even under the most taxing of conditions. A high diameter butt section will give an efficient power transfer, allowing the fly to be put down with precision and accuracy. Many copolymer leaders are also memory free, so they lie on the water perfectly and they are transparent for maximum stealth in clear water and bright conditions.

Fluorocarbon leaders offer low visibility enhanced by a clear finish that makes the line almost invisible. They have a high strength-to-diameter ratio so you can fish fine with confidence; also excellent knotting strength, with high abrasion resistance.

▼ Master of the cast
The light is fading as Hardy and Greys' Andy Sowerby punches out his salmon line. As the dusk settles, Andy knows fish will be running up his native River Tyne. He is focused, easy in his movements and totally prepared for the take when it comes.

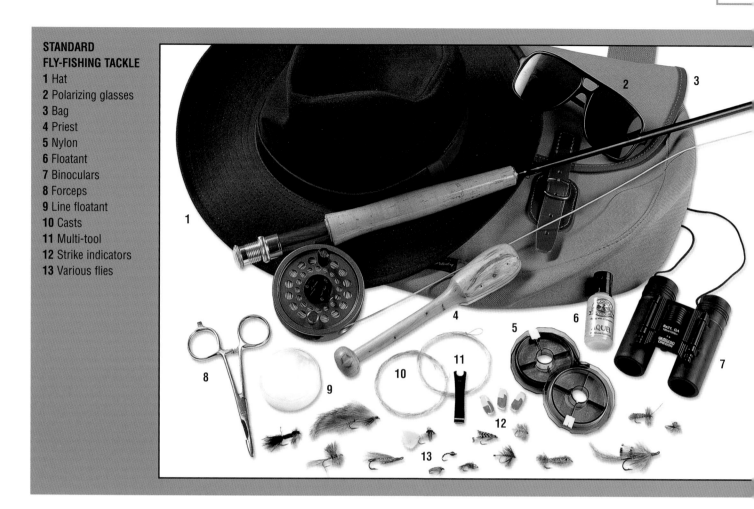

STANDARD FLY-FISHING TACKLE
1 Hat
2 Polarizing glasses
3 Bag
4 Priest
5 Nylon
6 Floatant
7 Binoculars
8 Forceps
9 Line floatant
10 Casts
11 Multi-tool
12 Strike indicators
13 Various flies

You might also consider buying braided leaders: these are expensive but they give ideal presentation. Choose a braided leader that is right for the job in hand. Some of them sink extremely quickly, whereas others will sit beautifully in the surface film.

Accessories

Sometimes, you want to make a leader float, at other times you want it to sink quickly. You can buy sprays, pastes and liquids to achieve these effects. You can also invest in one of the proprietary substances that help make dry flies float more perkily. A pair of sharp scissors is always a good idea, for snipping off unwanted ends and, you will need forceps to slip the hook from a fish's jaw.

You will almost certainly need a landing net, but in every situation you should ask yourself whether you need to use it. You can often simply draw the fish to you, kneel by it and flick the hook out without a net at all. This is much kinder to the fish.

Polarizing glasses are obviously essential to allow you to see what is happening under the surface. The reflected glare of the water is stripped away and now you can see where fish are lying and often on what they are feeding. Glasses are also an essential safety precaution when fly fishing, especially in winds or sneaky breezes.

Zingers are important. These are simply small, retractable reels that you pin to your jacket and on which you can hang scissors, clippers, forceps or whatever you are likely to need immediately to hand. Clippers are especially important. They provide a quick, simple way to trim all knots.

If you're also going to be deeply concerned with the biology of fishing, a marrow scoop is a good idea. With this, you can check the internal contents of any fish that you decide to kill for the table. Knowing what the fish has recently fed on can provide invaluable clues to the flies you need on your leader, which is the subject we turn to next.

The Fly Box

The more experienced you become, the greater the collection of flies you will accumulate. However, don't be bamboozled into thinking that vast boxes full of esoteric patterns are going to turn a bad fisherman into a good one. The great skill is in choosing the right fly for the fishing occasion and presenting it in the right manner. Many great fly fishermen have fished all their lives using just a handful of patterns. Take the ubiquitous pheasant-tailed nymph: you could probably use that in at least 60 per cent of fly fishing situations at any time of the year and catch fish.

▼ *Starting out*

If you've just taken up fly fishing, you likely won't have boxes full of every pattern man has devised. A basic selection, like the one outlined below, is a good starting point .

A FLY-FISHER'S SELECTION

1 STREAMER FLY
A large streamer fly is useful for big trout, steelhead or pike – anything that wants a large meal.

2 RESERVOIR LURE
A reservoir lure such as this is excellent for rainbow trout.

3 WET FLIES
Traditional wet flies are best fished on quick rivers for trout and grayling.

4 SALMON FLY
This is a good example of a fly that will attract salmon.

5 DRY FLIES
These are perfect for the summer and autumn trout river.

6 NYMPHS
Nymphs are the standard patterns for deeper-feeding trout and grayling, and for many coarse fish.

Nymphs

So what flies must you have? A vast percentage of what fish eat lives down deep amid the security of stone and weed on the bed of the river or stillwater. These creatures include freshwater shrimps, beetles, water fleas, tadpoles, waterboatmen, snails of all sorts and a huge number of nymphs. These latter will eventually ascend to the surface, shed their skins and transform into fully mature flies. All fish species love to feed on them as they're rising and hatching, as well as the flies into which they transform. It makes sense, therefore, to have a good selection of flies that imitate these small, generally dark coloured, foodstuffs. Don't be too confused by the welter of nymph patterns available because there are simply hundreds. The key is to choose flies that blend in with the surroundings – hence brown, green and black are generally successful – and retrieve them in a slow and life-like way.

Favourite nymphs include pheasant tails, Montanas, mayfly nymphs, various olives and black spiders. There's no magic fly, but there are expert ways of working them. Think how you can impart life and realistic movement. If you can, buy yourself an aquarium and install in it all manner of aquatic life. Spend time just watching how nymphs and underwater insects move – carefully, cautiously and in short erratic bursts. It's these movements that you are trying to imitate when you retrieve your fly through the water.

◀ *The moment of truth*
Your fly is on the water and you've presented it perfectly. In the crystal stream, you can see a big fish coming to inspect it. Be cool. Wait and watch and if the fish takes, don't be in too much of a hurry to strike. Delay until you know the fish is turning away and then you can tighten successfully.

Bugs, Shrimps and Beetles

If your nymph patterns really don't work, you can try imitating the other food sources already mentioned. For example, a chomper fly imitates a corrixa or waterboatman. Again, fish it in short, quick movements, generally not more than about 3 feet beneath the surface. Try various shrimp patterns in pink or green or even a hog louse imitation, best used on a floating line with a long leader. In summer, trout might well be preoccupied with feeding on water fleas often called daphnia, especially on large stillwaters. Huge banks of these tiny creatures drift round close to the surface in duller conditions but remain down deep when it is sunny. Small brown flies flecked with red can prove very effective in this situation.

Fish Fry

On many occasions, you will see large fish chasing smaller ones, because most fish species tend to be predatory at one time or another. This is especially the case late in the season when the urge to spawn is getting close. This is the time to use a fish or fry imitation, often rather inaccurately called a lure. The concept is to strip a fish imitation back quickly, and takes will generally be aggressive and hard-hitting. This is an effective way of exploring large areas of water on bigger lakes where location is a problem. Try flies such as Muddler Minnow, the White Fry, the Black Fry, the Minky, the Appetizer and the Baby Doll. Streamer fly patterns are also increasingly popular. Streamers don't look like much out of the water, but below the surface their movements are reminiscent of small fleeing fish.

We haven't even mentioned the traditional wet flies that are usually fished in quick, broken water. These flies are not meant to imitate any one food form exactly but to give

NEVER JUST ONE!
Always have at least two flies of any given pattern, size and colouring. There is nothing more infuriating than discovering at the end of the day what the fish are feeding on and then losing your sole example. You must always have a back-up to avoid this heart-breaking experience!

the impression of something small and edible. They are generally fished down and across the current and takes can be lightning fast. Top patterns include Butchers, Connemara, Blacks, March Browns and Peter Rosses.

Buzzers

In the evening, especially, you will probably see head and tail rises as the fish move through the surface film. You will see the head followed by the curve of the back, and the dorsal fin will frequently be held clear and sometimes the tip of the tail fin, too, before the fish goes down. Almost certainly, these fish are taking buzzers, and buzzer fishing is as exciting as it gets. Buzzers are small chironamid larvae that begin as blood-

worms in the silt and mud of the bed. These eventually turn into pupae, often red in colour, which rise to the surface and here they hatch out into the adult nymph. As the pupa – the buzzer – struggles in the surface film to slough its skin, it's incredibly tempting to most species of fish. Hatches are often prolific and it can seem that every fish in the water is feeding in the surface film.

Standard patterns have been around for years but new, shiny epoxy buzzers are proving dramatically effective. Fish all buzzer patterns on floating lines so you can work them either in the surface film or an inch or two beneath. Other flies make easy targets in or around the surface film as they emerge, so if your buzzer patterns aren't working, or if you see larger flies in the air, try other patterns. Hoppers, Floating Snails, Hare's Ears and suspender patterns are all productive.

The Dry Fly

Now, we've got to think about dry flies, and the most obvious of all are mayflies, seen on both rivers and lakes from the late spring onwards. These are large, beautiful, up-winged flies, which mean that their wings stand proud and look like mini-sails. There are endless mayfly patterns: the Green Drake and the Grey Wulff are favourites. Take a variety of sizes and colours with you and try to match your artificial with the insects you see in the air or on the surface.

Throughout the summer and into the autumn, you will frequently see flies looking like the mayfly but only a half or a third as large. These belong to the olive family. Olive duns are favourites, along with iron-blue duns and large dark olives. Make sure you have Greenwell's Glory and blue-winged olives with you.

Perhaps the flies in the air are sedges. Their larvae, commonly called caddis grubs, build protective cocoons from gravel, sticks, sand or shells in which they shelter on the bed of the river or lake. You will find most sedges hatching out in the afternoons and evenings and you will recognize them by their large, roof-like wings, as well as by two large forward-pointing antennae. Artificials such as the Goddard, the Caperer and the Grouse-wing all imitate sedges.

You certainly won't miss a hatch of damselflies – those beautiful creatures with their distinctive, electric-blue bodies and wide wing span. Damselfly nymphs are often more popular with the fish but the dry damsel pattern is always worth a go. Don't strike too soon at a rise because trout will often drown large flies before eventually taking them in. Once you've seen the rise, count slowly to three or four before tightening.

Terrestrials

You should also have imitations of what are known as terrestrials – flies that are blown onto the water from the surrounding bankside. These include hawthorns – so called after the bush and flower that these flies really seem to relish. They have black bodies, long trailing black legs and white coloured wings. Many will be blown into the water on a breeze and feeding can be frenetic. As the summer progresses, you will find more and more craneflies, or daddy-long-legs, blown onto the surface of both rivers and lakes.

Of course, there are all manner of specialized flies for specialized types of fishing and species. Steelhead flies, pike flies, bass flies… the list is a long one and your fly collection will build up according to the variety of challenges that you experience. Remember virtually every fish that swims can be caught on the fly so the scope is endless.

◀ *A fish's eye view*
A mayfly pattern hangs in the surface layer. Does it look like the real thing to the trout? And what about that hook? Is the fly copying the natural perfectly, or just giving an impression of something edible?

▲ *Will it or won't it?*
A big rainbow comes to inspect a nymph. This is the moment of truth – what you do next with your retrieve will decide whether the trout takes it or not.

◀ *Deception*
A fly is just about to be sucked in. Deceiving trout is one of the great fishing skills. The next big step is to actually detect the take. Many, if not most, takes go completely unnoticed, so watch hawkeyed for the slightest indication.

Winter Fly Tackle Care

You won't want to spend half the winter fussing over your tackle but it still makes good sense to devote a little time to its care in this slow period of the year. After all, tackle these days is astonishingly well made but doesn't come cheap, so it's worthwhile looking after your investment. Possibly even more important than monetary considerations are those of efficiency: come March or April, or a winter outing, you don't want your lines sticky or coiled, your flies rusted up or your reels sounding like bags of spanners. To fish well, you must have gear performing to its maximum.

▼ Moving parts

Your reel and your rod's reel seat will take a real battering through the course of a season. They spend a lot of time in the water, and are frequently dropped on sandy banks. Grit can get into the mechanism and foul up clutch systems and screw threads. Winter is thus a time for washing and oiling and making these items as good as new.

Rods

Clean them thoroughly with warm water and clean, scratch-free cloths. Check the rod rings for grooves, and replace any that are nicked badly. Make sure you get any grit or sand out of spigots or ferules and screw reel fittings. It's crucial to wash these if you've been using gear in saltwater. It's also a good time to wash out those rod bags, which could well be going musty. A drop of oil on the zips of your Cordura rod tubes could save frustration in the months to come.

Reels

Clean these in warm water and leave to dry completely. A gentle re-greasing can also be a good idea. Store your reels in a warm, dry environment throughout the winter months.

Lines

Take all lines off the spools and give them a really good clean in warm, soapy water. This is also the time for a little bit of fly-line treatment. Rather than putting your lines back on the reels, it's a good idea to store them on an old bicycle rim with the rubber tyre removed. You can get 15 to 20 lines on one rim and you'll find that this irons out any tight loops that tend to form when the line stays on the spools. Treat your lines carefully: come spring, they'll cast like new and they won't groove those rod rings.

Flies

Again, keep these in a warm, dry place, well away from moisture and dampness, which could lead to rusting. Check all your flies and make sure they are stored in a warm, dry cupboard and there's no leftover water in the boxes. It's a good time to check the hook points for sharpness and discard any flies whose whippings are beginning to look dodgy. We hardly need to add that winter is a great time to get down to tying your own flies ready for the next season.

Bags and Nets

Again, give these a good wash – you'll be amazed how much dirt the average fishing bag attracts during the course of a year. Don't store bags and nets in an outside shed or garage unless you are absolutely sure these are totally rodent free. A nest of mice over-wintering in a tackle bag causes absolute mayhem.

Chest Waders

Store these correctly, preferably indoors in a stable temperature. Hang them from a wader rack rather than leaving them crumpled up on a shelf. It's a good time to check and mend any leaks. Now, too, is the time to give them a wash. Don't use normal detergent but try Nickwax Tech Wash. Once the waders are dry, spray them with Grangers XT, a water repellent spray for all synthetic and breathable fabrics. Treating your chesties well during the winter can give them a whole new lease of life come spring.

Wading Boots

Pay particular attention to these: are the laces frayed and in need of replacement? Look carefully at the soles. Perhaps it's time to replace them or to restick a sole that is coming loose. Give them a good wash to get out ingrained dirt and grit, and then store them in a warm, dry environment.

▼ *Hardy and Grey's experts*
Andy Murray and John Wolstenholme are enjoying the summer. Andy is hard at work and John is taking it easy after an early start, but a large part of their pleasure derives from having the right gear in perfect condition.

Choosing Bait-fishing Tackle

Don't get carried away too much with the business of tackle. At its most basic, tackle is designed purely to put out a bait, register a bite, play a fish and land it. There are lots of buffs in the bait-fishing world who have a very technical approach to tackle. Good luck to them. Listen and indulge them if you wish, but it's often far simpler to stick with the basics.

▲ **Box of secrets**
A look into the tackle boxes of carp fishing experts can be mind-blowing. Carp learn very quickly indeed, and so rigs must always be one step ahead, and their intricacy is astounding.

The important thing is to choose your tackle with care, look after it and make sure that it's always in tiptop condition. If you treat your tackle badly, the chances are it's going to let you down, often at a critical moment. Also bear in mind that the tackle world never stays still. Companies are constantly forging ahead with new developments so, through the magazines and tackle dealers, try to keep in touch with what is happening.

Bait-fishing Rods

Don't rush into a purchase. Take your time and, if possible, test a rod out. It's always best to have used a rod on the bankside before deciding to buy it. Friends, fellow anglers, dealers, fishing magazines and, to some extent, company brochures can all help you to come to a decision.

Make sure that you're absolutely clear in your mind about what you want your new rod to do. Sometimes, you will be forced to compromise, but don't sacrifice your ideas entirely. How does the rod feel? Does it balance nicely with your reels? Don't just waggle the rod or let its tip be pulled down by the salesman (a trick as old as the Ark). Put line through the rings and see how it copes. Find out what guarantee is being offered on the rod – some companies now offer a no-quibble lifetime guarantee – a real bonus. Does the rod come with a travelling tube, always a nice accessory? Do you think you need one of the four- or five-piece models that can be broken down and stowed away in an aircraft locker?

Carp Rods

With carp rods, the choice is particularly mind-blowing. Let's look at the most common lengths and ratings. A 12-foot, 2.5-pound test curve rod offers plenty of power, is comparatively light to hold and, therefore, will probably bring added pleasure to the fishing experience. However, don't expect it to cast vast distances or haul really big fish from dangerous areas. If you want to cast that much further or you expect to contact very big fish indeed, then a 2.75- or 3-pound test curve will give added power. A 12-foot, 3-pound test curve rod will cope with short to long range fishing, along with method feeders and PVA bags. It's a rod for most situations. However, you can go heavier still: a 12.5- or 13-foot rod with a 3.5-pound test curve rating will offer maximum casting distance and really good line pick up when you are striking and playing a big fish. Rods like this are often the choice of anglers fishing for the biggest carp and even catfish.

Marker and Spod Rods

If you're serious about carp fishing, you will probably also want a marker rod. In the modern carping age, a marker rod is considered essential kit. Using a marker rod will give you a better understanding of the lake bed and enable you to find features such as depression, gravel bars, weed beds and silt gulleys. Most marker rods are around 12 feet long and will allow you to throw the big float and lead required for the job vast distances.

▲ *The perfect set-up*
Three rods baited, cast and ready to go. The angler can feel secure in knowing that he has the gear for the job.

CASTING WITH A CARP ROD

Pre-launch
Peter has baited up at the 100-yard range and lots of carp are out there feeding. Now is the time to get the bait out. A powerful 12- or 13-foot rod, a big reel loaded to the rim and a heavy enough weight are all necessary. The line must be flawless as a big cast like this piles on the pressure. Pete is gauging where he wants to put his bait and preparing himself for the cast.

The launch
Peter sweeps the rod forward, bringing his forearms in front of his face, his hands in the direction he wants to cast. Gathering speed, the rod will propel the bait to the baited area. This is a powerful cast, but Peter is in control. The terminal tackle, just visible in the top righthand corner of the photo, is about four feet from the rod tip: the perfect distance for maximum control..

Re-entry
Notice how Peter's hands and the rod are still in the same true line to the feeding area. The bait is about to land, and he is feathering its fall by controlling the line off the spool with his fingertip. By slowing the line, the cast force is diluted and enters with minimal splash. Once the bait hits the surface, he will keep the bait arm open to give line as the lead falls through the water.

Spod rods are now a common part of every carp angler's armoury and enable the angler to bait up well beyond catapult range. Choose a blank that is progressively compressed by the spod in order for the rod to work properly and propel the spod into the distance. Choose a rod that is happy working with small, medium and large spods, so you can cope easily with different situations.

Of course, not all carping work involves casting at the horizon and it's a good idea to have a stalker-type rod – something shorter, lighter and better adapted for mobile fishing to carp that you can actually see. Look for an anti-flash, matt grey finish so that the carp aren't alarmed. A rod between 8 and 9 feet in length is good, so you can use it in the tightest of situations. However, the rod must have power. Make sure it will be able to hold a big fish in snaggy conditions without danger.

Leger and Float Rods

Beyond this, you will probably want a general legering rod between 11 and 12 feet in length. Look for a test curve of around 1.5 pounds, which will make it suitable for most types of fish, including small carp. The rod should also have a screw-in tip attachment for a selection of quiver tips.

You will probably want a float rod, too. For most situations, a 13-foot rod suffices, both on rivers and stillwaters, for trotting work and for fishing at distances on lakes. If,

however, you're trotting a really big river, then 15 feet may be a preferable length, because it will give more line control and better line pick-up. It's very important to decide how you will be using your rod. For most float fishing situations, a rod with a test curve of around a pound is acceptable. However, if you're thinking about big carp, barbel or massive tench, then it's wise to go heavier.

Choosing a Reel

The vast majority of reels used in the bait fishing world are fixed-spool reels of one type or another. For carp fishing, big pit reels now rule the roost, with huge line capacities and a bait runner facility. There is, however, a tendency to use reels for every type of work that are on the large side. A heavy reel only increases the general weight of what you have to hold and frequently makes the rod unbalanced. Nearly all fixed-spool reels these days have sensitive, smooth clutches. Most have rear drag adjustments, which are fine, but my own personal favourite is a front adjustment mechanism. For me, it makes everything just a little bit smoother. Do try any potential reel out on the rods that you own to make sure that the complete package feels right in the hand.

The Centre-pin Reel

Centre-pin reels are an absolute joy. You don't have to own a centre-pin to relish your

▲ *Meaning business*
Mitch Smith and Lee Collins lay out their gear at the start of a major expedition after big Russian carp. Serious gear for serious fish.

▼ *Reel control*
It doesn't matter if you're using a centre pin (left) or a fixed-spool reel (right), you want the reel to balance the rod comfortably, and to fit your hand.

◀ *A river fisher's delight*
The beautiful barbel seen here was caught on a float trotted with a centre pin reel. This represents the high art of river fishing, and is a skill to aspire to.

▼ *At his master's bidding*
This is the best moment of the day. His Indian master is sleeping off lunch, and this gives the boy a bit of fishing. Does he wake his master if there's any action? Well, would you?!

river fishing or close-in carp and tench work, but you are missing a fantastic way of fishing if you never try it out. Centre-pins give you a measure of control that you could never previously imagine, and the thrill of playing a big fish on a pin is something you will never forget. Perhaps, however, it's for river work that the centre-pin really comes into its own. You won't be able to cast huge distances – nobody can with a pin – but that's not the point. When it comes to trotting, control is absolute, and while a centre-pin is not as easy to master as a fixed-spool reel, the benefits are immense.

The Multiplier Reel

For really heavy work, a multiplier reel is the tool you'll need. Perhaps you're trolling for pike on vast waters or fishing for huge catfish. These are situations where the reel will be subjected to immense pressures and must hold vast lengths of high-diameter line. This is where the multiplier comes into its own. Of course in addition to this we have lightweight multipliers designed to flick plugs, spinners, spoons and rubber jigs with highly-focused accuracy.

Fishing Line

There have been huge advances in the design of lines in just the last few years. Diameters have come down and strength has risen. A lot of the ultra-thin lines are of copolymer construction, which gives amazing strength to diameter possibilities. Some of the older copolymer lines were susceptible to abrasion and could break unexpectedly, but these problems are increasingly a thing of the past.

For some situations, braid is a good option, having many advantages. It is limp and easy to cast, and it's also very fine considering its incredible strength. However, like copolymer line, braid can snap very quickly and most unexpectedly, especially in rocky situations. Indeed, if the swim that you are fishing is very snaggy, particularly with hidden boulders, it's probably best to stick with the old-fashioned but very reliable monofilament for most purposes.

▶ *A near run thing*
Look carefully at this photograph. You will see the line is frayed almost to breaking point, and the hook is bent totally out of shape. This is what a big Spanish barbel did to me a few years back. Another couple of minutes and it would have been gone. Nothing highlights more clearly the need for tackle that can stand up to the job.

Lines also now come in a bewildering array of colours. After many years of fishing in India, I've grown to think that the more closely the line merges with the water colour the better. In India, green lines that blend in with the turquoise-coloured waters of the river seem to do far better than white lines. It may be mere coincidence, but why take chances?

Never be tempted to use too fine a line for any fishing situation in the hope that you will buy more bites that way. There's no point in getting bites if you lose the fish. Check your line carefully after any major battle, especially the last few yards, which take a lot of strain. If you are in any doubt, take the line off and re-spool. Store line away from sunlight and make sure knots are always secure.

Hooks and Other Terminal Tackle

There is a bewildering variety of hooks on display at any good tackle shop, but make sure that the hooks you choose are exactly suited for the purpose in mind. Supply yourself with a wide range of hook sizes, because you don't know what the successful bait of the day is going to be. It could be a small maggot or a great lump of sausage-meat, and it's stupid to be caught short. There are all manner of different hook designs on the market, but the over-riding concerns are strength and sharpness. Don't pursue any fish in a situation where the hook you are using could bend and straighten.

As for sharpness, many hooks these days are chemically etched and keep a point very well. To check the hook is sharp, just run the point over your nail to see if it makes a slight impression. A bigger issue is whether to go barbless: there's little doubt that a barbless hook is best for the fish, so for that reason I would recommend barbless. Alternatively, go for a micro-barbed hook or simply flatten the barb down on a normal hook with a pair of forceps or small pliers.

Weights and Floats

When considering leads and feeders, think carefully about what a swim needs and what will be your best approach. Sound travels extraordinarily clearly through water, and a heavier lead or feeder than is necessary will be heard and felt by fish many yards away. Some leads are silvery-coloured and flash in sunlight, and I'd say, as a diver, that it's best to avoid the more garishly coloured swimfeeders. Choose both subtle leads and feeders that merge as much into the background as possible.

▼ *Squeeze those barbs*
A barbed treble hook is always tricky and potentially dangerous to extricate from a fish's mouth. Lose the barbs and you won't lose any more fish.

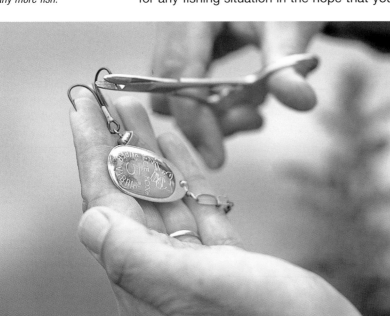

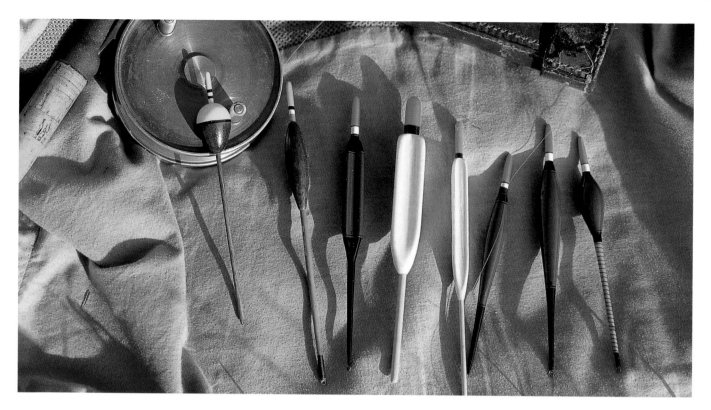

▲ *Ready for the river*

A selection of typical and traditional river floats. There is plenty of buoyancy in the bodies, which helps them ride the current and not get pushed under when it's rough.

Choose your floats with equal care. It's a common mistake to use such a light float that you can't control your tackle properly. However, bear in mind that a heavier float automatically creates a heavier disturbance. Think about the size of your float in shallow, clear water. You don't want too much of it under the surface, especially if the fish are wary, and don't make the mistake of thinking a transparent-bodied, plastic float can't be seen.

Long Stay Gear

I'm afraid it's beyond me to get into the confusing world of long-stay session accessories. If you look at some brochures, there is a totally staggering array of bivvies, umbrellas, bed-chairs, sleeping bags, cooking equipment, tackle barrows and even bivvy slippers for sale. Once again, my advice is to buy the best you can afford after due consideration. Aim to stick with tried and trusted brands.

FEEDERS

Swim feeders come in all shapes and sizes, designed for use on both still and running waters. The block end feeder (top) is perfect for maggots on any water. The other feeder (bottom) is open-ended and plugged with ground bait which explodes when the feeder hits the water. The feeder has the advantage of placing a carpet of bait very close to the hook.

THE METHOD

The method is very simple. The coiled feeder is packed tightly with stiff ground bait that is embedded with food items. The hook bait is pressed into the ground bait and the whole ball is cast out into the swim. Because of the weight, great distances can be achieved, especially on stillwaters. The idea is that the fish home in on the scent of the bait and a feeding frenzy begins.

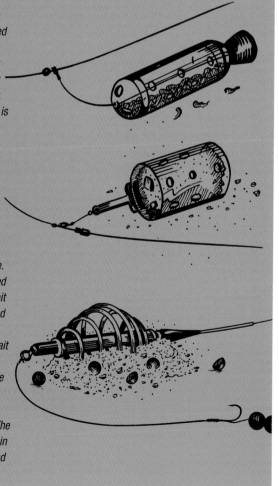

Choosing Lure Tackle

Many people start their lure fishing with an outfit that's adapted from their float fishing setup, which is a fine way to begin, but you'll get more pleasure if you use something that is designed for the job. With lure fishing, you will be casting and retrieving all day long, so you don't want a rod that is too heavy, or a reel that is bigger than you really need. The rod and reel need to matched, and they need to be right for the lures you'll be casting and the fish you're targeting.

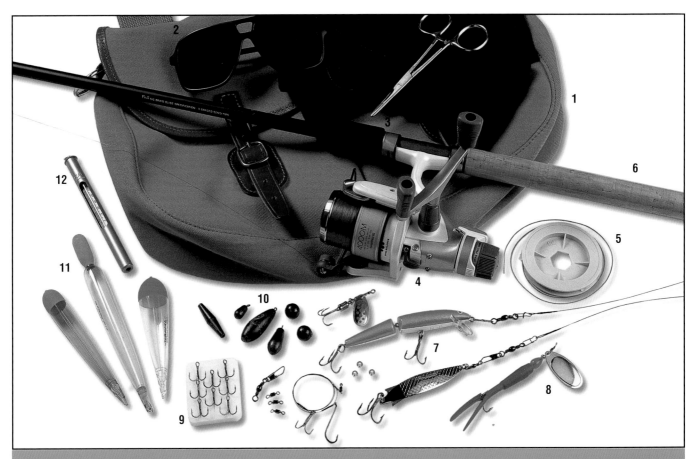

LURE FISHING EQUIPMENT

1 SHOULDER BAG When you're travelling light, this will carry all your gear.

2 POLAROID GLASSES These help you see the fish through the surface glare.

3 FORCEPS Forceps are necessary for removing hooks safely and easily.

4 FIXED SPOOL REEL A fixed spool reel is essential for trouble-free casting.

5 TRACE WIRE This is a must for all predators with sharp teeth.

6 SPINNING ROD Light and not too long, a good spinning rod should be comfortable and not too tiring on the arm.

7 PLUG A jointed plug gives out good vibrations as it wiggles through the water.

8 METAL SPOON A metal spoon has a good action in the water and catches the light. Note how both this and the plug are attached to a wire trace.

9 TREBLE HOOKS A selection of treble hooks for deadbaiting.

10 WEIGHTS Useful for taking a lure down deeper in the water, and for anchoring a deadbait on the bottom.

11 PIKE FLOATS A selection of pike floats in various sizes to suit different waters and deadbaits.

12 THERMOMETER The temperature of the water can be crucial. If it is very cold, then deadbaiting is likely to be more successful than a spoon or a plug.

▲ *The lure-fisher's gear*

A light, responsive reel with a delicate clutch mechanism is vital. Note that the rod in the photograph has a screw reel attachment for added security during constant casting.

The Lure Fishing Rod

For really taxing work, say salmon fishing in big, swollen rivers, by all means go for a rod perhaps 11 feet in length and capable of casting anything up to 4 ounces in weight. However, a rod this size takes its toll on the arm muscles, and it makes sense to go much lighter for a lot of spinning. For bass, sea trout, medium-sized pike, most steelhead and perch, rods of 7 and 8 feet are more than adequate, and often a 6-foot rod can give you the thrill of your life. Indeed, I've had some of my best ever fishing with a 5.5-foot wand with a casting rating of 1/10 to 1/3 ounce. Small summer salmon, pike to 15 pounds, a 4-pound sea trout, a black bass just under 5 pounds – tremendous, unforgettable stuff.

The North American and Japanese angling markets excel in light, technically-advanced rods that are designed for single-handed multiplier use. They're quick, precise and responsive but with real power in the butt. In cramped, overhung conditions, casting accuracy is massively increased with a shorter rod.

Casting Reels

As for your reel, most fixed-spool reels will do, providing they are not too heavy. A relatively small fixed-spool reel – one you would probably use for float fishing on stillwaters or swim feeder fishing on rivers – will be ideal, providing it can take a 100 yards of 8- to 10-pound line. If you are using a light rod, you don't want to use too heavy a reel with it. The whole outfit will feel cumbersome.

If you really want to get into the lure fishing game – and you certainly should – you will want to check out bait-casting reels. These are simply small, delicate multipliers,

▼ *Baltic beauty*

This lovely Swedish pike was caught in the bays fringing the Baltic Sea. It fell for a carefully worked rubber imitation, bounced along the bottom very close in to the reeds.

but they're ideal for accurate casting and careful retrieve. Most modern bait casters are cut from one-piece aluminium bar stock and are incredibly strong and light. They retrieve very quickly, perfect for the lure angler who wants to give his surface plug a quick spurt. The modern braking systems mean that over-runs when casting are now almost always a thing of the past. Drag systems are very precise on bait casters, and they can be loosened or tightened with lightning speed – very useful in a battle with a big fish in and around snaggy areas. They also have the ability to work efficiently with both nylon and braid, an important advantage for any lure angler who will probably want to use both lines in different situations. Many modern bait casters also feature a quick-release thumb bar that disengages the spool and makes for very rapid casting. This is vital when you're fishing shallow, clear water and you see a quickly moving predator.

Always look after your bait casters and keep them well oiled. Take care of them on the bankside, too: never put them down on a sandy beach, for example, lest particles get behind the spool and into the mechanism.

Suitable Lines

Braid is very much the line to use with a bait-casting reel. It's very thin for its strength, extraordinarily limp, and it therefore casts like a dream. It seems to have absolutely no disadvantages and will probably be the answer for 90 per cent of your lure-fishing. However, under extremely rocky conditions when a fish is expected to fight long and deep, braid can be exposed. Modern braid is

tougher than the material on sale just five or 10 years ago, yet it still cuts quickly and unexpectedly if rubbed under pressure against a sharp rock edge.

Under these sorts of conditions, nylon monofilament can be the material of choice. Modern nylon is much less springy and more durable than it used to be. The strength to diameter ratio is also much improved.

Knots and Traces

Whether you are using monofilament or braid, take care with your knots. You will nearly always have a wire trace at the end of your line. Of course, in certain circumstances, the need for a trace is obviated – if you're spinning for salmon, steelhead, trout or black bass, for example, and you are absolutely sure there are no other toothy predators in the water, wire is not necessary. However, in any water where there may be pike, zander, dorado, tiger fish – anything with teeth capable of cutting braid or monofilament – then, for the fish's sake, you should use a wire trace.

Many shop-bought wire traces tend to be too short. A big pike, for example, can easily engulf a small lure right down to the back of its throat in an instant. A wire trace that is just 6 inches or so in length is absolutely useless in this case. My advice, in nearly all circumstances, is that a wire trace should never be less than 12 or 15 inches long. Also, as with your knots, make sure that all swivels and snap links are 100 per cent up to the job in hand – far too many fish are lost by links, especially, opening out under pressure.

▼ *The fish and the fisherman*
A beautiful zander like this one, below, must be fished for with a wire trace, as it has the sharpest of teeth. The photograph on the right shows both the peace enjoyed by boat fishermen, together with the intensity that the fishing demands.

Spinners and Spoons

Both of these artificial baits provoke a response from predators, either because the fish are hungry and they mistake the lures for small fish or because they are territorial and are angrily protecting their patch. On a spinner, a vane or a blade always rotates around a central bar as you are retrieving the lure. Some patterns have life-like plastic worms made of soft rubber attached. This makes the spinners more attractive and also encourages the fish to hang onto the lure longer once it has been engulfed. Buzz baits have plastic skirts over their hooks, which imitate swimming crayfish. Spinner baits can go through the most weeded of waters and they are best for searching out fish holed up under lilies or deep down in undergrowth. Flying condoms have taken the world of the salmon angler apart. These lures produce a heavy throbbing action and have proved effective for all manner of species.

Spoons wobble through the water with a slow, erratic motion, making them look like a wounded fish. Spoons can be trolled behind boats, as well as being cast and retrieved, and their weight takes them down to great depths. The action of a spoon in the water often depends on the style of retrieve and, if you vary this, it can give the impression of a wounded or sick fish in distress. It's also possible, if the water isn't too snag-ridden, to fish spoons very slowly indeed. Cast them out, let them sink and hit bottom, then twitch the spoons back a yard at a time, letting them grub along the bottom and lie static for anything up to 30 seconds before pulling them on their way again. Working a spoon

this way creates a dramatic impact. The bottom suddenly erupts with puffs of silt and the predators see a crippled, silvery shape scuttling along the bottom, looking for cover, seemingly terrified.

Plugs

A plug is simply a wooden or hard plastic lure designed to look and move exactly like a small prey fish. The advantage of plugs is that you can choose one for whichever depth of water you want to explore. There are all sorts of plug designs and you may find them bewildering at first. However, as a rough guide, it pays to buy a selection along the following lines.

Start with a few shallow divers that work from just under the surface down to 6 feet or so – ideal in weedy, summer waters.

Buy a few top water plugs that work exactly where their name implies, right in the surface film, where they splutter and splash and really cause a commotion.

▲ *Less is more*
Okay, this probably isn't the biggest perch you'll see in your lifetime of fishing, but it is nonetheless an exquisite pearl of nature. Look at those bars on its side. The colour of its fins. This is a beautiful little fish.

▼ *Lures of all sorts*
Lures are made from many different materials: metal, plastic, rubber, wood, bone and even mother of pearl. The big questions are how they work in the water and how realistically you retrieve them.

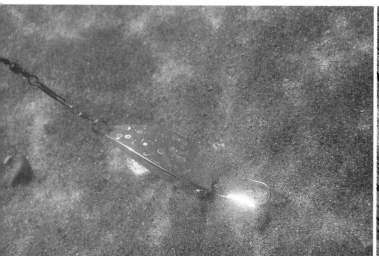

▲ Who's hunting whom?
As you can see, the author has caught a fine Mongolia taimen on a plug. But look carefully at that taimen itself and note how it has in its own turn been hunted by a much bigger fish.

▼ Plugs galore
Plugs come in endless sizes, shapes and colours. Some are jointed, some work on the surface, some in mid-water and others, deep.

the angled vane – or lip – that is at the head of the plug.

It's essential to build up a collection of plugs with different colourings, different sizes and different actions. It's just like fly fishing: one day only one type of plug will catch anything and the rest of your box will provoke no response whatsoever.

Jerk Baits

Jerk baits are the beasts of the lure jungle, and these baits have built up quite a reputation for catching big fish. Most of them float. If you are going to jerk bait successfully, go for a stiff rod designed for the purpose and a solid leader that will avoid tangles. A braid line helps to ensure that the action you impart through your rod tip is transmitted all the way down to the lure and isn't softened by the stretch of monofilament. Really work the rod tip. Crank down fast to rip the jerk bait deep. Occasionally let everything go still so that it rises with an enticing wobble.

Your main consideration is the depth of water you will be fishing and the level at which you think the fish are feeding. For this reason, it's important to know the sink rate of every jerk bait in your box. If it's cold and you know the pike are down deep, go for a jerk bait that sinks perhaps a yard per second and can get you down to where you think the fish are lying.

Think about colours, not just with your jerk baits but with all your lures. If the water is murky, you need to use a plug or jerk bait that is brilliant and flashy. When visibility is

You will also need a few deep divers that work at depths greater than 6 feet and can go down as far as 30 feet. These tend to be bigger lures and they're mostly used in deep lakes throughout the northern hemisphere. They are especially useful in winter or in very hot weather when the fish go down deep to escape the sun.

Floating plugs that dive when retrieved are very useful, too, because the speed of the retrieve determines how deep they dive and this means that you can explore a wide variety of depths. These are particularly good when fishing close to any sort of structure. The diving action is produced by

less than a couple of feet, go for fluorescent, white or the shiniest silver. Sometimes, in very clear water in bright conditions, black lures are the only successful ones.

Fishing the Jig

The jig is a simple concept that uses a large, single hook with a lead head moulded around its eye. Then a soft, plastic body is impaled around the hook. The size of the lead head is important, because it determines how deep the jig will work. However, it's the plastic body that is vital. These come in endless combinations of shape, colour, size and action. Some are like snakes, others frogs, others small fish. It's a fantastic world of piscatorial imagination.

A jig is ideal for working along or near to the bottom, and is especially useful when conditions are difficult, perhaps in cold or coloured water when the fish are reluctant to stir far. Jigs are versatile and you can retrieve them in mid-water, vertically or even trolled behind a boat.

I love rubber crayfish for black bass... let it twitch its way down through the water to the bottom and then pull it back slowly in short, scuttling motions. I love all shad patterns for good-sized pike. Make sure the rubber bodies are tough enough to resist the attention of innumerable sharp teeth, and accept that many a tail is going to be completely nipped off.

Build up a wide selection of body colours. As a rough guide, in clear water

HOW A PIKE LOCATES A LURE
A pike has sharp eyesight, especially in decent light and clear water when it can probably see its prey up to 20 yards away, but in low light or muddy water it resorts to vibration and smell for prey location. A moving lure – especially one that rattles – attracts predators by the vibrations that it sends out through the water. These are picked up by sensitive detectors along the fish's lateral line.

vibrations from the lure allow the pike to home in on it

eyes are set high in the head

lateral line

start out with natural patterns such as rainbow or brown trout. If the water is slightly more cloudy, look for patterns that have stripes or bars. Fire Tiger is a good starter here. If the water is coloured, then contrasting patterns and colours often make an impact. If the water is really clouded, go for vibrant colours and jigs with a really powerful action that send out strong vibrations through the water for the fish to pick up on.

Bear in mind that the deeper the fish, the heavier the lead you will need to keep in contact. Think about currents, which can lessen your contact and make the jig work less effectively. Try jigging vertically if you're in a boat, letting it rise up and flutter back towards the bottom. If your jig is coming back constantly covered in weed, then you're fishing too deep, so use one with a lighter lead head.

▼ *Red for danger*
A selection of rubber baits ready to work their magic. Red is an attractive trigger for most predators.

Sea-fishing Gear

Fishing the seas and oceans offers huge possibilities for different angling techniques. The fish themselves can be huge – perhaps a 1,000-pound marlin – or they can be small and discriminating, yet still as exciting to catch. A bonefish, for example, weighing just 3 pounds, can run off a 100 yards of line with ease. A sea bass can pull like a small salmon, and a pollack never knows when it's beaten.

▲ **At home on the seas**
John Wolstenholme is an internationally renowned angler from South Africa. In the seas around his home, many dramatic fish species are there to be caught.

Sea-fishing Rods

Any sea rod has to be of good quality – the saltwater will test any weakness in the finish or the materials – and must be able to withstand the rough treatment that it's likely to receive.

Boat Rods

These are arguably the bruisers of the sea scene. Boat fishing itself is all about blood, sweat and tears, particularly if you're after big fish deep down in bad weather. Any boat rod has to be tough, of high quality material and finish, and has to be able to stand up to devastating punishment. However, a boat rod needs to have two subtler characteristics: it has to have power but it also needs a

measure of feel. All power and no give, and you might as well fish with a broomstick. Also, unless the rod has some flexibility, it will reach a point where it can go no further and will simply snap. More and more anglers are using the uptide rod now from a boat. This has a longer casting butt and a longer, softer tip, which helps in casting, bite detection and playing a fish.

Look for good quality rings, screw reel seats, comfortable handles, strong spigots, good quality whipping, top line guides and end rings incorporating large rollers.

Shore Rods

Rod designers probably face the biggest number of challenges with shore rods. Today, there are endless materials, lengths, tapers, styles and blank designs from which to choose. Each individual shore caster will also have his own style of casting and his own whims and fancies. Again, look for a rod with comfortable, well-spaced handles and the strongest rings. Make sure that you buy exactly the right shore rod to go with the style of fishing that you will be doing. Think how heavy a rod you need: are you fishing a storm-battered cod beach in the winter or casting for flatties on a gently sloping sand beach in the summer?

If you're spinning, normal freshwater gear will generally suffice, but do hose it down after use lest the reel fittings and eyes begin to rust. Also, clean out the spigot joint very

▲ **Working the shoreline**
Notice how calm the water is, perfect for watching predatorial fish like bass in action. I'm travelling light so I can cover a lot of ground. A pair of binoculars will help me pick out surface activity in the distance.

▶ **Punching it out**
Fishing the surf for species like sea bass is a big thrill. An 8-weight outfit is ideal for most conditions.

◀ **Amidst the bergs!**
Here I am off the west coast of Greenland, slightly above the Arctic Circle, perking for giant halibut. I am also keeping a wary eye open for polar bears!

▲ *The fly and the sea*
Saltwater fly fishing is the most exciting development in fishing today. Rods and reels are being designed that are perfect for the challenges of the tide and the surf.

carefully to avoid sand and grit getting in there and spoiling the tight fit.

Saltwater Fly Rods

Increasingly, rod makers are designing purpose-built saltwater fly rods as the numbers of fly anglers hunting fish in saltwater is growing all the time. In general, saltwater fly rods have low-profile blanks to cut through the heavier winds with ease. However, the blanks also have to be strong because fishing in the sea will generally put them under more pressure than fishing in freshwater. Furthermore, it is a good idea to go for at least one large diameter butt ring, if not two. These allow rapid clearance of slack line, which is vital if a bonefish is making for the horizon. Some of the meatier saltwater fly rods offer an additional fighting grip handle with which to play big fish such as tarpon with greater ease. A saltwater-anodized reel fitting will completely eliminate any problems of corrosion.

Rods of 6-, 7- and 8-weights will be ideal for fish up to 20 pounds or so – bonefish, sea bass, pollock, wrasse, codling, permit and the like. The 9-, 10- and 12-weight options are necessary for tarpon and the exotic big game species.

Sea-fishing Reels

As with rods, the emphasis here has to be on quality and strength, but careful cleaning and maintenance will go a long way towards increasing the life and efficiency of a reel that is expected to take the punishment of sea-fishing conditions.

Boat-fishing Reels

Just like the rods that go with them, boat-fishing reels have to be tough and expect to have the guts ripped out of them. A boat reel will be expected to haul up heavy fish, often from massive depths and frequently in heavy swells. Virtually always, the reel for this type of work will be a multiplier, and it must be strong and well-made, with a large spool capacity. Good gearing is also essential, and this has to be precise, strong and completely reliable.

Shore Reels

Shore reels also have to work hard. Once again, the multiplier reel is the strongest option available and helps with really long casting. However, if you are contemplating lighter work, especially light bait fishing from rocks, piers or groynes, fixed-spool reels will be up to the job. You can also use

fixed-spool reels for practically all sea spinning work. Make sure sand and grit doesn't get into the works, and be sure to always wash them down after you use them in order to prevent corrosion.

Fly Reels

There are now many saltwater-compatible fly reels on the market, anodized to prevent corrosion. They should also feature sensitive and robust drag systems, as the fighting power of sea fish is frequently extraordinary. Large arbor reels are particularly applicable to saltwater work, as they have the capacity to store at least 300 yards of backing.

Lines and Rigs

Choose your lines with great care. Make sure they are heavy enough for the job because they will take a severe pounding. Check lines frequently: the wear and tear of fishing over rocks, through heavy weed beds and over sharp sand and gravels takes its toll. Braid might well be an option but remember, just as in freshwater fishing, it can be suspect in very snaggy conditions.

Choose your hooks and leads carefully, too. With hooks, especially, do make sure they do not corrode or lose their point.

▲ *Nothing wrong with tradition*
Whilst the buzzword is saltwater fly fishing, millions of anglers worldwide still enjoy more traditional forms of saltwater fishing either from the beach or from piers.

▼ *Use your lead!*
A selection of sea-fishing leads all designed to hold different types of ground. Some leads hold better on sand, whilst others are designed for shingle, mud or boulders.

Clothing

Modern-day angling clothing is light-years ahead of what was available even 10 years ago. Modern fabrics and designs have revolutionized life for the angler, whatever his or her discipline. Now there is adequate protection against all weather conditions anywhere in the world. In the past, reliability and efficiency in breathable clothing has come at a high price, but modern technology has allowed great strides forward in efficiency, durability and – importantly – cost. Always buy the best you can afford. Look after it and you will fish through anything the world's weather systems can throw at you in complete comfort.

▲ **Black beauty**
A Spanish-caught black bass. You'd expect the weather down south to be uniformly pleasant, but it wasn't on this day. Howard was happy for his hat and his waterproofs.

▶ **The hats have it!**
Christopher West holds a Mongolian taimen. The sun is shining now, but there's another snowstorm on its way, and Christopher will be glad of the wolf on his head as the temperature plummets.

Cold- and Wet-Weather Gear

For the most atrocious weather conditions, you will need an outer shell that is tough, durable, fully breathable and totally waterproof. You will also need a hood system that is adjustable and comfortable to use. A lightweight mesh lining inside the hood makes for a great fit. The lining will also follow the movement of your head, allowing for clear, unobstructed vision.

Also, look out for well-designed pockets – and plenty of them. Reinforced elbows and shoulders are also desirable, as, too, are hand-warmer pockets and 'D' rings for attaching nets and wading staffs. Full length will be necessary, unless you're wearing chest waders, in which case a short or medium length will suffice.

The Layer System

In foul conditions, it is important to wear a base layer system next to your skin. A fully breathable top and trousers provide a vital link between the skin and outer garments, which will keep you dry and comfortable in all temperatures. Look for garments that are thin, warm and lightweight. They should dry quickly and be fast-wicking for maximum transport of moisture away from the skin.

In between, you will need good-quality fleeces. These will double as a top layer in mild conditions and a middle layer in cold months. They should be lined, with interior pockets.

Gear for Mild Weather

In milder conditions, lighter jackets and trousers can be used. These should still be totally waterproof, windproof, durable and breathable, however. Always ensure that the zips are strong and of good quality. Test the cuffs for adjustability and ease of movement. Always try clothing on to ensure complete comfort and effortless movement. Practise casting, too, so you know there's no tightness around the armpits or shoulders.

Hot Weather Gear

Pay special care to blocking out the the sun's rays. Never be tempted to fish shirtless, and be careful about fishing for too long in shorts. Many modern, lightweight, quickdrying shirts offer technical sun protection.

Wading Gear

Breathable waders are great. However hot the weather, you can wade and walk long distances in comfort. Even in the cold, you can use them over base layer thermal pants – just double them up if it's a few degrees below!

Wading Staff

If you're going to do any serious wading, I would recommend a wading staff. These give an amazing amount of extra support in a heavy current or if you're moving over an unstable bottom. A wading staff retractor is also vital so that when you reach your fishing point you can begin to cast unhampered.

Lifejackets

Automatic lifejackets that inflate within seconds of water immersion are also highly recommended. They are compact, light and also they won't interfere with your freedom of movement.

Useful Accessories

Never neglect headwear. Hats will keep you warm in cold conditions, dry in wet ones and will shade you from the sun in the tropics. A brim also cuts out reflected light and works in conjunction with your polarized shades to let you see the entire picture. In many situations around the world, you will need a midge-net hat for warm weather work.

Gloves can really save the day when it's cold and wet. Neoprene is a great material for gloves. Check that cuffs are elasticated for an easy fit. A flip back forefinger and thumb will help with intricate work. Thermal socks are essential for cold weather work.

Fishing Vest

A fly vest is useful for the angler on the move. Most fly vests have enough pockets to cope with the majority of fly-fishing situations. Check that your vest is light, breathable and pleasant to wear daylong. Stretchable, load-bearing shoulders add to the comfort. You will need retractors for tools, and pockets both inside and outside the garment.

▲ *Keeping cool on the flats*
Here, under blistering sun, you want clothing that's going to protect you from harmful rays and keep you cool. Nothing tight fitting. Everything quick drying. Shirts and trousers so light you hardly know you're wearing them.

Chapter Three

Skills In Practice

You may be perfectly competent in theory, but it's when you're actually waterside that theory becomes practice, and your results will tell you exactly how good you are. Naturally, skills that are learnt away from the water can only be honed through trial and error. You'll never get anything right the first time, probably not even the second or third times. I still make lots of mistakes, but it's all part of the fun – and the challenge.

Skills In Practice

So you're there. The water faces you. The challenge, whatever way you are fishing, is about to unfold. The next few hours can be a triumph, a disaster or anything in between. How do you maximize your chances of success?

▼ *Country idyll*

Don is an old friend and a very skilled fly fisherman. Look at him. His concentration is intense as he keeps perfect contact with his nymph as it trundles back towards him. He's looking for the nymph, and he's also looking for a take. If any trout makes a move across the current, he'll be onto it. Any twitch of his leader and he'll react.

▶ *Happy days*

Peter is my one-time Spanish carp mentor and a fine fisherman, willing to put endless time into research and preparation of new waters. Spain is a big place, and Peter has pioneered his own successes here.

Take What You Need

Firstly, check that you've got everything that you are likely to need with you. This isn't meant to sound patronizing, and I know it sounds overly simple, but it's not. Many fishing techniques demand mobility and flexibility, so you don't want to bow yourself down with a huge amount of unnecessary kit, but at the same time you don't want to miss out anything that's going to prove essential. Finding the balance is important. Think everything through very carefully and make sure that you've got the rods, reels, lines, accessories, baits and clothing that you're going to require. My own tackle shed is something of a junk store and I rarely keep rods in their individual bags. This can lead to a considerable problem on the bankside when I find I have the top section of one rod and the bottom section of another and the two fail to bond, however hard I try! As a result, I've got into the habit of quickly putting rods together before ever leaving the house, just to make sure.

Check Your Mind Set

It certainly pays not to set your expectations unreasonably high. Don't go out lacking in confidence but, equally, don't be upset if you fail to break records. Draw pleasure from everything that happens around you – and that doesn't necessarily have to be the capture of an enormous fish. Rejoice in the surrounding landscape, the wildlife and, best of all, true companionship.

Don't panic if events don't unfold as you were expecting. Sometimes waters can be higher or lower or clearer than you anticipated back home and you've simply got to cope with what the elements throw at you. Always bear in mind that fishing is supposed to be fun, a sport, relaxation – it's not a matter of life or death. It's very rare in this day and age that what you can catch is destined to keep you and your family alive.

Be Adaptable

I've already stressed this, but always take the time to assess the situation in front of

you properly and don't rush headlong into setting out on a preconceived plan. It could be that conditions are not what you had expected, and it is wise to take the time out to observe the water, see what is happening and, if necessary, reassess the situation totally. Success is not dependent solely on how many hours your bait, lure or fly is in the water. It's much more important to make every minute as effective as you can. A football manager once said that it only takes a second to score a goal: the same is true of fooling the craftiest fish in the water.

Horses for Courses

Don't give up hope even if conditions are wildly against you. Sometimes you can arrive at a river and find overnight rain in the hills has raised the level several feet and the colour has gone to chocolate. It's tempting to shrug your shoulders and head for home, but don't. Perhaps a brighter fly will do the trick, or a bigger lure or a smellier, larger bait. Perhaps you'll fish in a different part of the river, or perhaps you'll just have to experiment until you hit on a winning combination. Just keep going in situations like this and anything can happen – often good things.

Let's say conditions are fine, you put a good plan into practice and you stick with it, but still nothing happens. At what point do you decide to swap horses and change your approach? Sometimes the answer might be obvious – it may even come from a fellow angler giving you a bit of good advice. At other times you just have to go with your instinct. If you have a definite feeling that it's time to move on or to change approach, then you're probably best going along with that, providing you don't chop and change too frequently.

Learn As You Go

It certainly pays to keep a record of your expeditions. Note down the weather and water conditions, the exact places that you fished, what you were using at the end of your line, how you fished and how you faired. If you can be bothered to take water

temperatures with a thermometer, this information, too, can come in handy. You might not see any patterns emerge overnight but over the course of a few years even the sketchiest of notes will begin to form a coherent record that can teach many lessons. Also, your notes will certainly help you remember what you have learned.

▼ *Visible entities*
Al and Tim are on a beautiful piece of wet fly water as it gushes through a mill. There won't be much fishable water, but at least the fish will be easy to locate out of the current's full force.

Freshwater Fly Fishing

There's little doubt that, if you're going to succeed, fly fishing demands the most critical presentation. If you're casting a lure and make a mistake, it may hit the water with a resounding splash, but sometimes that in itself can be a benefit. If you're bait fishing and the bait is big enough and attractive enough, the temptation to eat it can often overcome a fish's wariness of your poor presentation. Fly fishing is less forgiving. If you present dry flies, nymphs, buzzers and all the rest in a clumsy fashion, you are doomed to failure 90 per cent of the time. You may have some successes on a very heavily stocked water or a water that is coloured, but if you move onto wilder fish in clearer water, you might as well forget it.

▼ Asian gold
Grayling are beautiful fish on any of the three continents they inhabit. But it's hard to imagine any grayling more beautiful than this Mongolian specimen. Difficult to catch the world over, grayling can take, sample and eject a fly in a fraction of a second.

Fly Presentation

I used to teach at a boys' school, where I ran the fishing club. Over the years, it was interesting to watch them learning to cope with the skills of fly fishing. A boy who could only present a fly badly would generally catch next to nothing. Let's say his skills were at around about the 50 per cent level. If he improved by 10 per cent, he'd catch one or two. When his skills reached 80 per cent, he was perhaps catching three or four fish in a session. By the time those skills reached 90 per cent, the boy was proving successful in virtually every situation. The improvement was nearly always due to better fly presentation.

The Leader

The leader is critical, too. If it is not tapered, then flies, dries in particular, often won't turn

over satisfactorily. If there are knots in the leader and you're retrieving it across the surface, you will invariably create a wake and alert the fish. Decide whether your leader needs to sink or to float, and make sure it does whichever you choose with complete efficiency. This means buying commercial floatants or sinkants and not just leaving things to chance.

The use of fluorocarbon in leaders has proved one of the greatest advances in fly-fishing tackle for a long time. Fluorocarbon really will help your presentation skills. The material is three times heavier than water, so, when using buzzers and nymphs particularly, it soon reaches the desired depths. When using dry flies, the sinking fluorocarbon leaders leave the dries suspended in the surface film and looking far more natural than they would if attached to normal nylon. Moreover, fluorocarbon has the same refractive index in water as the water itself, making it the most invisible line available. It also has a smaller diameter than standard nylon and this, again, helps your presentation no end. The fact that it gives superior knot strength is an added bonus. These qualities mean you can fish a heavier breaking strain than you would with nylon and still get away with it – an obvious bonus if you are pursuing big fish.

Make sure your leaders are straight and not kinked. This will help the flies in their passage through the water. Make sure your leader is long enough: there are times in heavy conditions when you are forced to use short leaders of 6 or even 4 feet, but if conditions are favourable, if the water is crystal clear and if the fish are very spooky, then the longest leaders that you can handle will give you the best possible presentation.

The Importance of Fly Lines

Fly lines are often not given the attention they deserve. A good fly line casts more easily, which means you cast with more control and the line is much more likely to land gently. A good fly line, too, will possess little memory and so will not lie coiled and kinked on the water's surface. Instead, it will lie limp and straight and retrieve with little or no surface disturbance. The fish's survival depends on being critically aware of what is happening in and upon the water around it. If you disturb its personal zone, the chances of success plummet. So don't worry unduly about what fly pattern and size you are going to use: it will be much better if you present the first fly you pick out in as natural a way as possible.

◀ *Dreamland*
A shot to get any true fly angler salivating. Dave is fishing a crystal-clear Slovenian river. There are lots of trout hunting for food amongst those big boulders.

▼ *Poetry in motion*
A big river. A long cast. Perfect control. Notice how Simon has let go of the line at exactly the right moment, letting the loop run through the rings and narrow out to the far side of the river.

Dry Fly Tactics

It's late evening. The stream is placid and a big trout is rising steadily on the fringes of a willow tree. A dry fly is tied on the tippet, and the current takes it down towards the surface-skimming branches. A wagtail hovers dangerously close, but then the big, black neb of the trout breaks the water. The line is tight, the rod hoops and the reel screams.

▲ Dry fly heaven

An English chalk stream in the early summer and the lucky angler is fishing the upstream dry fly for very visible brown trout. The art here is to not scare the fish, and to place the right pattern exactly in the taking zone.

your artificial to the natural in three important areas: shape, size and shade.

Many patterns of fly are broadly generic and can suggest many things to a feeding trout. Quite what the fish sees and why they reject one fly but accept another will always remain something of a mystery. Moreover, it's not just the choice of your fly that is so vital – presentation is at least as important. As a general guide, always carry a selection of Adams, in both standard and parachute dressings in a range of sizes, along with CDCs, olives, sedge patterns and, in the months of May and June, mayflies.

No wonder the dry fly is the world's favourite tactic. Dry fly fishing is the most visual of all river fishing, and provides a mixture of both efficiency and excitement. There are several variations on the dry fly theme and most are based on a single fly cast upstream or, on occasion if rules allow, downstream.

Choosing a Pattern

Whereas fish can be fairly relaxed over patterns of nymph, they are frequently much more picky when it comes to the taking of a dry fly. 'Match the hatch' is an adage as old as fly fishing itself, but that doesn't mean it's lost its relevance. When choosing a pattern, you just have to look at the naturals that the fish are feeding on. It's important to match

Using Floatant

Floatant will keep the fly perky on the surface. Rather than smearing floatant on the whole fly, put it on your fingers first and then apply to the part of the fly that you wish to float. This will improve presentation immensely, and also helps to degrease the leader. A floating tippet can drastically reduce the number of takes you'll get when fishing the dry fly. Degreasing ensures that the leader tip sinks, making it much less obvious. Talking of leaders, it's worth the extra expense to buy one that is tapered. This ensures the accurate casting and good turnover of the fly that are both so important when fishing dries. Get everything right, and you'll substantially improve your catch rate.

1 RUN OF FAST WHITE WATER
Better for nymph or wet-fly fishing, or for using small dry flies fished close in.

2 DEEPER, SLOWER POOLS
These will often need a bigger fly pattern to draw fish up from 10-15 feet down. Fish these slowly and let the fly drift in the eddies and surface film.

3 STEADY RUNS
Three to five feet deep over gravel and sand. This is perfect dry fly water.

The Upstream Dry Fly

Upstream dry fly fishing is considered the standard approach to rising fish and, on many rivers, is the absolute rule. Always approach from behind the fish, to ensure that you remain concealed in the fish's blind spot. Its cone of vision does not extend directly behind the head, so, providing you move your feet quietly, you can approach undetected. On crystal streams, this is even more important because you need to get into casting range before the fish is aware of your presence.

When fishing the upstream dry, you can achieve a realistic, drag-free drift quite easily as the fly line will drift towards you with the current. What's vital, however, is to retrieve the slack line at the same speed as the drift of the fly.

The first rule is to make your cast so that the line lands three or four feet upstream of the target. When rising, a fish will often drift back on the current to intercept the fly and then return upstream to its habitual lie. Casting too short will meant the fly lands behind the fish's chosen position.

▼ *Mayflies: real and imitation*
Early summer in the northern hemisphere sees the mayfly hatch, a thrilling phenomenon. Mayflies are big and beautiful, and trout just adore them. Yet despite their size they can be hard to imitate, and there are many patterns to choose from. Perhaps the most important consideration is the presentation.

As the fly drifts downriver, track its drift with the rod tip while retrieving slack line and slightly lifting the rod tip. You can mend the line again if you need, to extend the drift further. All this makes the fly look unattached to the line – an essential factor in this method.

When the fly is past the fish's position, make a roll pick-up and quietly lift the fly off the water. Don't bother letting the fly drift for more than a few feet past the fish as it's a waste of fishing time. Recast gently, and try the fish at least a few times more.

The Downstream Dry Fly

This is a somewhat underused tactic, but you must check the rules of the water being fished first. If allowed, the downstream dry can be one of the few ways of approaching that hard-to-reach fish. With this method, the fish sees the fly first but can't see the tippet until it is too late. Downstream dry fly fishing also allows you to drift the fly in the dead centre of any fish's feeding lane without lining or scaring the fish. On very heavily pressured water this can be the only method that will produce results – even though you rarely get more than a single chance.

Preparation

Stand well back from the water when fishing downstream. The vision of the fish is much

▲ *In the wilds*
Howard Croston has walked a long way into a mountainous area to fish this clearwater stream. He's working his nymph close to the aquatic vegetation, confident that big, shy fish are lurking nearby.

IMPORTANT POINTS TO REMEMBER

● With all dry fly tactics, keen observation of the fish and insect life is essential. Don't rush to tie on any fly, but consider each and every rising fish carefully. What is it feeding on? Where is its preferred lie? Where is it taking food? Where are you going to position yourself for the cast? Where should the line and the fly land? What bankside cover can you use? How close do you need to get to the fish? Once the fish is hooked, are there any dangerous snags that could spell ruin?

● When you are upstreaming, try to land your cast three to four feet from the target. Allow the fly to travel slightly to either side of the head of the fish. Aim for no more distance than six inches from the fish's head. If your line goes over the fish, you will simply scare it.

● As with every fishing method, there are variations on the technique. Sometimes, it's good to use a pair of dries. One is tied directly by a short length of nylon – 12 inches or so – from the bend of another, generally larger, fly. This technique helps you spot rises to a tiny dry that may otherwise be almost impossible to see, especially in low light. You can even hang a small nymph off a big dry using the dry as a perfect sight indicator that can often attract a fish itself.

● Absolute accuracy is one of the major keys to successful dry fly fishing. A few hours spent casting at targets on the lawn at home will lead to many more hooked fish on the river. You are never so expert that practice won't make a difference.

better in front than behind, and you'll be spotted much sooner. Carefully check the length of the cast needed. If you are going to wade, before you enter the water and cast to the fish, mark its position in relation to a prominent object such as a rock or a bush.

Now you're in the water and know where the fish is lying. Make your first false cast off to one side of the fish while you judge the cast length and the angle. False casting over the fish itself will cause it to spook. What you're doing is preparing that perfect first cast, which is by far the most likely to be taken. Next, make your presentation cast high over the target and then stall it to create lots of slack in the line. This gives you the drag-free drift that you're want. To perfect this, practise as often as possible. The first cast must count.

The fly and line are now in the water and you have to ensure that the fly reaches the fish first. Control of slack line is the key to downstream dry fly fishing. If you give too little line, the fly never reaches the target. Too much line leads to disturbance on the water and so much slack that setting the hook is difficult. If you've judged the cast accurately, the line should just be starting to straighten as the fly arrives at the target. You will only get this one window of opportunity, so make the absolute best use of it.

▲ **Under the trees**
It's high summer, with blue skies and a blazing sun. Trout will still feed, but often only where the light is subdued and they don't feel threatened.

◀ **The moment of truth**
This trout is approaching a mayfly pattern, and now it's decision time. Any sign of drag and the fly will undoubtedly be rejected.

Dry Fly Fishing in Action

There's a river anything between a couple of yards and 20 yards across. It's clear, with deep pools and shallow ripples, and the day is sunny with patchy cloud. Brown trout are the quarry. They're probably wild, but even if some have been stocked, they're still very alert and not easy to fool. So, before anything, watch your approach. Once you're close to the river, stop, look and listen. Alarmed fish don't always flee. They might just sink to the bottom and stay quiet for half an hour. Just because you can see fish doesn't mean to say that you haven't spooked them.

Look for Clues

Before you start, stand and watch from a spot where you can observe a lot of the river. A bridge is good, but so, too, is a bend. Look for cobwebs on that bridge and see what the spiders have been catching over the last 24 hours. You'll probably find sedges, midges and a host of other flies. See if you can find similar in your fly box. Look in the fields around you. If the pasture is dominated by sheep, the dung flies will be black. If cows abound, those same dung flies will be coloured brown. That gives you a clue to the sort of colouring your imitations should follow.

Watch the insects hatch around you. Look for the duns emerging into the spinners with their long tails. Try to catch them in your hands or in a net for a closer look and a comparison, again, with what you've got in your box. Different styles of egg laying can help in fly recognition. For example, blue winged olives migrate upstream in clouds at walking speed. They're heading for specific areas that attract a huge proportion of the flies in any given area. Mossy areas are particularly attractive to olives. The fish will follow flies a good half a mile upstream to egg-laying spots such as this. Wild browns, especially, seem to know instinctively where to find them. Mayflies, on the other hand, are more like bombers when it comes to laying their eggs. Their nymphs can burrow into almost any river bed material and thrive there, making the adults much less specific

▼ *Calm control*

Tony Curtis (below left), a member of the England European team, works a stretch of fast water. Look at how he holds his rod high, and how he maintains contact with his fly. Howard Croston (below right) stalks a Slovenian grayling in crystal-clear water. Note how he keeps the stone bank between him and the fish.

when choosing egg-laying territory. All these signs give you a clue as to what the trout will be feeding on.

Watch the Trout

Non-feeding fish will show an almost total lack of movement, lying doggo on the bottom. You might have scared them, as I've said before, but more likely they're just not interested. Heavily feeding fish will take up to 10 insects a minute, feeding at all levels from top to bottom. That's why, if you haven't frightened wild browns, they can be one of the easier fish to catch. You'll also see random jumpers and flashers splashing out here and there. These are generally just knocking off parasites, or sometimes taking bigger flies well above the water's surface. Watch them carefully. If you see trout with their heads down and their fins splayed out, then these are probably fish asserting their territorial rights and they might not be easy to tempt.

Study the rises fish make. The water displacement indicates the size of the trout responsible. It's true that the biggest fish may sip in a fly with hardly any fuss, but they generally have trouble disguising themselves all the time. Listen for big splashes – the biggest fish don't survive solely on insect life but mice, frogs, shrews and crayfish, too.

This is what a day dry fly fishing the river is all about: taking your time, watching everything going on around you and trying to read the signs that nature is giving off.

Avoid Being Seen

On smaller streams, don't wade unless it's really necessary. In the majority of cases, you can reach fish easily from the bank, especially if you use a 10-foot rod. The trend is often for 8- or 9-foot lengths, but a 10-footer can get a line round corners, trees and reeds that defeat smaller rods. A matt finish to your rod is a great idea because the flash of varnish in the sunlight is a killer giveaway.

So you've found your fish and you know what it's feeding on, you've got your imitation and now it's time for you to make a move. Approach low down, Apache-style. Don't go closer than a rod's length from the water. False cast as little as possible and remember that a dark fly line flashes less than a bright white or yellow one. Now cast a foot above the water so the line, leader and fly all settle like thistledown. When you recast, be careful of spray landing over your targeted fish. It's good to throw your line to the side to get rid of the water droplets before dropping the line back in the fishing position.

▲ **A good fight**
A rather beautifully spotted and well-proportioned brown trout is held for a second to the camera. It sipped in a nymph and fought well at close range.

▼ **The wonder of nature**
A true fly fisherman always keeps his eyes open and notices the many minute miracles happening all around on the bankside. Damsel flies are particularly remarkable.

Wild Brown Trout

Wild really does make a difference. A fish that's been brought up in a hatchery and stocked into a water when mature will learn lessons quickly, but it's never going to be as perceptive and instinctively brilliant as the true, indigenous, wild fish. I don't know why; probably nobody does. Perhaps the redd-born egg that develops into a parr in the river and grows into a mature fish there has a oneness and a bond with the water that can never be replicated.

▼ **The old mill**
The biggest wild browns on any river are often found close to mill ponds where there is depth of water and a large quantity of prey fish.

The Wild Brown's River

It's not just the wild brown trout themselves that are so special and so demanding; their habitat, too, can be exacting, and requires special skills if it is to be conquered. A wild brown trout river, in particular, is almost certain to be a devil to fish. It's likely to be crystal clear, it might not be very deep, and it's probably going to be made up of a series of diamond-bright pools and dashing, well-oxygenated rapids. There are likely to be overhanging trees, probably good weed growth, but almost certainly prolific insect life. All this adds up to clever fish in a crystal environment where competition for food isn't going to be too stiff. As any angler of experience knows, that's a combination to freeze your blood.

The Subtle Approach

Firstly, let's analyze the best approach to a wild brown trout river. It's dawn and you're at the riverbank. You need to be the first on a water such as this to stand any real chance of success. Every time you or anybody else casts over a wild brown trout, the odds of it being caught diminish significantly.

Sound is intensified by approximately a factor of five underwater. So, if you can, choose to fish from grass or mud rather than gravel. Above all, watch your footsteps. Women often have the advantage here, as they tend to have smaller feet and be lighter in weight. Moreover, they don't show that same self-defeating urge to hurry to the waterside and destroy their chances before they've even begun.

You'll obviously be walking upriver, simply because you're approaching fish from behind, but think how you walk. Become aware of your shadow, and be especially conscious that the shadow lengthens as the sun sinks. Even a quickly raised pointing finger can spook a fish. Avoid scaring small fish at the margins because they flee and trigger off a chain reaction of fear throughout the water. Most brown trout rivers are clear and shallow, so it's best to creep and crawl and make yourself as unobtrusive as a water vole.

Keep your voice down if you're fishing with a mate. In skinny water conditions, a wild brown can hear an excited voice or bragging tones yards and yards off.

The colour and texture of your clothing are also important. Think drab and soft. A hat's good, if only to shield the flash thrown when the sun strikes your pale face. Put on a tackle vest rather than encumbering yourself with a bag. Wild brown trout rivers are all about mobility.

Casting for Browns

Above all, on a wild trout stream, make every first cast count. Don't be impetuous. If you've got a guide, listen to him. Watch the lie, watch your fish and take your time until you've worked out a strategy. The more casts you put over any piece of water, the further your chances fall. Wild browns are

expert at seeing you, so you need to learn to see them first. Obviously, you need polarizing glasses (although a horrifying percentage of anglers fail to use them).

On thin, clear water, you must learn to cast a long leader if you are to avoid putting the fly line itself over a fish. Put a fly line over a wild trout and it's goodbye. Practise casting lying down on your back, or at a crouch, or on your stomach. Learn to roll cast and spiral cast, so that trees are no problem. Cast slowly and methodically, not jerkily, and

▲ *The challenge*
Wild browns can take up lies in highly inaccessible places, making it vital to work flies into tiny pockets of water.

◄ *The art of concealment*
On crystal waters like this, the tricks are to make yourself as small as possible and cast a good distance to far-off fish.

▲ *Hooked!*

A wild brown has made a mistake and is headed off downstream.

think about your silhouette all the time. You only have to strive for distance when you've spooked fish, and by striving you spook them more and more. Don't become that human windmill. Don't false cast on a wild trout stream more than you have to. If you can put out the line required in a single flick, do it. Try to cast a foot above the water, so that your fly and line fall lightly.

Natural Cover

Use any natural disturbance to help mask your own unnatural intrusion upon the fish. For instance, fish close to a feeding swan – but not so close that you run the risk of hooking the poor bird. If you see drinking cattle, get close to them and flick a fly immediately downstream. You might even kick up a little silt yourself, to colour the water, if you're sure that you're not going to get shot by the bailiff or owner!

During the day, you're going to be spending a lot of time fishing in the surface zone with small olives or light Hare's Ears or similar small, nondescript offerings. Everything is light and tight with short cast dead straight across the river. Let the fly swing downstream a rod length or two before arrowing them over the water again. Keep constantly on the move, seeking out new pieces of water and visible fish.

On most wild brown trout waters, it will become easier later on in the day, and bigger fish come up around dusk, especially when sedges are out. Keep on the lookout for big, splashy rises.

Fishing Deeper

If you want, you can go heavier. Goldheads and heavier nymphs fish deeper, so cast them upstream to get them down, bouncing the bottom. Fishing true wet fly is different; fish them down and across, very near the surface. Always fish on short lines, searching behind boulders, in amongst tree roots and snags. True wild brown trout fishing on streams is really inquisitive and searching. You need chest waders or thigh boots to get close to the fish – small, quick browns and long lines aren't a good combination at all.

Think Quick, Travel Light

This is a a demanding sort of fishing, and casting accuracy is essential. So, too, are quick reactions. Wild browns – smaller ones especially – take faster than almost any fish alive. Never let your eyes stray from your tippet. Strike at anything – a zip forward, a snatch in the current or a brief hold against the stream. If a trout dimples where you think your olive might be riding, then strike and the fish will probably be on. Trust your instincts, and hone your eyesight.

There probably isn't a more physically or mentally demanding form of fishing. The wild brown trout and its dancing streams ask the utmost of you. You're always moving, watching, thinking and planning. Every piece of water is different and throws out a new challenge. You might decide to use some floating weed to break up the silhouette of your fly line. You might want to dull down your leader and rub it in the dirt if necessary. If you decide a strike indicator is necessary, then a piece of twig or a sliver of reed is less likely to alarm a wild brown than a shop-bought blob of polystyrene.

Don't fret about tackle. A couple of boxes of flies, some spare tippets (you're likely to lose a good few to the endless variety of snags) and you're really set for the day.

To get more fun than you'd ever believe possible and to lay down the lightest line that you've ever cast, think about fishing lightweight. It's for the flitting, wild brown trout streams that the 2-, 3- and 4-weight rods have been designed. Not only are these rods light; they can also cast with great accuracy.

▲ *And released*

A fish as fine as this just has to go back. It's only been out of the water for a second, and it will take a very short time indeed to recover. Stocks of wild brown trout need to be well preserved if a fishery is to retain its health.

◀ *Crystal clear*

Paul Page – the England team manager – fishes a deep run over large boulders. He's aiming to work the fly as close to the rocks as possible where he knows fish are lying.

Nymph Fishing

Fishing the upstream nymph is a classic way to catch trout. The river doesn't have to be alive with rises for you to know that you're fishing effectively, targeting trout beneath the surface that are taking food close to the bottom around weed beds and amongst stones. Upstream nymphing demands several different skills. Most importantly, you've got to find the fish, and this involves spotting them individually, often deep down, or deducing where they will be lying in the river. For this, you need to think how the current is working, where food could be pushed and where the fish will be taking up vantage and ambush points. Recognizing all the factors that make up a trout's lie are of vital significance. As ever in the fly fishing world, don't rush when you are nymph fishing. Immerse yourself in the pace of the river and become one with its flow.

▲ *Summer days*
A perfect stream scene. Water glistening in the background, thick weed growth, a pleasing rod and reel and a nymph all ready to go. This is precise, demanding fishing but also something very much to be enjoyed.

▲ *The strike indicator*
Some people like them, some loathe them. Whatever your view, these strike indicators, or levellers, do make seeing a take that much easier. They can also act like a float in bait fishing by controlling the depth at which a nymph works, particularly useful in deep water.

Reading Trout

Once you've seen the trout, look at its body language. Is it moving from side to side? Do you see the white of its mouth as the lips part to sip in food? Is it rising and falling in the water column to intercept passing food items? If so, this is a feeding fish. If, on the other hand, it's lying doggo, close to or on the bottom, then probably it's not.

Let's say it's feeding. You now have to choose the right nymph and, more importantly, where to place it so it's at the right level in the water when it gets into the vision of the feeding fish. If you put on a heavy nymph and cast too far upstream, it will simply hit bottom and stay there, yards above your target. Equally, if you put on too light a nymph and don't cast far enough above your trout, then it will simply skate away downriver, unseen and untouched.

Nymph Behaviour

One of the most important nymph-fishing skills is to know your flies. It pays to test them out in clear water, either at home or on the bankside, so that you can determine the sink rate of each item in your box.

The weight of the nymph is, of course, vital. The rest you can treat more casually. In most cases you don't need to worry too much about specific patterns. Providing the nymph is brown, green or black and of a reasonable size – generally between 10 and 14 – you're in with a chance. Most of the time, trout aren't targeting specific nymph types but are simply feeding off the food items drifting in the current, and drab colours represent a multitude of food types.

Spotting the Take

So, you've found your fish, you've got into position without scaring it, you've made your cast, the nymph is in the feeding zone, but how do you know if it's been taken? This is the other great skill of nymph fishing, and it's probable that the majority of takes go undetected by most anglers. You think you know roughly where your nymph is but you're simply not sure. The deeper the water and the further away your nymph, the bigger the problem. Grease your leader so that you can see it lying on the water as it drifts back towards you. If it stops or shoots forwards or moves from side to side, strike at once. The take will sometimes be so strong that your fly line will jab upstream.

If the rules of the water allow, you may want to use a strike indicator. This not only gives a supreme signal of a taking fish but, importantly, allows you to select exactly the depth you want the nymph to be. The deeper the water you're fishing, the more advantageous this becomes.

Signs of Feeding

If you're fishing for a sighted fish, the game becomes even more exciting. When you think your nymph is in the zone, watch that trout for all you're worth. Note if it moves forwards, or from one side to the other. Does it suddenly rise up in the water or drop down towards the bottom? Any such deliberate movement suggests the trout is on the fin and moving quickly to intercept a food item, very possibly yours. If you're especially lucky, you might even see the mouth open. You'll see a gleam of white as the lips and inner mouth are revealed. That's sure proof that a food item has been sucked in and, if the leader moves at all, strike at once. Don't strike wildly with force. Simply lift the rod and tighten, and the fish will be on. However, you need to be direct to your fly and herein lies another skill. It's vitally important to keep in touch with your nymph at all times as it moves back towards you with the current.

This means well-practised hand-to-eye co-ordination. You've got to strip line back at the same rate that it is drifting along with the current. If you retrieve too slowly, you will end up with slack line. If you retrieve too quickly, you'll be pulling the nymph upwards through the water in a totally unnatural fashion.

Many skills are needed here, but the satisfaction is immense when you suspect your nymph is in the zone, feel it might have been taken, and tighten into an angry trout. It's a moment when everything conspires to create a piece of fishing magic.

*◀ ▲ **Horses for courses***
The type of nymph that you fish can vary hugely depending on the season. Rebecca and Nick (on the left) are choosing a nymph for a summer trout. On the right, the angler is fishing for a winter grayling and might well choose the most minute patterns. In fact, he was successful with little black nymphs tied on size-20 hooks.

NYMPH FISHING IN ACTION

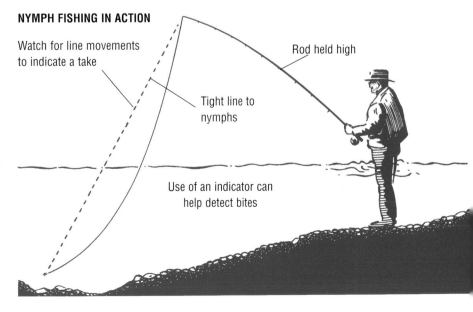

Watch for line movements to indicate a take

Rod held high

Tight line to nymphs

Use of an indicator can help detect bites

Czech Nymphing

This close-in, intimate and intense form of fly fishing began in Central Europe in the Czech Republic, Slovakia and Poland. The method is exciting and extraordinarily efficient. In these countries, at least until the last ten years, catch and release was rarely practised and fish caught represented important additions to the family menu. Fishing might have been fun, but it also had a supremely practical nature.

▲ ▼ *Absolute control*
Czech nymphing is all about total control and knowing exactly where your fly is. If there's any suspicion of a take, the strike must be made at once.

The Basic Principles

In a nutshell, the angler is fishing a team of nymphs close to the bottom and attempting to imitate as closely as possible the natural insects upon which the fish feed. To make this imitation totally convincing, the angler has to get close to where his team of nymphs is fishing so that he can control it with absolute accuracy. The method, therefore, almost always demands that the angler wades. Long casting is not part of the skill, which depends almost entirely on working the nymphs with supreme mastery and reacting with lightning rapidity when a take occurs. Very often the fish will be seen, so it's important to move cautiously and dress in a drab fashion. And always watch how you wade: caution is a good thing.

The Right Gear

A 10-foot rod gives a greater measure of control than one of 8 or 9 feet. It has, however, to be light and delicate so that the angler can wield it all day long. A quick tip action helps an instant strike the moment the indicator slips under the surface. The reel is not too important, as there is not a great deal of casting to be done, but the line must be a floater and preferably 4-, 5- or 6-weight, with 5-weight being the favoured option in most circumstances.

Leaders are generally 10 to 12 feet long with a heavy fly on the end and two imitations tied to droppers a foot or so apart. Leaders should be between 3 and 5 pounds breaking strain, depending on the size of the fish being pursued.

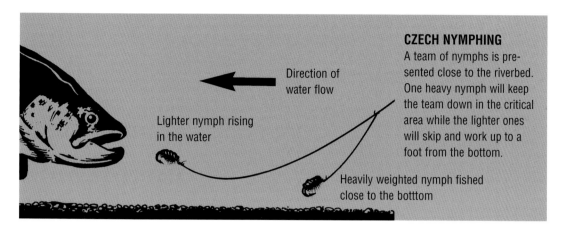

CZECH NYMPHING
A team of nymphs is presented close to the riverbed. One heavy nymph will keep the team down in the critical area while the lighter ones will skip and work up to a foot from the bottom.

Direction of water flow

Lighter nymph rising in the water

Heavily weighted nymph fished close to the botttom

A strike indicator is also a vital piece of kit. This must be large enough to support the weight of the flies, and it is set close to the depth of the water being fished so that it can hold the flies fractionally off the bottom. The strike indicator is also important for just that – indicating the minutest take. Frequently, bites are very fast indeed and the vast majority would be missed without this visual indication.

The Necessary Flies
Of supreme importance are the flies themselves. The technique depends on flies tied to imitate the tiny natural foodstuffs that trout and grayling eat in their natural habitat and are looking for in the general drift of the river. Caddis imitations are extremely important. So are nymph patterns, shrimp and any of the small foodstuffs that live close to the bottom amongst stones and gravel. The flies must look and act as naturally as possible and that is where one of the major skills of the method lies.

The Water and the Fish
Czech nymphing is almost always a method for rivers. A perfect piece of water will be between 3 and 7 feet deep. It will be easily approachable by wading, and the main run of water to be attacked will be no more than two rod-lengths away from the angler. The current should be neither too fast nor too slow – a nice easy pace is ideal. It is important, too, that the nymphs can ride serenely down with the current without becoming fre-

▲ **Strike indicator**
A strike indicator is an essential part of Czech nymphing because it determines how deep the flies can work. The strike indicator must be buoyant enough to carry the weight of the flies beneath it. Experiment with different sizes and colours.

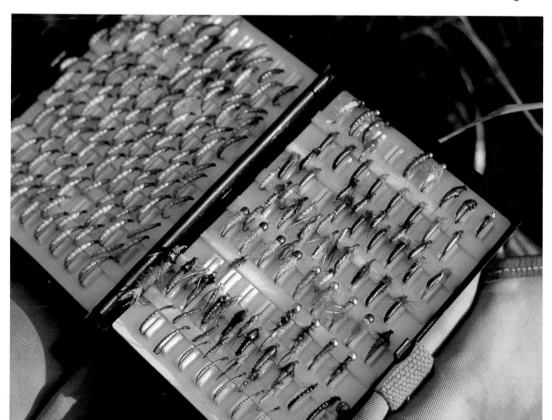

◄ **Different patterns**
A well-stocked, Czech nymphers box. These patterns might look similar but they're not. They will all work in individual and quite different ways. Also, they will all be individually weighted so that they sink at different weights.

▲ *A classic upstream*
Stuart Crofts, a leading
member of the England fly
fishing team, fishes his
nymphs upstream. Notice
how he is working to main-
tain constant contact with
them as they come back
towards him.

quently snagged around boulders, weed, fallen trees or other obstructions. For this reason, Czech nymphing is best practised over a gravel or sand bed that is comparatively level, with few sharp depth changes or contours.

The two main species targeted by the mid-Europeans themselves are the trout and the grayling. Both fish respond supremely well to the technique, and grayling in particular are very difficult to catch any other way, except when they come to the surface and take dry flies. However, the method is also extremely successful with members of the cyprinid family such as bream, roach, barbel and chub. In Greenland, it has proven a fantastic method with Arctic char, and in the States the few anglers who have tried it have found it to be a winner for black bass. In short, the method works with any type of fish

looking for a small invertebrates such as snails, caddis, shrimps and beetles that live close to the bottom.

The Czech Technique
So how do you do it? The angler gently wades out to where he suspects fish are going to be lying. Some 4 or 5 yards of line are stripped from the reel, and the strike indicator and team of nymphs is flicked a little way upstream. The flies sink quickly and the angler must be immediately ready for a take. The rod is held high as the strike indicator floats down the current, past the angler and then away beneath him. This is so that he can keep a tight line and respond instantly to any movement on the strike indicator. As the strike indicator and nymphs move on some 4 or 5 yards downriver from the angler, he lowers his rod until he can let them travel no

further, then lifts them out and rolls the line back upstream to repeat the process.

If there is absolutely no action and no fish can be seen after five or six casts, the angler might well move down a few yards and begin the process all over again until he locates some fish.

Intense Concentration

Because all the action is taking place so close at hand, the angler has got to move gently and remain unobtrusive. He has to watch his strike indicator like a hawk for any movement. All the time he is thinking how his flies are working deep down, very close to the bottom. The angler's job is to make them behave as naturally as is humanly possible. The action is tight and intense: it's literally eyeball to eyeball with the fish at a handful of paces. Polarizing glasses are essential in allowing the angler to see through the surface film and scan for any fish that might be present.

The All-important Indicator

The strike indicator has a major role, both in holding the flies at the right depth from the surface and also indicating any take. If the strike indicator goes under, moves upstream or simply momentarily holds stationary,

strike at once. Another of the big skills of the method is actually recognizing takes that can be very difficult to decipher.

The strike indicator has to be buoyant enough to carry the weight of the flies easily and must not be sucked down by the strength of any currents. It must also be very visible: it's a good idea to take different coloured strike indicators so they can be changed according to the reflections on the water. Red and yellow, and occasionally black and white, are favourite colours.

▲ ▼ *Ladies of the stream*
Fish don't come any more beautiful – or wary – than grayling. Perhaps the above photograph does them the most justice: that gorgeous dorsal fin means that besides looking good, they also fight well in strong currents.

Wet Fly Fishing

▼ *Total focus*

Juan is oblivious to everything around him, except for how his wet fly is pulling across the current towards the fish that he can see moving.

When you're nymph fishing, you are trying to imitate a real-life food item as accurately as humanly possible. Traditional wet fly fishing, however, is a little bit different. A traditional wet fly is more an impression of a life form than an exact replication. This isn't true of all wet flies – the Connemara Black, for example, does look somewhat like an insect being pushed by the current – but most traditional patterns, such as the Dunkeld or the Silver Invicta, fall into the category of attractors. Although they look a little like food items, it is the flash in the water that catches the fish's attention and teases it into an attack. With flies like these, it is all about exciting a fish's curiosity.

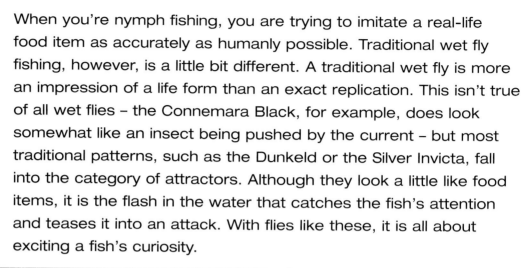

Fast Water Fishing

These flies work well because they are generally fished in shallow, rough, quick water where the fish don't have much time to make up their minds. The light, too, is being refracted and the current is whirling food around here, there and everywhere. The fish see your flies, find them interesting and make a grab.

In general, wet fly fishing is carried out on wilder, untamed rivers, most frequently over stony or rocky bottoms. This isn't the correct method for the placid, weedy chalk stream. You're looking for quick, riffly water that is between one and four or five feet in depth. You will often be wading, getting yourself into positions that you couldn't hope to reach from the bank. To some degree, you're fishing blind, covering as much water as possible and keeping very mobile. However, as with all forms of fishing, there are various skills involved. For example, you'll need to read the water thoughtfully, looking for the little pots and holes behind larger rocks or the creases between fast and slower water. Fish in quick water will always be looking to conserve their energy by hanging out in places where they can find some sanctuary from the current. They still need to be able to see what is happening around them, though, and they need to keep a beady eye on what's trundling past.

The Wet Fly Method

Wet flies are fished across and down rather than upstream, which is more typical of a nymph or dry fly. The cast is made at about 45 degrees downstream, across the river towards the far bank. What you're doing is allowing the fly, or your team of two or three flies, to follow the current down, gradually moving across it to end up on your side of the river. The major skill here is to avoid the current catching the fly line and pushing at it, making the flies work unnaturally quickly across the current or even causing them to skate across the surface. You must slow your fly line down to give the wets time to fish at the right depths and at the right speed. To accomplish this, mend your line to prevent the current dragging it. Mending is an essential technique in most forms of river fishing, but never more so than when fishing the wet fly.

You won't miss takes when they come, because your flies will be moving quickly, forcing the trout into fast, decisive action. You'll either feel a take with your fingers or you'll see the line tighten quickly and positively across the stream. The fish is generally self-hooked, and almost the first thing that you'll know is that your rod is bent and the line is ripping steadily through the water. This is undoubtedly an exciting, dramatic and effective method.

Wet fly fishing may not have all the sophistication of the dry fly or the nymph – after all, you're not imitating food forms precisely and you're not targeting specific, sighted fish – but wet fly fishing does demand a good reading of the water and that all-important skill of constant line mending. Finally, fishing the wet fly keeps you physically fit. Good wet fly rivers are often in wild, hilly terrain, and this method will keep you constantly on the move, forcing you to walk, to wade and to stretch yourself physically.

▲ ▶ *Working the fast water*
Both Al and Simon know that the wet fly works best where the water quickens and falls away, often with crests of white and nearly always working around rocks.

Dapping

The art of dapping is traditionally associated with large waters, generally in the late spring or early summer when the mayflies are in the air. This method was pioneered on the great loughs of Ireland, where it is still practised with fierce enthusiasm. However, fishermen worldwide have realized that dapping is effective and exciting, often catches the biggest fish in the water and is a real skill to be mastered. Dapping is really a boat-fishing method, although it can occasionally be done from the bank.

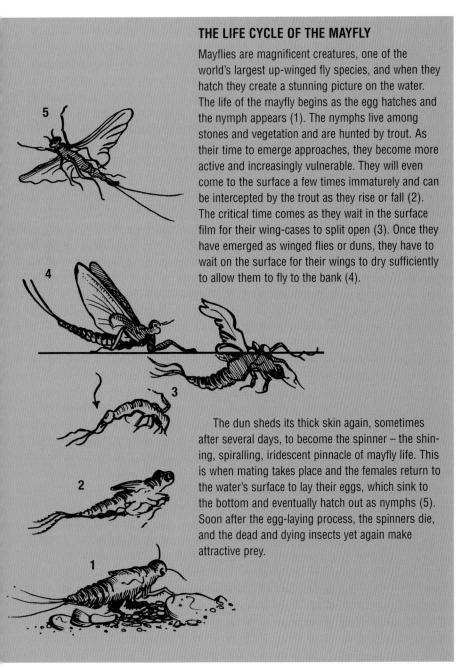

THE LIFE CYCLE OF THE MAYFLY

Mayflies are magnificent creatures, one of the world's largest up-winged fly species, and when they hatch they create a stunning picture on the water. The life of the mayfly begins as the egg hatches and the nymph appears (1). The nymphs live among stones and vegetation and are hunted by trout. As their time to emerge approaches, they become more active and increasingly vulnerable. They will even come to the surface a few times immaturely and can be intercepted by the trout as they rise or fall (2). The critical time comes as they wait in the surface film for their wing-cases to split open (3). Once they have emerged as winged flies or duns, they have to wait on the surface for their wings to dry sufficiently to allow them to fly to the bank (4).

The dun sheds its thick skin again, sometimes after several days, to become the spinner – the shining, spiralling, iridescent pinnacle of mayfly life. This is when mating takes place and the females return to the water's surface to lay their eggs, which sink to the bottom and eventually hatch out as nymphs (5). Soon after the egg-laying process, the spinners die, and the dead and dying insects yet again make attractive prey.

Dancing on the Water

In essence, dapping consists of drifting with the wind in a boat across comparatively shallow, rocky ground where the mayflies proliferate, and dancing your own mayfly on the surface of the water. Long rods are used, together with silk or floss lines that catch the breeze. In Ireland, at the end of the leader, live mayflies – anything between one and six of them – are commonly attached to a hook size 8 to 12. Collecting mayflies has become something of an Irish tradition. At times during the mayfly hatch, the trees and bushes around the shores of lakes such as Corrib literally heave with the insects. For generations, boys have set out to catch the living mayfly to sell to anglers. However, perhaps thankfully, imitation mayflies serve just as well.

The Dapping Method

Let the boat drift, sometimes for miles on larger waters, holding the rod vertically, paying out the dapping line until it clears the tip ring, then lower the rod so the mayflies are skipping on the surface of the water. Don't drag them about unnaturally. The aim – and the skill – is to make them appear as lively and natural as possible, and that's particularly important with the artificial. Twitch the rod tip from time to time, so that the flies skit from one side to the other. Make use of the wind, to keep telltale line off the water and to impart as much life as possible to your flies.

When you get a take, don't be in too much of a hurry to strike. Sometimes a trout

will submerge the flies before sipping them in, sometimes it will merely splash at the mayflies – real or artificial – in an attempt to drown them before taking them. In this case, do nothing, as the trout will probably return. Delay your strike until you see the line going out and tightening, then merely lift in to the hooked fish.

This isn't simply a method for the mayfly season. You can dap with any large naturals such as grasshoppers, sedges and daddy-long-legs. Equally, try the same method with imitations.

A decent breeze is generally considered important for dapping, as you do need a bit of a wave. I've dapped in terrifyingly strong wind conditions when my guide has only just been able to keep control of the boat. The fishing has been fantastic during these conditions, but do bear in mind that no trout, however magnificent, is worth risking your life for.

The Tackle Box

Traditionally, rods are 14 to 16 feet long. Telescopic models are favoured as they can be extended or shortened according to conditions. However, a long trout or light salmon rod can also be used if you don't want to make a special investment.

Centre-pin reels are generally used in Ireland, with 100 yards or so of 15-pound nylon backing in readiness for a really big fish taking off. To this is attached a length of special dapping floss, designed to catch the wind. The length of the dapping floss varies according to the state of the wind and length of the rod, but 10 to 12 feet is generally considered about right. To this is attached the leader – 4 to 8 feet of 6-pound nylon monofilament. It is unwise to go lighter than this because you're likely to catch some very big fish. All these measurements can be changed according to the weather conditions. In a very stiff wind, you probably won't need the floss at all, as it's only there to help catch the breeze when there isn't much of it about. Equally, use a heavier leader if you see some really big fish moving, as very little of it ever touches the water at all.

◄ ▲ *Mayfly madness*
When the mayfly are hatching on the Irish loughs everybody goes mad, not just the trout. It's a scene of general rejoicing because life around the lough side doesn't get better than this.

▼ *Dancing the fly*
Dapping is generally carried out from boats but if there's a decent breeze it's possible to dap from the shore if you keep your rod high.

Fishing The Popper

Poppers are simply flies constructed to float on the surface and make splashy, noisy movements on the retrieve. They are designed to look and behave like a small creature that has fallen into the water and is struggling for its life. The aim is, obviously, to trigger the predatorial instincts of a wide variety of species into making an attack. Poppers can be made to look and behave like almost any creature you care to think of – frogs, newts, small snakes, lizards, water rats, mice, even fledglings. Just imagine the number of baby birds that must fall from the security of their nest and perish in the water and you'll understand why many bass, trout and pike make a living that way. Indeed, one fisherman I met up with in southern Europe specialized in tying flies to look like baby swallows, and he did very well indeed out of the deception.

Popper-Fishing Tackle

Poppers are generally made from a variety of materials. The tails are usually fluffy and wildly coloured, while the bodies are made out of wood, plastic, cork – anything and everything that floats. Vitally, the head is scooped out so the face is saucer-shaped. It's this concave front that makes the popper 'pop' along the surface so efficiently on the retrieve.

If you're fishing a popper, and it's definitely one of the most exciting of all fly-fishing techniques, then a 7- to 8-weight rod is probably going to be ideal in most circumstances. If you are popper fishing for pike with really big flies, you might want to go heavier. Poppers are not very aerodynamic, and large ones are particularly hard to cast, especially when they get wet, so you need a powerful rod if you're going to achieve distance and accuracy consistently. Most popper-caught fish aren't going to scream off line, so huge amounts of backing aren't generally necessary, but you will need a sensitive clutch. You will be using floating lines almost exclusively with poppers, so a 7- or 8-weight line will match your most commonly used rods. Don't go too light with your leader – takes on poppers can frequently be true smash-and-grab affairs.

When and What

Poppers are best fished in warm, calm conditions, especially at dawn and dusk. For black bass, for example, poppers are not effective when water temperatures fall below 15°C (60°F), especially if the surface is

▼ *Big for bass*
Poppers and surface lures are generally great for black bass (right), which will often come up 10 feet to intercept them.

rough. Poppers work well at night for many species, when there is a big moon and little cloud cover, and they can be the only way to put a fly to fish hidden under mats of weed or lilies. Black bass, particularly, will come out for a well-placed popper.

Don't be afraid to go large – black bass will consume flies half their own length – but big isn't always best. Sometimes a species will go for a popper so small you'd think it would be overlooked.

the surface, leaving it closer to the structural zone you are fishing towards.

Watch the popper carefully for signs of an emerging fish. When one is close, only pop the fly if the fish is undecided or turns away – many species prefer to take it stationary.

If a few of you are fishing together on the bank or from a boat, try a popper race: cast them side by side and retrieve them close in tandem. This multiple disturbance is a great fish attractor.

◀ Let it lie
Don't be in too much of a hurry to retrieve a popper. Fish, bass especially, are happy to intercept one that is quite unmissable.

Popper Control

Think about how to work your popper. On landing, let it settle and don't move it for 30 seconds or more. Straighten up any slack line until you're tight to the fly, give it a sharp 6-inch tug and leave it again for up to 30 seconds before repeating the process. Many fish will be lying deep and need time to sense that your popper is there, to focus on it and make their minds up to attack. If you 'pop' back too quickly, a lot of fish won't even know you're there.

Poppers always fish best around any sunken structure, whether it be vegetation, masonry or old ironwork. Keep your rod tip low to the water, or even sub-surface, when you make that pull. This way the popper pops enthusiastically but you pull it less far across

Coaxing Difficult Fish

If fish, black bass especially, are cautious, make the retrieval tug just a twitch so that the commotion is reduced. Spooky fish of all species can be scared by a loud pop.

Hard-bodied poppers are durable and stand casting against structure, so you can get in really close to those fish afraid of open water. However, if fish are taking gingerly, a hair or fur-bodied popper feels more like real food and will be held onto fractionally longer.

If the fish are still spooky, keep changing size and colour, or change shape to a frog, lizard or mouse. A fish will often be angered into attack if you keep popping him in his own stronghold. Although he might not be hungry, territorial instinct will take over and he'll just have to do something about the intruder.

▼ Belt out that popper
Poppers aren't easy to cast, so make sure that your outfit is heavy enough to cope.

Pike On The Fly

John Horsey is a long-term consultant for the leading UK tackle company Hardy and Greys. He has a long list of competition honours behind him, and has represented England for many years on the international scene. He is also the acknowledged UK expert on fly-caught pike, and I feel very privileged to have him pass on his secrets to us in this fascinating piece.

▶ *Safety first*

Notice the wire trace here. It's absolutely essential to use a wire trace – and not too short a one at that – when you're fly fishing for pike. Failure to do so will often mean a nylon leader being severed and a pike being condemned to a slow and lingering death.

▼ *Endless patterns*

Pike fly anglers will argue endlessly over patterns. True, some colours, sizes and materials work better than others, but all aim to achieve one objective: to imitate a small, struggling, vulnerable prey fish.

A Worthy Quarry

Most of my pike fly fishing is carried out on the big stillwater trout fisheries. A lot of these places in the UK were stocked illegally by very naughty pike anglers wanting to further their sport. Pike, nowadays, are hugely well established, so there's no point complaining about it, especially as they are such mighty and worthwhile creatures in their own right, particularly in the autumn and winter months when the trout fishing tails away. Today, thankfully, there's a very enlightened attitude towards pike, even in big trout fisheries. It's generally accepted that, providing that the big fish of 12-15 pounds and above are released, there's very little chance of an explosion of jacks, which is the major concern.

Tackle for Pike

Let's look at tackle first. I go for a 9-foot, 8- or 9-weight rod with enough backbone to put out large flies and deal with big fish. Don't worry too much about fly reels: an 8-weight can easily be pressed into service, or

go for a 9-weight if your budget stretches that far. With a reel, the main thing is to look for a really efficient braking system.

You need three basic fly lines, so that you can search as much water as possible. You'll need a floating weight-forward line, a clear intermediate and a fast sinker. These three cover the basics, although, if you really take to your piking, you might very well find you want to branch out and explore a range of different line types.

Pike Flies

The main difference between piking and trouting is in the bigger flies that you'll be using. Most of them will be between 3 and 9 inches long! Many manufacturers try to turn their saltwater patterns into freshwater pike ones, but that's simply not good enough. The important thing is that your flies are tied with EP fibres, because this very mobile synthetic material gives the fly masses of movement. The other major advantage is that the fibres don't hold water. As soon as you've

lifted the fly out, it's all but dry, and that means even the biggest fly is light enough to cast with ease.

To some extent, the bigger the fly, the bigger the fish, but that's not a cast iron rule by any stretch of the imagination. What you do need, especially if you are tying your own flies, is really good quality hooks. I generally squeeze the barbs down on all my own flies. You just can't afford to take the risk of a big pike sucking a fly in and having a barbed hook go deep in an instant – pike of 15 pounds and above are too precious.

Special Gear

The other major difference with pike fishing, as opposed to trout, is that you must use a wire trace of some sort. I like the Rio Toothy Critter. This is an all-in-one tapered leader with a wire trace connected. It's smooth, it works well and it's extremely convenient. Increasingly, I'm using Pro Leader, which consists of an inner core of Dyneema covered with a stainless steel mesh coating.

Unlike conventional wire, this can be knotted – a great advantage – and if it does kink after you've caught a fish, you can pull it through your fingers and it will straighten out at once. It comes in 10-foot spools and is expensive, but it's worth it.

You'll need a long pair of forceps, an unhooking glove and a very large landing net. Scales and a camera are also useful. I should recommend unhooking mats – especially if you're fishing on a boat or hard stony banks – but I like to unhook my fish as often as possible in the net itself and let them go without lifting them from the water at all. However, if they are really large and you want records, then that's a little different.

You will also need polarized glasses, because a lot of success comes from spotting the fish and watching them take. On my favourite lakes, we chase them in just 2 feet of water. It's almost like bone fishing, and you can get really, really close to them in the boat. Once the shadow of the boat goes over them, however, they're off in a flash. For this

▲ *Wow!*
This is one of the most stunning pike I personally have ever seen. It weighed over thirty pounds and fell for a surface-fished fly.

▲ *Team work*

Ian manoeuvres the boat into position whilst Neil hammers out a big pike fly.

they cover vast amounts of open water looking for prey. They're young, incredibly fast-growing fish and they learn – for example, you'll often find feeding fish around the usual stocking points.

The Retrieve

The retrieve is important, and it pays to change styles all the time. I like a stuttered retrieve, a jerky figure-of-eight retrieve and a sink-and-draw type of action. These are my fail-safes, and I tend to switch from one to the other through the course of the day.

You'll very often get fish following. They simply ghost from the depths and follow the fly, keeping a few inches behind. If you stop retrieving, they stop. Start retrieving and they start up again. Infuriatingly, they won't make that last lunge. You can try taking the fly out of the water and flopping it down hard near the fish. This can trigger an instant take. Frequently, it's best to change fly, try a different colour and size, and retrieve it in the general area where you last saw the fish. Swapping flies is made easier if they're attached with links, but these have to be very strong indeed to withstand the continual punishment of casting.

The moment when a pike takes a fly is absolutely critical. Don't strike. I describe a pike take on the fly as a clunk-click type of action. At first, you have a pull and feel something like a metallic tug. That, I believe, is the clunk, the fly being sucked in and hitting the pike's teeth. Then, there will be a moment when the line goes slack. This is when the pike is actually following you and the tension decreases. The pike will then close its mouth – the click – and you'll feel a long, steady pull. How do you react? Well, keep pulling on the line, almost as though you are strip striking. It's nothing wild, but a calm, measured response. Don't forget, if you strike at the first pull, you'll lose the fish every time by just pulling the fly out of the pike's open jaws.

I play my pike as hard as I can to get them in as quickly as possible. A long fight, especially in warmer water, simply tires them

reason, concentrate on scanning the water close to you rather than looking too far afield.

Pike Fly Techniques

When it comes to methods, I've generally found that surface lures can be slow fishing, and I usually go subsurface. Pike fly fishing is all about location, and unless you can see the fish you just have to search as much water as possible. Often you'll need a sinker to get down really deep, but I tend to start close to the surface, work the middle zones and then, if all else fails, dredge close to the bottom. I like drifting on the drogue, too, as this allows me to cover even more water. So, you can see that searching the water really is the key. If you catch a pike, be immediately prepared for another, as you'll often find them clustered in specific areas.

You will find pike hotspots, but not in the conventional sense. Forget the usual recommended structures – tree roots, drop-offs, reed beds and water towers. Big reservoir pike aren't like other populations. Pike don't lie in wait, they don't mount ambushes, but

enormously, and a pike at the point of exhaustion is in a dangerous condition. I find that I can play a big pike with a 9-weight rod far harder than I can with a traditional 3-pound test curve dead-bait rod. I know that takes some believing, but it's absolutely true.

Fierce but Fragile

Pike are at the head of the food chain in waters such as those described here, and the only creature they really and truly have to fear is man. For this reason, I recommend single hooks, crushed barbs, forceful playing techniques, long pliers and unhooking procedures that take place, as often as not, in the water. Pike grow big and can certainly look menacing, but in actual fact they are very susceptible indeed to bad handling, and a bleeding pike is inevitably a dying pike. I love my trout but I adore my pike, and the mothers of 15 pounds and over – sometimes way over – are a welcome addition to any fishery. Catching these beauties on the fly is efficient and exciting, and once you've become used to it, dead baits will be a thing of the past.

◀ ▲ *Baltic bonanza*
Areas that have extensive weed growth and are crystal clear make for perfect pike fly fishing water.

▼ *Swedish beauty*
These big Swedish fish can be caught on lures and flies alike in crystal-clear water.

Summer Salmon

Summer salmon fishing on smaller spate rivers presents a great challenge. The fish tend to run during periods of heavy rain, when the river rises and colours. As it falls and fines down, the fishing can be excellent. However, the time window is brief and the fish soon wise up. An angler really has to strike when conditions are hot, but this doesn't mean to say that the usual rules of fishing go by the board. There's no room for the impetuous here. I was fortunate to meet up with the renowned Irish angler Ken Whelan on one of his favourite rivers, unfortunately when it was just a shade past its best. However, watching Ken was an object lesson in how anglers should approach these smaller, broken salmon rivers all over the world.

▼ Times of plenty

It's now on smaller, summer spate rivers, when the water is the colour of melted chocolate, that the salmon begin to flood up from the sea. The water is still too coloured to work a fly, but the salmon will be arriving – once the tinge falls out of the water you'll be in business. When you can see a bright orange or black fly a foot or so down, it's time to start fishing.

Setting Out

'If only you'd been here yesterday. I got here last evening and walked a mile or two of the river, just soaking it in, thinking how lovely it all was and looking out for fish. I helped a couple of lads land one, and we all enjoyed seeing it swim away again. There certainly were plenty of fish in the river just 15 or so hours ago, so we've got a chance, I guess.'

Ken's gear was heavy trout kit – a 9-foot rod, an 8-weight floating line, a 12-foot, 10-pound breaking strain leader, a sea trout fly on the dropper and a small shrimp on the tail. He would, he said, probably scale down the size of flies steadily throughout the day.

So, off we went, stopping first at a deep, slow piece of water that looked dead, dark and lifeless, the sort of place you usually associate with spinning.

'In places like this, you've really got to work the fly, because you can't get the current to do that for you. My advice would be to search out the tree line and to cast as far as possible under the branches on the far bank. Fish like to hang in the shade there. Look really hard for your fish and you'll sometimes see them hanging in mid-water. Keep your nerve when they come after the fly – don't strike or pull it out in your excitement. Wait for them to catch it, turn and move the line before you lift into them. Water like this is frequently overlooked and it shouldn't be, because a lot of fish like to rest up out of the white water.'

Faster Water

From there we moved down onto a perfect pool. The flow was channelled between the far bank and a rock outcrop on our side that served as a very tasty fishing platform. A line of alders and oaks hung over the main current, and Ken flicked his flies downstream under the branches. He fished the killing point as the flies swung round in the current and hung for an instant with devilish intensity. We both sensed the moment when a take was most likely and tensed. The sun was

continuously, keeping in direct contact throughout the entire cast and then, right at the very end of the retrieve, he held the rod high and skated the fly hither and thither in the current. You just never know when an intrigued salmon might be following to your feet.

◀ ▲ *Ready now*

The water now is in perfect shape falling, clearing with the fish steadying their run upstream and settling into pools. It's now that Ken can target them.

Testing the Pools

On the next pool downstream, an alder craned helpfully over the river and I climbed it to watch. That orange fly certainly had a life of its own, flicking across the current like a small anguished fish looking for sanctuary. As my eyes grew accustomed to the water, I

▼ *The perfect run*

Ken moves quietly, confidently and continuously. He fishes one good piece of water after the next, trying each place for 5-10 minutes before moving on.

out, glistening off the dancing water, piercing the tree canopy with darts of light. Squadrons of damselflies crisscrossed the river. A perfect day.

Next we came upon a very quick little run, really nothing more than a thimbleful of water bubbling between two rapids. It was the size of a small sitting room, about three feet deep and quite probably a holding pool for three or four fish. Ken decided on a single fly on the point for such a tiny little pot, coloured orange to suit the still peat-stained water. Then he fished it beautifully. You'd have to say he was flicking the line out rather than casting it, just bouncing the flies down with the flow and twitching them back, searching intently. The retrieve was all done with a neat figure-of-eight action – it's not good to have a lot of loose line out in a situation like this in case a hooked fish manages to make the downstream rapid and you've got to follow at a canter. I noticed, too, that he put a lot of rod top work into the retrieve, constantly jiggling the fly into life. He mended the line

▲ **Straight from the sea**
A summer grilse is truly a thing of beauty; a good fish will weigh five or six pounds, and it will be spirited. It will fight very well on normal trout gear.

▼ **Practise your stalking skills**
To be a successful summer grilse fisherman you must be able to pick out the fish that you are targeting. Sometimes you will be lucky and they will splosh out of a pool, but more often than not you'll just see glimpses of the fish, perhaps as their flanks catch the sunlight.

sensed the presence of salmon. Two of them. One was around 6 pounds and almost certainly not a taker. Its head was down and its body language was all dullness and sulkiness. The fly passed just a foot or so away from its head but its fins didn't even flicker. The other fish, however, seemed in half a mind to take. There's no doubt it could see the fly – whenever it got to within a few feet, the head would come up and the body would angle provocatively. The fins would work and you could almost sense the muscles flex. On one occasion, the fish even moved forwards in a short burst towards the fly, before easing off and dropping down in the water. There was obviously a third fish in the pool, too, because Ken had a strong, solid pull on the far side of the run where the tree shadow divided the water into light and dark. He was unlucky to miss it.

Anyway, another pool, slightly larger this time. 'There just has to be one at the tail there.' Ken waded more deeply, fishing the tightest possible line, determined not to miss another take, and just dibbling the fly back over where salmon had to be lying. 'I'll be flabbergasted if there's not, the water's just perfect…' Ken was a magician of action and movement, making his fly seemingly impossible to resist, but nothing.

Ken gave every one of these small pools around 15 minutes of very hard, concentrated fishing. Every nook was searched: these small river fish aren't big and they can literally melt into the tiniest pocket of water. You've got two chances: a new fish could enter the pool and be instantly vulnerable, or a resident fish could finally be needled into making a mistake. So, while it's tempting to keep on the move, don't sacrifice thoroughness on each and every pool.

The Final Pool
At last, we reached the end of the stretch and found a proper pool by normal salmon fishing standards. It lay around 80 yards long and Ken dibbled his flies over the neck and then worked the main body of the water, moving fast. He cast at 40 degrees or so downstream, the flies all but kissing the far bank, and then pulled them slowly a foot at a time across the flow. There was nothing mechanical about this. He varied the retrieve rate and action constantly. Watching his hands was a revelation: sometimes fast, sometimes slow,

a pause, a twitch, a jab and then a long, steady heave. He worked quickly: a cast and then a good pace downriver. The process was repeated again and again with caution and concentration. It was a lovely pool – all moving water, no big slacks or back eddies, and not too deep. Once again I could see salmon whenever the sun broke through the cloud and glinted off their bodies.

He was done. Fishing like this is completely exhausting – you're not only working hard physically, but mentally too. Ken decided on a couple of hours' break and then he'd fish the dusk when salmon are always more active, stimulated by the coming night. We walked upriver towards the fishermen's hut, fishless but happy after a hugely satisfying day.

FLIES FOR SALMON

Salmon flies do not generally attempt to resemble food forms. They are frequently created on a whim or around a theory, often with no real natural pattern involved.

Size, Colour and Dressing
The first consideration is going to be size of fly and this is heavily dependent on the water temperature and the time of year. In general terms, the colder and murkier the water, the bigger the fly should be; the warmer and clearer the water, the smaller it should be. For this reason, for example, if you are fishing water that is below 8°C (45°F), then a fly of around 3 inches in length is probably best. As the water temperature climbs, scale the fly down to 2 or 2.5 inches. Once the water temperature is above about 10°C (50°F), things change dramatically and you might be looking at a fly tied on hook sizes 4 to 8. If the water becomes warmer still, let's say 13 to 16°C (55 to 60°F), you want flies between sizes 6 and 10.

Next, I want to give you a rough guide as to colour. Actually, I'm far from convinced that salmon pay much heed to colour whatsoever, but whenever the water is clear I've always been recommended to use a fairly sombre fly that does not look too out of place. If the water, however, is murky, then a rather more colourful fly is needed to stand out from all the silt, sediment and floating rubbish.

The third consideration is the dressing of the salmon fly. Older patterns were generally dressed with feathers and, if you watch them work in the water, they somehow look stiff and unnatural. Modern flies tend to be tied more sparsely, often from fur, and they work much better in the water.

Temperature and Depth
Temperature also affects the depth at which they will work. The colder the water, the deeper you want the fly to move and when temperatures are below 8°C (45°F), it's best to keep the fly as deep as possible, perhaps even touching bottom. Boddington tube flies are excellent for this type of work. You can move them along slowly, almost feeling them rub the bottom silt and debris.

As the water warms, you'll want to fish with a floating line and a lighter fly that swims somewhere in the surface layers. This means that for warmer water fishing you will be looking at flies that are lighter and will sink less quickly.

The size of hook on which the flies are tied is another factor. In all probability, the big flies of the spring and cold water are going to be tied on trebles or at least double hooks. As the water warms, single and double hooks begin to take over.

Always Ask
A final consideration is the most important of all – local knowledge and advice. On any new water, the first job should be to ask the owner, the guide, a fellow fisherman or the local tackle dealer what flies they recommend and use. Local knowledge is not always accurate, but it would be arrogant to ignore it and it does give you some confidence when you're starting out.

Breaking New Ground

The vast majority of us face similar fly fishing challenges and have developed broadly the same range of skills. For example, most of us know how to fish a dry fly, a nymph or a team of buzzers with a certain amount of respectability. We've probably fished wet flies in broken water from time to time. We might even have learned to spey cast or certainly to roll cast. All these abilities will take us a long way in our fly fishing lives; we probably won't want – or even have the opportunity to – progress much further. Yet, should we so desire, there is an absolutely limitless array of challenges and difficulties waiting to be mastered, and this is where the fascination and eternal complexity of fly fishing comes in. I don't care how experienced or well travelled a person may be, no one can be a master of all the skills that fly fishing demands in every situation.

▼ *Impossible beauty*
Sometimes travel brings you to the most extraordinary places on the planet. This river in Greenland flows five miles or so from the Ice Cap to the sea, and is startling in its purity.

Greenland

Personally, I have been extraordinarily lucky in my life to have travelled a fair bit with a fly rod in my luggage. I've encountered many complex situations that have, on many occasions, defeated me. I want to look now at just a handful of situations where you really have to pull out some very special skills indeed if you are to succeed.

Let's take Greenland as an example. Many of the rivers there flow straight from the ice cap, and they can be startlingly clear and freezing cold, often with chunks of ice swirling past your feet. Many of the best pools are deep, sometimes 20 feet or so, and the Arctic char, the primary species here, can hang at any level in these icy torrents. They're willing to take a fly, but they're not willing to move up or down to intercept one. This means that your challenge is to put the fly at exactly the right level, so that it literally brushes past the char's nose. This is extremely difficult: in water as clear and as deep as this, it is often hard to judge even approximately whether a char is lying at 13 feet or at 17 feet, and those 48 inches can make all the difference between success and failure. Even when you've made an accurate assessment of depth, you still have to pres-

ent your fly at that level regardless of currents, cross currents, eddies and shrieking winds from the ice cap. No wonder the biggest Greenlandic char can be almost impossible to catch.

A Challenge in Asia

In Mongolia, one of the most demanding skills is to raise a big taimen into accepting a mouse pattern fished across the surface. The problem is that often the biggest fish are the sulkers. If you haven't encountered them on a feeding spree, they lie doggo in the fast-moving rapids, simply holding position around the boulders. You must incite a taimen into action. You must annoy it, drive it wild. Often, you need to cast 30, 40 or 50 times over an individual fish to rile it, to make its temper boil, and, of course, this demands complete accuracy of casting. It's not as though you're casting a nymph – you're hurling out a fly that could be six inches long and it's soaking wet. Then there's a wind cutting like a knife from the plains of Siberia to the north. There's probably snow in the air and fallen larch needles are coming down like a golden carpet over the river. This is a challenge of skill and determination, but the explosion of water when a taimen takes is ample reward.

▲ *Impossible fish*

These Arctic char live and feed in the sea and run the freshwater each year to spawn. They're extravagantly coloured, take flies and fight like Dervishes.

▼ *A cracking selection*

These taimen lures were created especially for a trip deep into the heart of Mongolia.

▲ *Brother Batsokh*

Of all the people in all the world to whom I stand in gratitude, Batsokh heads the list. He has saved my life on more than one occasion, and has led me to many extraordinary fishing spots, such as this. He holds an enormous taimen.

The Southern Hemisphere

Then, we have Argentina. Here your aim is to hunt dorado in vast marshlands riddled with clearwater creeks and rivers. Locating the fish is hugely difficult, and the dorado themselves can be incredibly spooky within the crystal-clear waters. Alternatively, you may be on one of the big sea-trout rivers with a massive wind belting into your face. It's a wind that can flatten houses, but you know sea trout of between 20 and 30 pounds are running in front of you and somehow you batter that fly out.

I remember fishing once on the northern island of New Zealand, on a river that runs into Taupo. I happened upon three enormous rainbow trout, obviously long-term residents in a small pool. These fish were all in the 15- to 20-pound bracket, and over four solid days I absolutely failed to interest them in a fly. First, my approach was wrong. When I got that right, my presentation was wrong. When I got that right, my fly choice

was wrong. I never did get it right because I had to fly home. Mind you, those three Antipodean monsters were no more difficult than tiny wild brown trout have proved on crystal clear rivers such as the Barle in Exmoor. The fish there may only weigh a few ounces but they can drive you crazy.

European Waters

Imagine a golden sunset over an ancient Irish lake. Chironamid are hatching into the air and big, golden, red-finned rudd are swirling under the surface, taking the ascending buzzers. Catching them should be easy, but it's not. Whereas trout will jag the leader forwards, these rudd sip in buzzers so discreetly there's barely any evidence of a take. You've got to watch like a hawk and, more often than not, strike purely on sixth sense and highly tuned instinct.

It's like fishing for big European barbel in clear, vast water, full of wavering ranunculus. You have to pick exactly the right fly, guide it

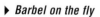

Casting for gold

The freshwater swamps of Argentina hold extraordinary fish, none more wonderful than this Golden Dorado. These are big, aggressive fish that hit a fly with ball-like force.

▶ **Barbel on the fly**

Just a few years ago it would have seemed unlikely that catching big barbel like this on a nymph or even a dry fly was at all possible. However, the world of fly fishing is constantly changing, and such an event is no longer remarkable.

▲ ▶ *The Indian experience*

Fly fishing in India was originally practised more than a hundred years ago, and it's now coming back into fashion. Indian mahseer up to thirty pounds or so are eminently fly catchable.

to exactly the right place and hold it there, in the current, long enough for an ultra-clever barbel to make up its finicky mind.

My own biggest humiliation was with some grayling in a river in southern Austria. The river and the valley were astoundingly beautiful and the grayling were gobsmackingly large. Many of them were around the 4-pound mark. There were many of them, but that didn't mean I could catch them. For six days I tried and for six days I failed, unless you count a baby of a pound as a success. I tried them with dries, nymphs, shrimps, corixa – everything – and not once did I make a single one turn its head. I came to believe they knew I was coming the moment I left my hotel a quarter of a mile from the water!

Playing the Big Ones

Even if you can hook a fly into a fish, there are times when it's almost impossible to bring them to hand. I remember Simon Channing's epic journey to the Brazilian rainforest after arapaima, and what Herculean skills he showed in extracting fish of a 100 pounds and more. However, let's say you're

fast into a mahseer in one of the furious, whitewater rivers of India. It's a 60-pound fish hooked at the top of rapids three-quarters of a mile long. How on earth do you hold something like this? If you can't, how do you follow it? The toughest salmon gear in the world simply gets shredded. I've even seen rods used for marlin just buckle.

Are there some fish in some situations that nobody's skill can subdue? How about big, northern pike in the Baltic Sea – yes, living out there in the salt. During the summer, the biggest of the females lie some three miles offshore around large, sunken plateaus and islands. The water here is deep, and the currents are ferocious. The areas are a jumble of massive, jagged rocks and heavy forests of weed. How do you get your big, silver streamers down deep in these places and work them so the pike think they are herring adrift from their shoal? Even if you do hook one of these pike in a boat so far from the shore, how do you land it? These are fish that can grow in excess of 60 pounds in weight.

Thoughtful Patience

I once watched a man discover a nest of

bass in a clearwater lake. There were three big fish lying over the scooped-out area about four feet down. He managed to wriggle himself into position without scaring the fish, and he put out a cast. They ignored him. He changed fly and cast again. Again, he was ignored. The angler made 30 different casts with 30 different flies, but the three bass didn't blink. On the 31st cast, using the 31st fly, he hooked and landed the first bass. With the next two casts, on the same fly, he landed bass number two and bass number three. A perfect piece of fishing. Then, there's Radim, a member of the Czech national team, who worked himself into position in the margins of a raging river and, in 50 casts, landed 50 grayling. And how about Bob, working a fly on the Kwinimass River in British Columbia mending the line at just the right moment so that his fly paused right in front of the nose of his chosen steelhead? Eighteen pounds of fresh-run silver was his exciting reward.

Skill upon skill upon skill. You could live to be a hundred years old and not master a fraction of the fly fishing challenges the world has to offer.

▲ **The rarest of them all**
This is a photograph the likes of which you might never see again. It's of an angry arapaima deep in the Amazon rainforest, hooked by one of my most respected friends, Simon Channing. This fish was lure-caught but they are – just – legitimate targets on the fly if you can locate them.

▶ **A sporting chance**
My friend James Ellis holds a super fly-caught pike. No wonder fly fishing for pike is all the rage. It's clean, it's fascinating and it's exciting. And a single hook in a pike makes release so much easier and fish-friendly.

A Year in the Life of Big Stillwaters

Howard Croston is an England International fly angler, game product development manager for Hardy and Greys, the leading UK tackle company, and an expert on large stillwaters. In this section he discusses some key moments during the course of the year on these inland seas, looking in detail at early season fishing, two different types of buzzer work, fishing for daphnia feeders and autumn techniques. These truly are some of the most essential skills to unlock the secrets of these daunting venues.

Early in the Season

Spring sees many of the big stillwaters – artificial and natural – opening for the first serious trout fishing of the year. These can be difficult, dour places when the wind is up, the rain is falling and temperatures are dropping. So, the first thing that you need to take into account is your clothing. From head to toe, you've got to be warm, snug and bone dry, and any of the outer shells from the leading manufacturers will guarantee you that.

Springtime Fly Gear

Generally, at this time of the year you won't be fishing imitative patterns. Ninety per cent of the time you'll be pulling lures back deep, and at speed, and often casting them out into squally winds and flurries of rain. This isn't, therefore, the time to pick up a 3- or 4-weight kit! Rather, you are looking at a rod between 9 and 10 feet, capable of putting out a 7- or 8-weight line, hour upon hour.

As for your leader, make it as long as you can, depending on the conditions. You don't want to get into a muddle, so although 9 or 10 feet is ideal, 5 or 6 feet will do happily in really grim weather.

Choice of lure is always an issue, but don't let it worry you unduly – all you really need are a few lures of differing sizes that are basically black, white and orange. Think about it: if the sky is black overhead, full of rain and wind and you're fishing deep, then you'll probably be better off with something bigger and brighter, such as a Marabou. If you've seen fish moving in shallower water, then perhaps it is better to use something a bit smaller and a bit more sparse.

Find the Fish

At this time of the year, fish aren't spread around large waters evenly but are nearly always shoaled up tight, and it is down to you to find them. Keep your eye on what

▼ *Reading the lakes*
It makes no difference whether a lake is in the southern (left) or the northern hemisphere (right). They are all readable so long as one knows how to decipher the clues.

Contours
Try and build up an impression of important contours on the lake's bottom. You'll often find fish feeding along the ledge where the shallows drop off to the deeps.

Rocky outcrops
Always investigate rocky outcrops. They harbour extensive food supplies and fish will hang close to them.

Shallow bays
Always investigate shallow bays carefully, especially early and late in the day. If you are the first on the water you'll often find that fish that came in during the night to feed in the margins are still there at dawn.

Spawning streams
Not all inflowing streams attract spawning fish, but local knowledge will direct you to those that do. You'll often find fish amassing near the mouth of spawning streams near to the end of the season. They're very catchable then.

Rocks
Look out for rocks, weeds, fallen trees, sunken boats – anything that breaks up the contour of the lake bed. Find a feature and you're sure to find a fish – especially if it's black bass that you're after.

The deeps
Search out the very deep holes in very warm or, alternatively, very cold conditions.

Feeder streams
Feeder streams are often favourite places because they can bring extra food stocks into the water. In very hot conditions the incoming water might also be cooler and contain more oxygen.

other people are doing, and if you see fish being caught, move that way – always observing fishing etiquette, of course! Above all, if you're bank fishing, keep on the move, covering the water quickly and systematically until you run into fish. If you've got a boat, so much the better, especially as you can moor 50 to 70 yards from a bank, with the wind behind you, and cast easily into waters that bank fishers can't reach. You will almost

always be casting to the bank, and it will almost certainly be empty bank, because there are very few anglers who really like to fish into the teeth of a gale.

Early Summer Buzzer Fishing
Here, I'm going to talk about early summer buzzer fishing on big stillwaters. You can fish them effectively with the buzzer from the bankside, or drift in a boat, if possible.

▼ *Going afloat*
A boat gives much easier access to taking fish, but the stealthy shore-angler need not be outdone if he wades carefully and doesn't disturb the margins.

FLAT-WINGED FLIES

There are thousands of species of flat-winged flies, for example, houseflies, mosquitoes and crane flies. They're characterized by their six legs and their two flat, short wings. Many are land insects, but there are several hundred aquatic species as well. Buzzers or midges are among the most important for the fisherman. Buzzer fishing can be useful in almost any month of the year.

ADULT BUZZER

The adult flies often sit on the water for a while where they are vulnerable to the fish. So, too, are the females when they return to the water's surface to lay their eggs. The adults can be imitated as well as the pupa. Try small Grey Dusters, for example.

HATCHING BUZZER

Escaping the pupal case can be a drawn-out process and the hatching buzzer is very vulnerable to preying trout. The cast-off skins are sticky, and when there is a great deal of hatching activity you'll sometimes find them clinging to your fly line when you retrieve it.

THE LARVAE

The larvae of the buzzer are commonly called bloodworm and they can be anything up to an inch long. You'll find them in the mud of the river or lake bed or among bottom vegetation. At this stage they're of little use to the fly fisherman, although coarse fish feed on them heavily, blowing up the bottom to get at the tasty morsels.

PUPAE

Buzzers hatch generally from early spring onwards. At first, you'll find them hatching in the day, but as the season progresses they become more active towards evening. The pupae rise through the water but have quite a problem getting through the surface film. They hang there very exposed in the top layer before hatching and it's at this time that you'll see the distinctive, bulging rise forms.

Buzzer Tackle

For standard gear, I would recommend a 10-foot rod, because it allows you to fish three or even four flies, widely spaced, but still giving you perfect presentation.

The leaders will generally be level and not tapered. I find these drop through the water well, really searching the water column. Tapered leaders are good when the fish are really rising and you're targeting moving fish. Breaking strain can be anything between 3 and 8 pounds, depending on the size of the water, the size of the fish, the size of the buzzers being employed and the weather conditions at the time.

The positioning and choice of the flies is important. Put your heaviest fly on the point. In the early summer, I like a black epoxy or superglue on a hook size anywhere between 8 and 14. The middle fly will probably be much the same pattern, but generally lighter. On the top dropper, I'll put a buzzer made of seal's fur to imitate a hatching or emerging insect. In employing a team like this, you are effectively searching the entire column of water beneath you.

Buzzer Technique

As for the method, I generally employ a figure-of-eight retrieve, which is slow and

▼ *Aware!*
Notice how Leo stands a good way back from the open water – he is doing so in consideration of how crystal-clear the lake is. Bass are his target, but rainbow (right) are equally aware.

steady, but with short bursts of speed to make the flies dart up and down the water column, just like the real insect. Takes can be colossal. Believe me, I've literally had the rod taken out of my hand. However, just as likely is a sip-in that you've really got to be on top of your game to spot. Watch the end of your fly line closely, or the leader, or the loop of fly line beneath your rod tip. If you see any twitch or movement out of the ordinary, tighten at once.

Fishing buzzers with an indicator can be a superb method, especially from the drifting boat. If you're pleasure fishing, a straightforward strike indicator is fine. In a match, you might have to use a very buoyant top fly to give the same effect. The indicator gives many advantages. In an oily ripple, you'll find a wave action moves the indicator, bung or whatever you want to call it, up and down, which, in turn, imparts a perfect movement to the flies beneath.

There's more to it, however. I frequently employ a really fast figure-of-eight retrieve. The wake the bung produces attracts trout to investigate. They'll rarely be foolish enough to take the bung itself, and what you'll see is a boil, a flat swirl just underneath it. Then, nine times out of 10, the fish will turn down, see the conventional buzzers, and the whole rig will simply go away.

Golden Evenings – Buzzers and Stalking Fish

You know the sort of evening: a hot day has gone before and now the dusk is settling, the wind is probably dropping, buzzers are hatching and trout seem to be head and tailing everywhere in that slow, leisurely way that they adopt in these tantalizing moments. Unfortunately, if the fish are in a picky mood, periods like this can be enticingly difficult.

Stalking Tackle

I tend to use a shorter rod than normal when fishing buzzers at times like this. Nine and a half feet will probably suffice on a larger reservoir, with 9 feet being fine on a smaller commercial fishery. The reason is simple: with a shorter rod, you can change the casting direction faster and follow a quickly moving fish.

Line will be a weight forward, and 7-weight covers most eventualities, but if you really want to enjoy a true light sporting challenge, you can go down to a 5.

I use a steeply tapering leader, either ordinary mono or copolymer. It's important that the taper is a steep one because you have to turn your flies over in the dead air that is typical of evening conditions. You should keep your leaders short enough to be accurate, yet not so short as to scare fish. If it's very calm, I'll go as long as 16 feet but if there's a wind, I'll cut that down to 12.

You're only going to be using one, or at the most, two flies on your leader for this style of fishing. This cuts down on tangles – infuriating when time is tight – and improves presentation. This is very sophisticated fishing indeed, and each cast must be as perfect as you can make it.

▼ *Tight control*
Fishing dries and buzzers (left) in the surface film calls for the tightest control and the lightest of touches.

As for the buzzers themselves, I personally like Shuttlecocks and I try to match the imitation to the natural that is hatching. This means I'm generally using hook sizes 10 to 18. If you're tying your own buzzer patterns, you'll very likely lead the tail of a fly, perhaps with a couple of twists of wire. This means it cocks instantly when it lands on the water rather than settling on its side, which is disastrous. If you don't tie your own flies, test your buzzers beforehand in a glass of water and see how they behave. You're looking for flies that sit with their plumes straight up, imitating the natural as accurately as possible.

Targeting the Fish

Let's now look at moving fish. If your target is rising frequently, coming up every couple of feet or so, bear in mind that its window of visibility is exceptionally small. You'll almost have to put your buzzer between its eyes or it just won't see it.

Think about exactly which way your target is moving. One tip is to look very carefully at the rise. On one side of the rise there will be a bulge, a build up of water created by the shoulders of the fish as it submerges. This gives an indication which way the fish is going. You might also see the fish's tail disappear, again an obvious clue.

The real skill in stalking fish like this is to guesstimate how much lead to give a fish. You have to form an accurate impression of how deep and how fast your target fish is travelling. The key is knowing how far to put your buzzer ahead of the fish, so that fly and fish meet as close as possible head on.

Concentrate a lot of your effort on the wind lanes. These are great places, as there is more surface tension here and hatching flies can't get off into the air as quickly.

Problem Solving

Let's say that the fish, for one reason or another, are proving ultra difficult. Is there anything you can do? One step might be to use a floating line with an intermediate poly leader or, even better, a Greys' Wake Saver line. Then, put on a buoyant suspender buzzer. Cast it out, let the leader sink, give the buzzer a tweak so that it sinks fractionally. Let it pop up immediately in front of your target fish. You've created the perfect imitation of a buzzer coming off. It's a difficult technique, but if you get it right it's absolutely deadly and you can fool even the most sophisticated fish.

Let's look at another cunning trick. Let's say you are using two flies and you're tracking a fish that's moving so quickly that you're not exactly sure of its position. Straddle where you think the fish is with your two flies so that you are actually covering two options. Once again, this calls for fast, accurate casting, but it can knock a clever fish off guard.

Make sure that you always cover a fish with the point fly first, especially if it is coming towards you, whether you are in a boat or on the bank. Unless you really have to, you don't want to show a fish a leader at all.

The worst nights of all are when the buzzer hatch is minute, much too small to imitate realistically. Take your buzzers off, tie on a lure and whip it straight back along the

▼ **Irish mastery**
Basil is the master of the great western loughs. His knowledge of the fish, the fly life and their interaction is supreme.

top. Make as much commotion as you can and you'll often find this knocks the fish off their feeding pattern and provokes an immediate reaction.

Daphnia Days

Throughout the summer and well into September, daphnia are one of the major food items on our big reservoirs, and a large proportion of the fish will spend a vast amount of time feeding on them exclusively. So, if you're not going to miss out, you've just got to take the daphnia phenomenon on board and work with and not against it.

Where Are They?

I suppose the first objective is to locate where the daphnia blooms actually are, because then you'll be finding the fish – logical, but essential. The golden rule is that on bright days you'll find the daphnia down deep, but when there's a lot of cloud about, they'll be up closer to the surface.

When finding the clouds of water fleas, or daphnia, the wind is another important factor. The wind tends to blow the algae in front of it and it's upon the algae that the daphnia feed. What I generally do is position the boat well off the lee shore and then drift in, fishing hard as I go, until I locate the hot areas.

If the day is sunny, I'll start off with a fast sink line and work as deep as I can. If they're not there, then I'll move up through the water column. Alternatively, if the day is very cloudy, I'll begin with an intermediate line. If I don't find the fish up near the surface, I can always work down until I meet up with them.

TOP EARLY SEASON TIPS

• Don't go light on the leader strength. If you are stripping a lure back fast, fish will hit hard. Six-pound breaking strain is an absolute minimum, and consider 8- or even 10-pound if good fish are around.

• Even if you are not wading, consider breathable chest waders. They will keep you snug and dry, even in the most torrential rainstorms.

• Safety is a major issue at this time of the year. If you're out in a boat, don't think of going out without buoyancy aids, and never go out on water that you consider even remotely frightening. Don't become too absorbed in your fishing, and keep a constant eye on where you're drifting, especially around rocks. Beware, too, of slippery banks, and make sure that you've got good, sure-grip soles to your boots.

• Keep your eyes open and don't be purely lure fixated. At some stage in the day, it could be that trout will move onto buzzers or even come up to the surface. If you find a nice calm bay, perhaps with just a bit of a ripple, or if the sun comes out and the temperature rises noticeably, you can fish a buzzer with mounting confidence.

• If you are contemplating an early season trout trip on a large, stream-fed water such as Lough Corrib in Ireland, take a selection of imitative minnow-type patterns with you, such as minkies, glass minnows or small streamers. In winter storms, minnows and sticklebacks are washed from the streams into the lakes where the trout gorge on them.

▼ *Inland seas*
Be mindful of the weather, especially if the water you are fishing is rocky or is particularly exposed. Remember, no fish is worth your life.

▲ *Bass city*
Look carefully at the top end of this lake – you'll see that it's dotted with trees and submerged branches: a perfect bass location.

This way you have both issues covered: study the wind and you can find where they will be on the water. Take a variety of lines with you and you'll soon find their depth.

My favourite rod is, without any doubt, a 10-foot 7-weight that is a good caster and has a through action. It will be a top stillwater all-rounder, letting me fish nymphs, dries and lures with equal efficiency.

The Fly Set-up
As for flies, I wouldn't go out without orange and black Blobs tied to a size 10. I'd also want some boobies tied in bright colours. A sparkler booby is a good bet. If I'm using two flies on a leader, I'd probably use a booby and a Blob. The leader is almost invariably 20 feet long, and I'd fish them 12 feet apart.

Sometimes I'll fish four flies on a leader – a Blob, then a nymph three feet down, followed by another nymph and finished with a booby. The idea is that the trout are attracted to the Blob and, if they refuse that, they'll see the nymph and be hooked. Good nymphs include Crunchers and Hare's Ear.

I'd like to make two points about your leader. As I've said, it will generally be around 20 feet long, but ensure that there's only about 14 feet between your point and your top fly. This is because you've got to think about netting a fish if it's on the point and where the top fly will be in relation to the top rod ring. It's a simple point, but it's often overlooked with disastrous consequences! A long-handled landing net obviously makes the whole netting procedure easier.

The other point about the leader is that it's got to be heavy, and I generally settle on either 10- or 12-pound breaking strain. There's a good reason for this. You cast your flies out, count them down and then really rip them back as fast as possible, and the trout hammer them. It's like hitting a brick wall.

You might wonder why the fast retrieve works so well when the trout are grazing on daphnia as lethargically as cattle on a rich meadow. My belief is that the fast-moving flies catch their attention and somehow knock them off balance a little. It's something unusual, but attractive, and they make an instant, positive decision.

Autumn on the Big Stillwater
October can be a true mix of weather and it's not unusual to find yourself in a real Indian summer, especially when the true summer has been a bit unsettled. In fact, bear this in mind, and make sure that you go out with the requisite sun protection if the sun is shining. If you do hit a spell of good weather, it pays to approach the water like you would in the summer – get out early and stay on the water late. Fish down wind of aerators or search pockets of the deepest water with a fast-sinking line. There might well still be algae blooms on the water, so it does pay to look for areas of clear water where you will find the fish much more responsive and much more able to see your flies.

Fry Patterns

October often sees the real start of fry feeding. Many perch and roach fingerlings are now an attractive size, and you will find them hanging around water towers, boat docks, weed beds and any fallen trees.

Watch also for gull activity. If you see them diving, you can be sure that predators are driving the small fish towards the surface – and those predators could very well be big browns or rainbows.

It's a very good idea to have two different rods set up at this time of the year – your normal rod and then a slightly heavier one for the fry feeder. I suggest a 10-foot 8-weight, with a weight forward line allied to a floating fry pattern. Having this specialist rod already made up can save you very valuable time. Fry feeding is sporadic and it can be over very quickly indeed, so when you see fry feeding, you must capitalize at once.

General Tackle

Your normal gear can be a standard 10 foot, 6- or 7-weight outfit for nymphs and dries, but you can have a great deal of fun at this time of the year coming down in line weight. For example, consider a 9½-foot 6-weight combination. You will find this is altogether faster, and you can cover rising fish more neatly and quickly with a shorter rod that generates that extra line speed.

Choice of Flies

I'm often asked which flies I would recommend for this time of the year. I would probably include the Bibio Raider, the Amber Hopper and the Red Holographic Shuttlecock among my best dries. Buzzers are now fading off the scene somewhat, but black epoxy patterns can still do the job quite well. Moving on to nymphs, it's hard to beat the Diawlbach range, though I personally love Silver Thorax Pheasant Tails and Crunchers.

For lures, you can't do much better than Sparklers or white Boobies, while everyone has their own favourite floating fry imitations. Anything that imitates small roach and perch does very well, and that old perennial favourite, the Tandem Appetizer, performs as well now as it did decades ago.

▲ *At ease with the world*
Early morning. Flat calm.
Feeding fish. A good rise.
Find the dry fly. Heaven.

▼ *One man's vice*
Charles Jardine creates
exactly the right mayfly
pattern for a difficult
chalk-stream fish.

Freshwater Bait Fishing

I used to live very close to a large day-ticket bait-fishing water. I walked around it virtually every day unless the weather was absolutely foul or it was physically frozen over with ice. I watched some anglers succeed there, but the majority, however, failed. Why? On the simplest possible level, most of those that failed were just fishing the wrong places. It sounds very basic, but the vast majority of anglers would leave their vehicles, walk a short distance and then settle down in the nearest available place.

▼ *Mean and moody*
Magnificent pike like this are the reward for the bait fisherman that sticks it out in desperate conditions.

First Find Your Fish

More times than I can count, if they had merely moved another 10 or 100 yards, they would have physically seen evidence of many feeding fish. Over and over, they were fishing where practically nothing was happening, and they were doomed to failure from the outset. My basic, most logical advice, therefore, is to leave the tackle safely locked up while you walk the water and look for the signs of where fish are present and where they are feeding. Location is the key, and though it's an oft stated and obvious fact, it is frequently overlooked.

Do It Right

Of course, there were other factors, too. The anglers who succeeded were those who chose the best method for the particular swim on the particular day. If legering, swim feeding, float fishing or even free-lining was the best method, they'd choose it.

They were also the people who fished the best method in the best possible way – with calm control and consistent accuracy. Their feeding would be spot on, their casting would be pinpoint and their bait presentation would be immaculate. They would concentrate like hawks and strike at bites, however slight. Nothing they did was slapdash, clumsy or left to chance. It was an education and a delight to watch them.

Have another look at the section on bite detection in Chapter One. When you are bait fishing, bites can be exceptionally sensitive and might merely nudge a quiver tip, dip a float or tremble the line between your

fingers. There are some baits and methods that on some occasions might produce a bigger bite, but not always. Do not make the mistake of thinking a very slight bite is necessarily the result of a small fish taking interest. Frequently, the bigger the fish, the more warily they will actually pick up a bait.

Never be in too much of a hurry to leave the waterside at the end of the day. The increasing shadows and the darkening water almost always encourage non-predatory fish, especially, to move more and to feed more aggressively.

Some Useful Tips

Before we move on to look at all the many forms of freshwater bait fishing, let's just run through a few tips that could prove vitally important.

• Target shallower water in the early part of spring as the water begins to rise. Fish will often over-winter in deeper parts of the lake, but as their metabolism speeds up, they will come to feed on the fertile shallows.

• Target areas of the lake that get a lot of sunlight, especially in the colder months of the year. It's not just a question of temperature: the light itself stimulates many members of the cyprinid family in particular into greater feeding activity.

• Don't overlook the western bank of any stillwater in the dawn period. It will receive the first rays of the rising sun and the water will warm up more quickly there, encouraging serious feeding activity.

• Travel as light as you can. Watch the water and move on to any fish that are rolling or bubbling. A mobile approach is particularly important in understocked waters or when the fishing conditions are difficult.

• Never over feed - it is best to put in less free offerings than more. Until you get to know a water particularly well and have been successful enough to start experimenting, use baits in which you have confidence.

▲ *Pot of gold*
A rudd is one of the most beautiful fish of the European summer. Taken on either bait or fly they're an absorbing species.

◀ ▲ *Distance fishing*
Using a marker float like this can be a boon in telling you exactly where you have laid a carpet of bait.

◀ ▼ *On the pin*
This sleek, hard-fighting barbel fell to a worm bait fished at distance under a float.

▼ *Length for control*
A thirteen- or even fifteen-foot rod is very useful in conditions like this, when float control is imperative.

Float Fishing

Before we look at one of the most engaging skills in float fishing – long trotting – it's wise to look at the theory of floats in some detail. It's not at all uncommon to see anglers using totally the wrong float for the job in hand.

Size Matters

Make sure that the float you choose is big enough for the job. There's nothing worse than scratching around with a float that is too small, either to be cast the required distance or to hold out in the current in a wind. A big float can always be over-cast and drawn back into the baited area so as not to cause too much disturbance. A big float also gives you far more control than one that is too light.

Shapes and Styles

Floats are either basically long and thin or have a certain type of body. The long thin ones are probably the most popular, and are generally made of peacock quill, reed or plastic. The bodies on floats are often made of polystyrene and these can be placed down towards the bottom of the float to give stability in rough water. Those floats with bodies near the top are generally meant for streamy, fast water where surface stability is required.

A lot of modern floats can be rearranged by using a variety of different tips that can be inserted into the top. These tops can be of different colours, which will help with visibility if you change swims or as the light alters. Also, if you're having trouble registering bites, a finer insert tip can often help. Many floats are now made with clear plastic bodies, often called crystals. The idea here is that timid fish in clear water cannot see them so easily, and are not so likely to be alarmed.

The Avon Float

Let's have a look at the most common types of floats, beginning with Avons. These are good trotting floats for long distances. Some Avons are made as crystals, for shallow water, and some are made with wire stems to give greater stability in turbulent water. Loafer floats are similar, and designed for longer distances and bigger, heavier baits such as meat or bread. Loafers are perfect on fast- or medium-paced rivers and swims where the surface boils.

Stick Floats and Wagglers

Most river fishing is done with the ordinary stick float. Fish these top and bottom – that is, attached to the line in two places – and string the shot down the line evenly, shirt-buttoned, as it's called. Smaller stick floats are designed for close-in fishing and delicate work. Large stick floats are designed to cope with faster, deeper water, and they can also take bigger baits, but don't use them a long way out, or your control over them will suffer.

Probably the most common floats are the ordinary peacock wagglers, which should be attached to the line by their bottom end only. These are ideal for all general approaches in rivers and lakes. Baits can be fished on the drop, as they fall through the water towards the bottom, by pushing the weight up

▼ **Out in the stream**
If you can wade out to the line that you want to fish, you will find float control much easier because you are directly behind it and don't have to mend the line to anywhere near such a great extent. This way, you will find your presentation easier and it will invariably be more effective.

▲ **In the lilies**
A big-bodied float like this is particularly useful for a heavy bait – perhaps a couple of lobworms or even a dead minnow presented for a perch or bass.

towards the float. These floats are buoyant enough to allow a bait to be dragged through the swim without constantly registering false bites.

Crystal Floats

A popular modern float is the loaded crystal. This is a clear-bodied, large waggler with a bomb incorporated into its base. The bomb allows the float to be cast long distances on a very straight trajectory. The clear body means that shy fish, in gin-clear waters, are less likely to be alarmed. However, the loaded base does drag the float deeper on entry into the water. This means that you have to be careful if the swim is shallow and the fish are feeding warily. It pays to overcast and draw the float carefully back into the swim. Feathering the cast can also help reduce the speed of the float on impact.

Drift Beater

Another outstanding float, especially for stillwaters, is the drift beater. Stillwaters are never, in fact, still. The wind sets up subsurface currents that can drag many floats out of position and make the bait behave unnaturally. The drift beater has a long antenna that keeps it stable in strong currents. It also has a visual sight bob that stands out at a distance. This is a perfect float for medium- to long-distance fishing on lakes in rough conditions.

There are many specialized floats, but these are the most important. Note, too, that most of these floats can be fitted with a nightlight insert. These are frequently of the Beta variety, which can give out a glow for many years. These come in ratings of 300 or 500 micro lamberts. The 300 version is generally visible for five to 10 yards whereas the 500 version can be seen for at least 25 yards.

A Dying Art

Sadly, we are living in an age where the art of float fishing with a running line is being lost. This is partly because many match men use a pole with a fixed line, and partly because many specialist anglers are switching to legering and swim feeder fishing techniques. This is a pity, because fishing the float brings satisfaction and is an exquisite way of presenting a bait in the most natural of fashions.

▶ **All the floats you'll ever need**
The top photograph shows a selection of river floats. The ones with the fluted bodies can grip the current well; the non-fluted floats are perfect with big baits and streamy conditions. The middle photograph shows a second selection of river floats. The one on the left, a stick float, is perfect for fine work for smaller fish in clear water conditions. The yellow top float would be ideal for a worm bait, and the other two would work well in fast-flowing conditions. The bottom photograph shows a selection of stillwater floats. The two floats on the left are wagglers, and the two on the right are designed for lighter, close-in work.

◀ **Fooling the fish**
If a float is cocked, it will sometimes be seen more easily by a wary fish in clear water. Laying a float flat is often the best solution.

Long Trotting

There are many types of float fishing that require appreciable levels of skill, but perhaps the most demanding to master and the most artistic in action is long trotting. Long trotting is a term given to fishing the float downriver over long distances, certainly over 20 yards, and often up to 100 yards.

▶ *Pin appeal*

You can, of course, trot a river using a traditional fixed-spool reel, but a centre-pin is the tool that is tailor-made for the job. A centre-pin gives you perfect control all the time and leaves you in constant contact with the float.

Benefits of the Method

Long trotting is, first and foremost, efficient. It is an ideal way of finding fish in a feature-less stretch of river. If there is no response after the first dozen trots, then move down 100 yards or so if space permits and fish the next stretch of river. By travelling light and moving frequently, even a mile of river can be fished quite thoroughly within a morning.

The second major use of long trotting is to contact fish that are very shy and will not

1 THE POINT
A fishing position like this always works well because you are in line with the flow of the river, which helps your control immensely.

2 THE CREASE
There is a distinct line – the crease – between the slow water by the bank and the fast water in the main current. Fish love this area.

3 THE MIX
Water divisions always attract fish. They move into the cloudy water looking for food, then return to the clear water for extra oxygen.

tolerate close human proximity, particularly in fast, clear and shallow rivers where wild species are easily spooked.

The Long Trotting Technique

When long trotting, a longer rod is useful. Excellent reel control is necessary, whether this be centre-pin or fixed spool. The skills required in long trotting are many: the line must be mended continually so that control of the float is constant. If the current creates bows in the line, strikes will be missed and, just as bad, the float will be pulled off course and the bait will behave unnaturally.

It's also important to control the float, as it has to be guided towards promising areas and inched around snags. You can't simply let the float go with the flow and trust to luck. You've got to impose your own wishes on that small creation 80 yards away from you. You've also got to hold the float up occasionally so that the bait rises enticingly off the bottom, often prompting a fish into an induced take. Let the float travel out of control, even for a couple of yards, and you're risking calamity.

When the float does eventually go under at long distance, the strike needs to be instant and powerful, and must continue until the pull of a hooked fish is felt. Everything has to be done gently, but confidently and with a smooth assurance. Hitting a fish, especially a large one, at nearly 100 yards in a swift current can be quite a shock

▲ *Trotting the stream*
Note how these two anglers have put on chestwaders so that they can enter the main current. This means that their floats are trotting directly downstream, making it easier to mend the line.

HOLDING BACK

Holding the float back is a trotting art form. Remember that the current is faster at the top of the water than at the bottom, so if the float is allowed to drift down uncontrolled it will pull the bait along at an unnatural speed. By slowing the float, you will make it move at the speed of the water deep down. It's a good idea to stop the float periodically. This will lift the bait off the bottom and make the line and lead less obvious, tempting the shy fish to bite.

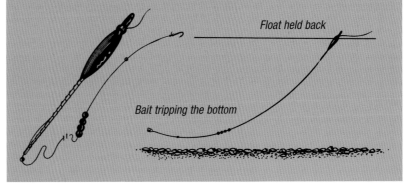

Float held back

Bait tripping the bottom

▲ Delightful control
Phil simply flicks his float out into the middle of the river with a gentle, pendulum-like underarm action. He exerts complete control so that the float falls onto the water with as little splash as possible, which is always very important.

to tackle and angler alike. Take no chances with your line, hook or knots.

Playing the Fish

After the fish is hooked, keep the rod low to avoid any splashing. Such activity will only alarm the rest of the shoal and make a hook slip more likely. Once the fish begins to come, keep it on the move with a steady, horizontal pumping action. Pull the fish several feet towards you, then reel line in as quickly as possible, repeating the process until you have the fish close. Now it's ready to be netted.

▶ The speck of red
Red is one of the most conspicuous of colours, and it shows up well even in dark water like this. Here Phil is holding the float back so that just the tip of it can be seen. The bait will be rising enticingly from the bottom.

◀ *A pearl of nature*
These are the perfect words to describe the beauty of a mint-condition roach. Beautiful scales, gorgeous shape and deep red fins are the hallmark of one of the world's most special fish.

Trotting Weather

Ideal conditions for long trotting are dull, overcast days when there is little wind to ruffle the surface. Bright sunlight leads to a lot of surface glare, which, in turn, makes seeing the float a long way off a headache-inducing job. Wind chop on the river is at least as bad, especially when combined with glinting sunlight. A wind of any strength, particularly across the stream, makes float control at long ranges even more difficult than it is normally. This does not mean to say that long trotting in breezy, bright conditions is impossible, but it does pay to build up experience on the calmer, duller days, when fish are more inclined to bite anyway.

Finding and Feeding

If fish have been located at a considerable distance and you think it unlikely that you will scare them, by all means move down closer to them. Long trotting can simply be used as a way of finding fish and, once located, you can move in on them and fish in a more tight, delicate way.

Loose feeding is a problem at long range, and it is best to feed in dribbles of mashed bread, possibly flavoured and possibly containing maggots, casters or even pieces of chopped worm. This concoction will gradually drift down the river bringing fish on the feed or even pulling them close up towards the angler. If the hook bait is large enough to make a real statement – say a huge lump of meat, bread or a bunch of worms – then loose feed is less important. Remember, a big bait could need a heavier float than you have been using for maggots or casters.

▼ *Taken at range*
This good chub succumbed to a lobworm fished under a float and trotted about 50 yards downriver. The bite was dramatic and the fight, protracted.

Legering

When you're bait fishing, there are many times when you really do need to strive for distance, and fishing close in under your rod tip isn't an option. Perhaps the water is very busy and the fish are pushed way out into the middle, or perhaps that's where the food sources lie and where the fish feed naturally. So, if you see activity at 30 yards out or further, the most successful and straightforward method to use is the feeder/quiver tip combination. You can use either a block end feeder with maggots or an open end feeder with ground bait and samples of the hook bait inside.

▶ **Feathering the cast**
Feathering the cast by slowing down the rate at which the line comes off the spool is the best way to consistently place a bait in exactly the same spot. Slowing the bait will also reduce its impact, lessening the splash.

▼ ▶ **Quiver tips and feeders**
On the left is a quiver tip rod with a selection of quivers. Some are glass, some carbon, each with different test-curve weights. On the right is the maggot-packed feeder disgorging its contents.

Feeder Fishing

Using a feeder is, essentially, a comparatively easy way to fish and I wouldn't rate its skill factor sky high. However, as in any form of fishing, feeders do have their own complexities. It's important when you are using a feeder to ensure that your casting is tight and accurate. It doesn't pay to cast a feeder into lots of different places, as you will simply break up a feeding shoal and have them scattered and wandering looking for your bait. The best way to make sure that your casting is spot on each time is to line up a feature on the far bank and cast to it repeatedly. You can even put a bit of tape on your spool once you've cast out so that you will be reaching exactly the same distance each time you cast.

In shallow, clear water especially, you

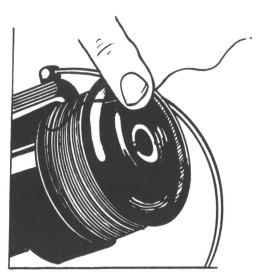

don't want your feeder to enter the water with too much splash, so use as light a feeder weight as possible and, just as if you were float fishing, feather the feeder down at the end of your cast.

Bite Detection

Detecting bites is a necessary skill when feeder fishing. Certainly, your quiver tip will sometimes be pulled right round, the rod nearly disappearing off the rests, and you will be in absolutely no doubt about striking. However, a word of caution – with a bite like this don't strike too wildly or you could have a break-off. On most occasions, however, the tip will merely flicker and nudge, and you won't be at all sure whether you are experiencing line bites or the real thing. Even the biggest fish can sometimes shake a quiver tip as though a gust of wind is blowing. It's up to you to experiment. If the tip quivers minutely, strike. If there's no hook-up, leave the next tremble and see if it develops. The more you strike unsuccessfully, the more you are pulling your feeder through a shoal of fish and unsettling it.

The next step is to experiment with your hook lengths. Go longer or shorter until you get a positive indication. Experiment with your hook baits. Try two maggots, or three maggots, or a maggot and caster combination until you find the answer. Perhaps the tip of a redworm will change everything around. Maybe your hook is too large, so drop a size. Perhaps it's even the wrong colour, so change that. There will nearly always be an answer. It's up to you to find it.

The method feeder has made a big impact on stillwaters all over the world. It certainly attracts fish and, in heavily stocked waters, can prove irresistible. Bear in mind that you are casting out a comparatively heavy weight and you need to step up your line strength accordingly or you'll risk snapping off on the cast. Bites tend to be positive using the feeder method, so ignore flicks and nudges and wait for the tip to go right round. Another ploy is to leave the reel on backwind, and don't even think of picking up the rod until you see the reel handle beginning to revolve.

◀ *Ready for action*
Notice how the quiver tip rod is held high so that as little line as possible falls on the water. This is the perfect day – little breeze, overcast conditions and the fish will be feeding well.

▶ **Feeder choice**

A cage feeder like this can be very useful in quick water. Once it has discharged its cargo of bait, its profile presents little resistance to the current so it is unlikely to be pushed out of its settling position. Note how the spool of the reel is filled right to the rim – perfect for accurate casting and for control of the fish.

▼ **Fast water problems**

Fish can spot an unnatural-looking bait, and the movement of the food item in the water can be a crucial factor. In a strong current, a light bait is likely to be swung around and may even spin wildly at the end of the line. A single shot pinched onto the line close to the bait will keep it down and increase the chances of a fish treating it as part of its natural food supply.

Simple Legering

The feeder is a very useful tool, but it isn't the only way to leger at distance. I've already said that if the water is clear and shallow and the fish are spooky, the swim feeder itself can prove a major deterrent to the fish. In these circumstances, it's better to fish a simple lead weight and mix particles of the bait you're using with ground bait and then catapult the balls out to the desired spot. On pressured waters, this can work well, because the lead is less obvious than the feeder and you can make the balls of ground bait so light that they don't enter the water with a huge splash.

The main problem with this method is that you've got to get your ground bait mix absolutely right. What you don't want is for the balls to break up in the air and scatter randomly over the water in front of you. Equally, you shouldn't mix the ground bait so that it becomes as hard as a stone and enters the water like a bomb. The ideal is for the balls to begin breaking up as they hit the surface and then carry on dissolving as they fall to the bottom. If you can manage this, you'll almost get a curtain effect as the bait streams down in a constant plume from surface to lake bed. Maggots and casters mixed in with the ground bait are perfect for this approach, casters particularly, because some will come free from the ground bait when it hits the bottom and will rise slowly towards the surface again, so that the visual attraction of what you're trying to achieve is even further enhanced.

The major skill with legering, then, is really to do with your ground baiting. This is where many anglers fall down. The whole secret to intelligent ground baiting lies in attracting the fish to the area and then holding them there. This is where the use of tiny particle baits comes in – grains of rice or hemp seed excite the fish, don't fill them up, are difficult to find and will keep them digging around your swim for hours to come.

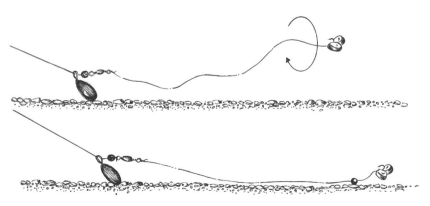

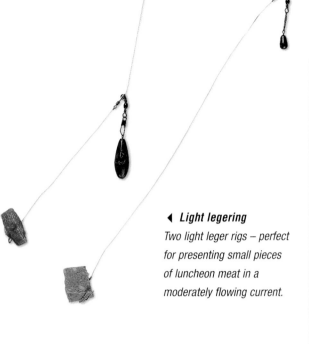

◀ **Light legering**
Two light leger rigs – perfect for presenting small pieces of luncheon meat in a moderately flowing current.

However, be warned, the use of very small baits such as hemp can create a rod for your own back. The fish become preoccupied and stop looking for any bait that's larger than a pinhead. Present a large bait over a bed of hemp and you can wait a long time for fish to show any interest. This means you will be forced to fish lighter and lighter with ever-smaller hooks. A hair-rig often becomes necessary.

Hook Bait Alone

You don't always have to leger with either a feeder or with loose ground bait. Indeed, for big fish on clear, pressured water where they are ultra wary, either of these approaches can be detrimental. The more stereotyped your approach is in any situation, the less likely it is to fool the cleverest of fish. An alternative is to set up a rod with a leger weight and a big-impact natural bait alone. Lobworms do very well for most fish species. If the water isn't too crowded, simply walk round it and cast the lobworm towards any likely looking spot. Fallen trees, extensive reed beds, close-in weed and man-

made structures such as bridges and boat jetties all shelter feeding fish. Pay particular attention to your sighting techniques. Binoculars will help you pick out areas of clouded water or even the tips of tail fins as fish feed in shallow water.

If you find fish feeding like this, cast your weight and bait some 5 or 10 yards beyond them. Then slowly retrieve until you're pretty sure that the bait is nestling in close proximity to the feeding fish. Don't cast right onto their heads in these situations or the fish will simply bolt or, at best, they may stop feeding and sulk until they sense danger has passed.

▲ **The winter river**
This is how the winter river looks: cold, lifeless and forbidding. However, maggots trickling through the dead and dying branches can provoke a reaction from the fish.

▼ **Lure of the dawn**
Dawn on most waters presents the best time to catch bottom-feeding fish, especially in hot weather.

Touch Legering

On one level, touch legering can be seen as simply holding the rod in one hand, holding the line in the other and feeling for a fish to take the bait. It's that straightforward on a certain level but, as you'll see, there's a whole lot more to it. It's also probably one of my favourite three or four ways of fishing. Just why is it so magical? Touch legering is not only an extremely efficient method. Much more importantly, it is wonderfully thrilling and takes you right under the skin of the river and into the very living rooms of the fish that live there.

▲ ▼ *A low profile*
Rob is well hidden here behind a screen of rushes. The barbel, seen below, are feeding close to the riverbed, but that does not mean that they are unaware of the movement above them.

An Electric Connection

When you're touch legering, your line is like an umbilical cord connecting you with another life force. Through his line, the experienced touch legerer can tell you almost exactly what is happening in the swim before him. For example, the touch legerer will eventually begin to realize the difference between real and line bites. Soon, the line bites will tell him the number, the size and possibly even the species of fish that are moving around in the swim. You will certainly begin to build up an almost completely accurate picture of what the swim contains and the make-up and contours of the riverbed. When you begin to get proper bites, touch legering will tell you exactly how the fish are regarding your bait and set up, whether they are confident, wary or even downright petrified.

Travelling Light

There's lots more. When you're touch legering, you don't need a rod rest. In fact, you shouldn't have one - belting the point of a rod rest into a gravel bank will alarm the fish even before you cast. Without one, you can also up sticks and move on in a fraction of the time most bank bait anglers need. Indeed, good touch legering is all about mobility and exploring the entire length of the river. Touch legering is rather like fly fishing in that you try here, there, everywhere, and in the process you find more new swims than you could ever imagine.

The method can tell you so much. If you're sharing a swim with a friend, and he casts in a swim feeder or a heavy lead and you immediately feel fish bolting into your line (line bites in the jargon of the touch legerer), you know that the fish are scared and scattering. It's just the same if your friend hooks a fish – you'll almost instantly get line bites as the shoal breaks up. You begin to realize just how spooky, how easily scared the fish in front of you can be.

The Real Thing

It can be like that when you're getting actual bites. (Don't worry, you'll always know the difference between a line bite and a real one: it's impossible to explain, but you'll feel instinctively that there is something live down there, that the line is shrieking a message to you.) Decent bites from confident fish are quite unmistakeable. These are slam-bang and you merely lift into the fish. One minute you're dozing, watching the kingfisher on the far bank, and the next your rod is hooped, your reel shrieking and you can't quite believe what a magical experience it is.

However, it's not always like that. Very frequently, you will feel bites that are merely a shake or a tremble. You can feel the fish pick a bait from the bottom, hold it between its lips and then place it back down again. This is not hocus-pocus. It actually happens a great many times, and it's fascinating. It's you and your fish at close quarters, both pairs of eyes bulging. It's showdown time at the OK Corral. The fish knows you're there. You know he knows. It's a total battle of wits.

As the fish pose their problems, your brain is racing. Do you fish upstream?

▲ *Comfort in all*
Good touch legering technique is all about comfort.

▼ *Legering the stream*
The anglers below are legering in quick water using worms as bait. They are holding the rod in one hand and the line lightly over the index finger of the other hand. Tucking the rod under the arm gives perfect balance.

▲ At the seaside
Touch legering is a very useful technique when fishing the coastline for species like bass.

▶ Reading the water
You'll find that if you get out into the river like this, you're much more at one with the pace of aquatic life. You'll see more fish, and you'll also begin to really understand how the currents around you are working.

Do you lengthen or shorten the hook length that you're using? Do you use a bigger or smaller bait? How about hook size? A change of bait altogether? A cocktail of two or three baits, perhaps? Have you put in too much feed? Too little? Do you rest the swim and come back within an hour?

Keeping You Thinking

In these sorts of ways, touch legering teaches you as much about the fish as it is possible for a human to know. For example, your first cast is absolutely your most important one, because the more you cast, the more the fish become skittish about your presence in their world. Make the first cast as perfect as you can to stand the best chance of catching fish off guard. The design and size of your lead are both crucial. The heavier the splash and the shinier the leger, the more damage you're doing to your swim. You begin to realize that even throwing free offerings into your swim before making the first cast can prove disastrous. Heavy baits have a shotgun effect that can blast a semi-scared

swim right apart. If you want to put in bait before fishing, why not do it the day before if possible? It should certainly go in a couple of hours before actually making that cast.

Touch legering demands that you approach every swim with the clearest possible plan of attack in mind. You've got to think exactly where to put your terminal tackle, where it's going to settle and from where you need to fish. Don't even think of casting out until you've got the best possible plan prepared. Your approach to even the same swim will differ session after session, depending on light conditions, water height, flow, visibility and weed growth.

The Basics of Touch Legering

You don't want a rod that's too long and heavy if you're going to cradle it all day. Lighter, more sensitive rods make it easier to feel what's going on down the line. A good rod should be between 9 and 10 feet long and light enough to hold all day long. Match this with as light a reel as you can find that will still do the job adequately. In most situations, we tend to use reels that are far too large for the job in hand. It's very rare that you need a reel with 300 yards of line on it!

Once your leger and bait are in position, hold the rod comfortably under your arm – that's where lightness comes in. Crook the line from between the reel and the butt ring around one or more of your fingers. I like to use the index finger, but I constantly vary this. Comfort is the over-riding issue.

Point your rod directly to where you think your bait is lying. You will have to consider the depth of the swim, the current and the weight of your lead to make these calculations. Try to eliminate as much slack line as possible between your fingers and your terminal tackle. This means mending the line busily until your terminal tackle holds bottom.

Wading is of great benefit when it's safe to do so. This cuts down the length of line between fingers and bait and, while touch legering doesn't have to be a close-in job, everything obviously becomes much more tight and intimate as distance decreases.

Find a relaxed position whether you are wading or standing, or sitting on the bank. Otherwise physical discomfort will soon become a nagging distraction and it's essential that you become as one with the river as possible.

You should feel so intimately in touch that one slight pull from your fingers will dislodge the bait and trundle it down in the flow. You should feel that if a fish even breathes on that bait you will know about it. If that sounds impossible, don't worry. You will very soon get to know the difference between a piece of floating weed on the line and a real bite. That proper bite is absolutely 100 per cent impossible to ignore. It's a life force that screams at your instincts even if it's comparatively gentle and doesn't wrench the line from your fingertips.

▲ ▶ *The author in action*

Touch legering is probably my favourite method of them all. It keeps me in touch with every whisper of action, and fine fish, like the barbel seen above, are often the result.

Free-lining

In many ways, free-lining is very similar to touch legering. The basic difference with free-lining is that the bait is kept on the move, so that it drifts downstream in a totally natural way. Many species of fish rely on the drift of the river to bring food to their doorsteps, and this technique exploits this method of feeding perfectly.

▲ *Going with the flow*
The perfect free lining setup: standing in the current and letting the river peel line off a centre-pin.

▼ *Use your loaf*
Bread is a great bait for most cyprinids. Tear a bit from the centre of the slice, push the hook through and squeeze slightly around the shank for a fluffy yet secure bait.

The Correct Bait

Free-lining can only really be carried out effectively with a heavier bait. A lobworm is good, and multiple lobworms also work. I've used up to five on a single, large hook. Dead fish, sausage, luncheon meat and bread flake also work. You might also want to use a large split shot to increase the weight of smaller baits, or to add weight to a large bait in a very fast current. Above all, you must always know exactly where your bait is and be in direct touch with it. This means using a bait heavy enough not to get lost in the current.

Free-lining Technique

To begin with, you need to be physically as directly in line with the current as possible. Unless you're on a very small stream, this will generally mean wading. If you're not in line with the current, you'll find that the push of the water creates big bows in the line and, once again, you will begin to lose the immediacy of contact that is so vital to this method.

Simply lower the bait into the water and then allow the current to take it away. Pay out line as it goes, but don't let line spill out too freely. Constantly check the line, lift the rod tip and ensure that you are always in direct contact with the bait. This might mean that you're constantly mending the line and ironing out any loops that the current is trying to create. The faster and deeper the water, the more often you will have to do this.

Why the emphasis on keeping in touch with the bait at all times? Simply because, if you're not tight to the bait, you won't know when you get a bite. Worse, if you do have a lot of slack line wafting in the current, it's easy for a fish to swallow the bait without

you being aware of the fact, and the fish will come to harm. You should always make the welfare of the fish a priority.

In slower currents, you may need to lift the bait off the bottom and let it go again with the flow in a series of hops downriver. You might also decide to use a smaller bait in slow, shallow water and certainly remove any split shot.

When a bait finally comes to a natural stop, try and hold it there for a few minutes while always maintaining that direct contact. Why? Well, in any stretch of river, food travelling in the drift – such as your bait – tends to drop to the bottom in one of several specific spots. Perhaps this will be a depression or behind a stone, or even at the tail of some weeds. Whatever the cause may be, the fish become used to visiting these places on a regular basis because they know that they will always find a reliable supply of food.

When you decide to retrieve the bait, don't reel in wildly but twitch the bait back slowly and erratically. For many species, this can be just as effective as the drift downriver. Trout and perch, especially, will hammer into cleverly retrieved baits.

The Free-lining Bite

What exactly are bites like with free-lining? Bites, in fact, can vary widely. You can have plucks, tugs or full-blooded runs, so be aware. Read each and every situation and strike quickly once you are aware that a fish has taken. Better a missed fish – which will probably come again – than a deep-hooked one that you want to return.

Overall, this is a great method for river fishing. It's very effective, wildly exciting and allows you to be extremely mobile so that you can search out all manner of promising water. It's relevant for any species – trout, salmon, perch, barbel, chub, even carp.

▲ *Making use of the current*
The angler has waded far out into the river so that he is fishing directly down the flow. This means he is in constant and direct contact with the bait and can feel any interest from the fish.

▶ *The surface bait*
Chub, in particular, like to come up and intercept food either on or just beneath the surface.

Carp Fishing

Throughout Europe, more people fish for carp than for any other species. Carp fishing is also becoming increasingly popular in the US. It's the size, power and undoubted beauty of the species that proves so attractive to the angler, and perhaps, above all, anglers like the challenge of carp because they are so very wary and cunning.

▲ *Easy does it*

Clive has taken a good five minutes to work himself into position here. From afar he saw a carp working under the old boat house, and now he's ready to swing out a natural bait. It never pays to rush.

▼ *Playing fair*

Dowsed with water, this gorgeous common carp is briefly displayed before being released back into the water.

An Intellectual Challenge

Even in their wild state, in waters that are hardly fished, carp show the deepest suspicion of anything unusual. In lakes subjected to angling pressure, carp quickly become wise to the anglers' ploys and seem to have an uncanny ability to get the measure of any new tricks within a very short time. It is a constant battle of wits between fish and angler. When the anglers invent a new method or a new bait, it puts them at an advantage for a while. Then, however, the carp become wise and learn to recognize the new tricks that have been fooling them, and stalemate is reached again until the anglers have another brainwave.

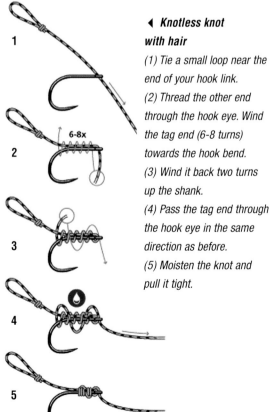

◀ *Knotless knot with hair*

(1) Tie a small loop near the end of your hook link.
(2) Thread the other end through the hook eye. Wind the tag end (6-8 turns) towards the hook bend.
(3) Wind it back two turns up the shank.
(4) Pass the tag end through the hook eye in the same direction as before.
(5) Moisten the knot and pull it tight.

A Wise Old Fish

Carp can grow to a great age – certainly 60 years or more. This long lifespan helps reinforce their instincts and innate facility for learning. They don't learn in the intellectual way that humans learn, but they are capable of registering experience and acquiring a store of responses to these experiences.

If any fish can be described as intelligent, then big, old carp are the first contenders. These fish lead relatively ordered existences with only seasonal and climatic changes in their environment. Anything unusual will be noted, and even when the fish seem totally preoccupied with feeding, they are constantly alert. Moreover, like many other creatures, carp have the ability to communicate unease or fear. This needn't involve surging off in panic flight. Carp seem perfectly capable of transmitting signals to other carp by the subtlest body language, indiscernible to any but other carp, and certainly not to the angler.

The Carp Community

Watch carp in the warm sunshine of a late afternoon when they are resting and at their

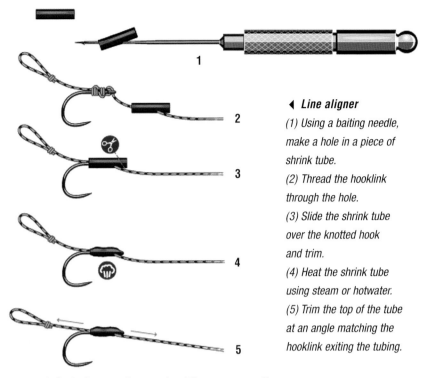

◀ Line aligner
(1) Using a baiting needle, make a hole in a piece of shrink tube.
(2) Thread the hooklink through the hole.
(3) Slide the shrink tube over the knotted hook and trim.
(4) Heat the shrink tube using steam or hotwater.
(5) Trim the top of the tube at an angle matching the hooklink exiting the tubing.

most infuriating to the angler. They may well have been basking for 12 hours, lying in the milk-warm water with their bellies caressed by beds of soft weed. They give every impression of contentment. You might see their eyes roll, and you can watch the languid

◀ Enjoying the day
This carp is simply wallowing in the weed, enjoying the sunshine that you can see reflecting off its back. Although it's sleepy and not feeding hard, a fish like this will sometimes be tempted by a bait. Try a piece of bread crust, a floating dog biscuit or even a worm cast just in front of its nose.

▲ Digging hard
When carp get their heads down, the bottom can explode. This fish has smelled the sweetness of sweetcorn and pellets, and is digging furiously. Watch carefully for bites – they can be surprisingly gentle as the fish simply sucks in the bait and doesn't move off.

▶ Searching the swim
Here we see two carp moving slowly across a silty bottom, looking hard for food. This is the sort of area where they will expect to find bloodworm.

movement of their fins. These are definitely not feeding fish, and they are almost impossible to catch in this condition. They are interested only in relaxing in the sunshine, perhaps even enjoying the company of their fellow shoal members. Occasionally, the sun will get too much for them and they will drift away into the shade of overhanging trees. It is there, in the cool, particularly as evening approaches, that the occasional fish will decide to begin feeding.

It might surprise a non-angler that carp exist as a real community. They really seem to know each other and the water they inhabit. Day after day, they will swim round in the same small groups, almost as if they were capable of forming particular friendships. Within each group, there is a definite pecking order, with a leader who seems to decide the pattern for the day.

Feeding Habits

In rich waters, the carp's diet consists almost entirely of small invertebrates – bloodworm, daphnia, shrimps, beetles and tiny snails. Their whole lake is a larder, heaving with juicy titbits. Unlike the fish in relatively barren, newly created lakes where there is real competition for food, these fish have no need for anglers' baits and are particularly difficult to catch.

Carp like these move slowly over the lake bed, grazing like cows. The fish are actually excavating the silt, creating quite noticeable hollows around them as they suck in huge mouthfuls of mud, sifting it for food and expelling it through their gill flaps. Bubbles of gas billow from the gills as well and break in a froth on the surface. These fish are probably only going to be tempted by a

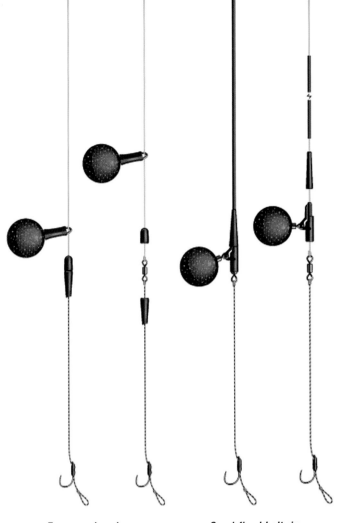

▲ **Free-running rig**
*This rig allows the fish to run
with the minimal resistance.*

▲ **Semi-fixed bolt rig**
*This rig holds the lead in place so
the hook can prick the fish without
causing it to bolt.*

▲ **Over the masonry**
*Fallen masonry like this
often attracts fish from bass
to carp to pike. This big fish
is intent on picking up bait
that is well-positioned
in one of its favourite
sanctuaries.*

completely natural bait such as lobworms, brandlings or a big, black slug.

The Carp's Senses

A carp's sight is surprisingly sharp, certainly in clear water. At a couple of yards or so, anything in the water stands out clearly. When a carp moves really close to a bait, details become pin sharp. The carp also has a good wide-angled view of the world above and gets a pretty useful impression of anything happening on the bank within a hundred yards or so. Shapes are blurred, but an angler moving without cover will alert a carp more than a football pitch away.

Carp also have a great sense of smell, necessary in the wild to detect bloodworms and swan mussels hidden under inches of silt. They also have a discriminating sense of taste. They can become really hooked on a particularly flavour of bait, for example, and then caution may be subjugated. However, they can also remember unpleasant associations, which is perhaps why baits fall from favour after a period of great success.

A carp depends a great deal on its powers of hearing, and every time a bait or a lead hits the water, it will register. I have seen carp shy away from a bait dropped 40 or 50 yards away. Even a gun fired half a mile off can cause a carp to sink out of sight and hide amongst the lily pads for an hour or more.

The tactile senses of a carp are also highly developed. They will be able to feel lines dragging across their bellies or rubbing against their fins. Their mouths are also extremely touch sensitive and will often detect things that are wrong with a bait. Carp can learn to mouth baits gently, testing their feel before swallowing or rejecting them.

Big Carp Adventure

Mitch Smith and Lee Collins are big names in the carp world, and also advisers for the tackle company Hardy Greys. Their position ensures that many mouth-watering propositions come their way each year, but few posed the challenges of a trip to the Volga Delta in Russia in the summer of 2004. Just arriving intact with all the gear proved to be an accomplishment in itself. Moscow airport takes some negotiating, and when they eventually arrived in Volgograd in the dead of a hot, mosquito-ridden night, they still had to find transport to the fishing grounds over 100 miles away. The intrepid pair finally arrived at their destination after 36 hours travelling and, as dawn was still some hours away, they put up a couple of bed chairs and crashed out until mid-morning.

▲ ▼ *Crazy carping*
Above we see one of the trip's great successes: a beautiful 50-pound Russian common carp. Below we see the village that Mitch and Lee created.

The Volga Delta

The delta of the Volga is absolutely vast, and the river begins to break up into innumerable channels 200 miles from its entry into the Caspian Sea. The main river itself proved to be an almost impossible proposition: perhaps a mile wide, endlessly deep and moving like a train. It definitely held carp, but location and bait presentation would both be a nightmare. Even the few miles of waterway that the boys had bitten off were bound to prove hard to chew. The arms of the river were pretty mighty themselves, often over 200 yards wide and anything up to 40 feet deep, but at least they had the features that Mitch and Lee wanted.

Scouting Around

Local fishermen were keen to show them some promising areas but, crucially, Mitch

and Lee took time out to search for an area with which they would both be entirely happy. Some 10 hours was spent afloat with an echo sounder and binoculars looking carefully for any features, any signs of fish down deep or on the surface. Little by little, the lads drew up a list of likely places.

In the end, they plumped for one of the bigger arms of the main river where it narrowed slightly to produce a deep bottleneck some 120 yards across. On the far bank, opposite the beach from which they had chosen to fish, stretched a morass of fallen branches and submerged trees. Over quarter of a mile of true aquatic jungle was formed and, to judge by the evidence of the echo sounder, there were many fish present. The fallen trees obviously gave the carp sanctuary from the flow of the river and from passing boats – the perfect place.

Pre-Baiting

Mitch and Lee spent hours preparing the bait – they were now into their second morning. Buckets and buckets of boilies were chopped painstakingly into halves so that they would not roll in the current and so that the flavour would be released more rapidly.

Huge amounts of seeds and corn were also added – a medium-sized supermarket had been virtually denuded of its stocks. When everything was ready, the buckets of prepared bait were ferried across the river and deposited with absolute precision over about 20 feet of water just out from the worst of the snags.

Getting Prepared

The pair were meticulous over their gear. Their big reels were filled to capacity with 20-pound breaking strain line and more. They rigged up with shock leaders, not just for casting, but to give extra security in the fight. Knots were tested. Hooks were needle-sharp. Leads were chosen to hug the bottom, and the rods were made ready – 3-pound test curve rods, which they knew would give them plenty of leverage.

The boys then set up pitch. Their bivvies were erected, along with those of the Russians who had come out to watch, learn and admire. Soon a whole village had t aken shape, with cooking and storage tents and a first-class kitchen preparing the first meals of the session.

In the late afternoon, Mitch rowed the

▲ *Safety inline lead*
The safety inline system is probably the most commonly used bolt rig. Used on hard bottomed, weed-free waters, it allows the lead to detach itself when snagged. The rig tubing prevents tangles.

◄ *Mitch's set-up*
Four rods, four reels, four rigs – everything has been meticulously prepared and is ready for nightfall.

baits across and placed them exactly over the baited area while Lee held the rods, played out the line and then clipped them up back on the bank. This in itself took almost three hours, and the light was failing fast. Mitch then spent half an hour with a throwing stick whirling boilies 120 yards across the river to top up on the bait deposited earlier.

Fish On

There followed four nights of steady action. Four rods each gave Lee and Mitch eight chances during the hours of darkness, and it was rare to see more than one or two rods still in place by the time dawn came. Between six and the full eight runs were the norm, and takes were simply electrifying. The pair virtually sat over their rods throughout the night so that they could hit runs as fast as possible and stop them getting into snags. Once the fish were hooked, huge power could be generated by the X-Flite rods and there was never a moment when they looked like being in danger, even though some of the fish were very large indeed.

One of the best fish of the session was caught by a young Russian disciple in full daylight. Mitch and Lee were obviously delighted for him, and they gave him huge moral support and constant advice throughout the battle. Again and again, the big common looked like winning the fight, but a mixture of side strain and swift, efficient pumping kept it moving away from danger.

On the bank, there was great rejoicing when the fish was landed, and Mitch and Lee quickly supervised the weighing – the fish scraped 50 pounds – and the photography session. Never once was the fish out of water for more than 30 seconds, and Mitch could frequently be seen pouring saucerfuls of water down its head, over its gills and across its flanks. Although the temperatures were in the high 70s and the fight had been a long and hard one, the fish went back without a wobble – real testimony to the careful regime the guys had imposed.

The Right Priorities

This extraordinary Russian expedition was a display of great competence. The pair settled on their plan, set out their stall and

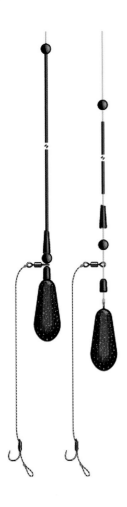

▲ *Helicopter rig*
With its aerodynamic and anti-tangle properties, this is an excellent rig for extreme distances.

▶ *A helping hand*
Big Mitch helps his delightful Russian carp-fishing friend sort out a few rig problems. That's the beauty of top-flight carp fishing: there are no secrets and no jealousy between anglers.

▶ ▶ *Into the distance*
Mitch used to be a top athlete, and it shows when he flicks his boilies out over a hundred yards towards the far bank. Carp fishing might involve sitting behind rods, but it can also be very physical.

◀ *The battle rages*

Downriver we spotted two Russians in an inflatable boat, and they'd been playing a fish for well over two hours. Notice how the 'assistant' is tapping the rod butt – this provokes the fish beneath into action.

▼ *What a pussycat!*

As expected, the enormous fish turned out to be a great catfish, well over a hundred pounds in weight. These are leviathans with mouths practically big enough to swallow their captors.

fished with clear-sighted intelligence. Above all, they showed care for their environment, for the Russians gathered around to watch and for the fish themselves. It is easy to write big carp fishing off as static and uninspiring, but it's not when you see it in action, not when you see the intricacy of the rigs and the accuracy of the long distance casting. Above all, when you have 40-pound-plus carp 100 yards away at night in a big, deep, swirling river, any single weakness in the angler's make-up will be brutally exposed. In short, Mitch and Lee left Russia having created a huge impression on their hosts.

Carp Off The Top

Surface fishing for carp is the most thrilling type of fishing imaginable. You see the fish, you see their reaction to your bait and presentation and you see the take. Truly, you are a participant in the whole event. However, it's a challenging form of fishing: true, you see the fish but, conversely, they see you. You're fishing right on the surface, so the line, hook, knots and all the flaws in your set-up are more clearly seen. You're often fishing very close in, so camouflage, stealth and the most expert use of cover are all essential.

Slow and Watchful

As with any style of fishing that demands consummate skill, don't rush carp off the top. Take all the time you need to walk your lake. Note any areas of scum where food will be trapped, making it easy for the carp to intercept. This includes scum lanes in open water, full of food pushed there by the breeze. Look out for cover, where the carp feel safe. Study areas of heavy weed, lily beds and thick reed margins. Never pass by thick, overhanging branches without first carefully studying the dark water beneath. Look for jungle areas where there are lots of fallen branches and tree trunks lying in the water.

You can also watch for specific fish. Often, you will be pleased if any fish comes along, but sometimes give yourself an added challenge by hand-picking your fish. Perhaps, it's special because of its size, beauty or a rarity of colouring or scale patterns.

Pre-Feeding

A great deal of the skill in fishing from the top comes in your ability to feed the fish up to a state of readiness. Don't be in too much of a hurry to introduce your hook bait. Instead, take your time and gradually build up the carp's confidence with free offerings. Often, you can use the wind drift on the water to

▲ ◀ *Something different*
Many anglers now are pursuing carp like this with floating baits fished on traditional fly tackle. It's a sporting and exciting way of fishing.

attract carp out of snaggy areas into open water. They will pick up the scent, begin to investigate and, hopefully, follow the moving food to where you can attack them more conveniently. Again, this takes time to achieve and you must exercise patience.

There are other considerations when it comes to the feeding process. Most vitally, don't overfeed. There are days when the fish appear ravenous enough to eat you out of house and home, but this isn't always the case. Sometimes you can push fish to a crescendo and then, quite suddenly, they'll begin to lose interest and drift back into cover and you've missed the opportunity. The key is to keep fish interested, looking and following the bait. If you get any impression the fish are tailing away and moving back to the weed beds, cut back on the feeding at once. Your aim is to build up competition and have them scrabbling for your bait. Fish in a hurry are less likely to take time looking for mistakes in your presentation.

Sometimes, when you have fish feeding really avidly, it's a good idea to cut off the bait supply altogether and starve them for 10 to 15 minutes. This achieves the effect of moving the fish around a great deal as they look for the last remnants of food. Then, when they see your hook bait, they'll often take it without their usual consideration.

Presentation is the Key

When you are fishing on the top like this, take great care over your presentation. Line

is the first problem. Thick line is very obvious when it lies on the surface, especially in bright light. Thin line, however, always runs the risk of being broken, and no caring angler wants that. Fortunately, modern lines are much thinner and more resilient than they were even 10 years ago, and some of the fluorocarbons are now excellent. Another trick is to sink your line an inch or so under the surface where it immediately becomes less obvious. However, if it then rubs along the back of carp, it will immediately spook them, and any advantage is lost. As the light fades, the carp can lose sight of the line and begin to lose caution, so don't be in too much of a hurry to go home early.

◀ ▲ *Reading the signs*
You can tell a huge amount by the way a fish approaches a floating bait. In the photograph on the left, the fish is moving slowly and confidently, whereas the fish on the right is obviously spooked.

◀ *Making use of the wind*
You can draw carp in from large distances by making use of the wind and drifting floater baits long distances down stillwaters. Here, floating bait are catapulted out from the bank opposite the angler and pushed through weed beds by the wind. Carp are attracted and follow the stream of bait.

▲ **The controller**

A controller float helps an angler cast added distances, and it's also very useful for signalling that the bait has been taken – especially if it's sitting amongst lots of similar ones. Be careful, though, as carp especially can become suspicious of controllers after a while.

Alternatively, fish in areas of accumulated scum. Carp enjoy these places and the scum does obscure the profile of the line. The line can also be hidden in areas where weed brushes the surface. In the same way, you can often lay line over the pads of lilies, so it's not actually touching the water at all. This really is the thinking angler's game.

If you can, fish close in, so the only weight on your line is the bait and the hook. Sometimes, you can even dap a bait with no line on the water whatsoever, and fish almost under your rod tip. If you must fish at a distance, though, you'll need a float to give some weight. A float also helps signal a take. If the fish are showing signs of caution around a shop-bought float, try taking a 9- to 12-inch twig and threading this on the line so that it rests against the hook. You can achieve this by attaching it with bands or, if you can, drill a hole through the twig and thread the line through the hole afterwards. The concept behind this is that the carp will come to the bait and all it actually sees is a small, juicy offering resting against a dead twig.

Disguising the Hook

Hooks, too, are a problem. Often the hook weighs more than the actual bait, which means that it lies under the water and is the first thing the carp sees. A heavy hook also pulls the bait down slightly compared with the natural, loose feed and, again, the carp are suspicious. A large bait, such as a piece of floating crust or floating paste, can be used to hide the hook and the problem isn't so great. The real headache begins when you are using small, floating particles. The hook can be hidden between several particles and this is a useful and long-lived method on many waters. Sometimes, the hook can be made more buoyant by gluing pieces of polystyrene to the shank or you can try hair-rigging a bait. Keep working, keep experimenting and make the shallows your laboratory where you can see exactly how your line and hook behave.

Bait itself is an important consideration. Years ago, all you had and all you needed was a floating crust. Today, there are numerous recipes for floating, boily-type baits available, but basically the use of baking powder and the oven can make virtually everything float. Floating boilies can be bought from most tackle shops, but most floater fishing these days is done with particles – especially any one of the many brands of dog and cat biscuits.

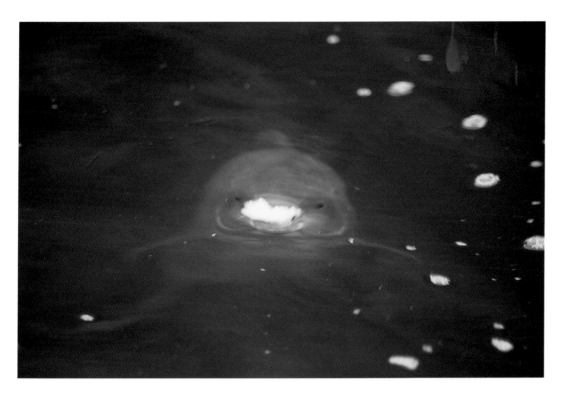

◄ *Lovely*

A very big fish this. It's taken some time to build up the carp's confidence, but now it's definitely approaching the bait with food in mind.

▶ *The take*

There's a moment of hesitation, but then the carp sucks the bread in. And then it panics. It bolts. The surface erupts.

Time to Strike

The question of the take must also be discussed. Often carp will rise to the bait, only to turn off at the last second, leaving a huge, splashy boil. Carp will also pick the bait up between their lips and test it, ejecting it as they surge away. It's tempting to strike at these occurrences, but all you'll do is pull the bait away from an already scared fish and spook it even further. All bait thereafter is treated with ever-growing suspicion.

The paramount rule, therefore, is to strike only when you're absolutely certain that the carp has taken the bait, and that has it has the bait properly in its mouth. Sometimes, if you're lucky, the line will stream off, but often it will just twitch and move a little way, very slowly, as the carp settles a few inches under the surface and begins to swallow it. If you're fishing close in, it is particularly important to keep your nerve when you see a fish come up and suck the bait in between its lips. If you strike now, all is lost. Always wait until the bait is taken properly into the mouth, as only then can you strike with confidence.

The Skill of Stalking

Stalking a big, wily carp that knows its way around the water and also the ways of anglers is one of the true tests of an angler's skill. This is a style of fishing that is intensely focused. A single, solitary mistake can blow any chance of success sky-high. Every single move has to be considered and carried out with painstaking care.

What to Wear

It may not be the first thing that comes to mind, but think about the clothing you wear. Clothes should be drab and designed to blend in with the surroundings. They should also be loose to disguise your own body shape. An extra layer of thorn-proof clothing is wise, as nettles and thistles can prove a hazard, and often you'll have to lie still for hours on end. Consider, too, your footwear: walking shoes or trainers are excellent if there's a lot of dead undergrowth around, but thigh boots, and even chest waders, may be preferable if there is a chance that you need to go into the water for a snagged fish. A hat is also a good idea, both to cast shade over the face and, more importantly, to keep glare off in sunlight. The sudden flash of a pale face can scare every carp within 100 yards. Polarized glasses are absolutely essential. When fishing early or late in the day and around marshy areas, insect repellent is vital if you're going to remain still, quiet and focused on the job in hand.

The Stalking Location

To stalk successfully, you need to be on your own, on a quiet bank, well away from the usual crowd of anglers. Almost certainly,

▼ *Tree tops*
It's good to get up a climbing post like this and look down onto the water – you can see what is happening much more clearly from above. Be careful though, especially in winter when the branches are damp and slippery.

these places will be in areas where it is diffi-cult to present baits easily. Good stalking banks will often be tree-lined, with lots of fallen bushes, branches and underwater snags. Islands, just a little way out, are good locations, too, and lily beds and channels are well worth investigating.

Carp use all these areas for sanctuary, to escape from the general hubbub of the lake and to enjoy the feeling of security afforded by the quiet surroundings. There is usually a great deal of natural food in these shallow, snag-ridden areas. Depth is not important; a carp is quite happy to spend hours basking with its back clear of the water, confident that there are no anglers around. They are particularly fond of patches of still water where the wind doesn't reach and where scum builds up on the surface, trapping trav-elling and hatching insects. You might well hear the carp slurp in a drowning moth or hatching midges.

Searching for Clues

Look carefully for visible signs, both through your glasses and, if you possess them, through a pair of binoculars. Even the biggest fish can give off the most subtle, most easily-missed signs. You need to examine every square yard of water in front of you before very carefully moving on to the next. Most obviously, you are looking for backs or for fins breaking the surface. Fins can be held out in the air for minutes, look-ing for all the world like a dead leaf, so watch anything suspicious for quite a while.

Bubbles, too, are a sure sign of fish. It's easy to dismiss those large single bubbles as escaping marsh gas, but a big fish may have stirred the leaves with its ventral fin releasing a single, oily bubble. Anything out of the usual should rivet your attention. Clouds of silt are an obvious giveaway; they're a comprehensive sign of feeding fish. Look very carefully, too, at the water's surface. Sometimes it rocks, eddies or wells up – not dramatically in any way, but slowly and smoothly, and it signifies fish on the move. Sometimes the water just seems

▲ *Into the rough*
Sebastian keeps a low profile as he approaches a sanctu-ary swim under a bankside bush. Just the sight of his head here over the foliage will send the fish scurrying.

▼ *Mobility*
Neil has fished massive lengths of river over the long day. He's kept on the move and has probably fished over forty different places.

▲ **Action!**
The water is colouring up as fish disturb the silt. Bubbles are rising. The waggler float lifts and sways as fish brush against the line beneath.

▼ **Nothing left to chance**
Rods can be seen on a shallow, clear lake. Camouflage is the answer.

▼ ▶ **Ambush**
A hair-rigged boilie is placed amongst the reed stems.

to be alive as if being pushed by a large body beneath.

Let's say you've located a fish. Think very carefully now about how to present a bait and just as importantly how you are going to land the fish. Don't be irresponsible, and if the carp is in an area that's totally impregnable, simply let it pass.

The Right Gear

Forget all the normal carp rods out there on the market. Long rods simply get hung up in the branches of trees and are difficult to make a swing cast, certainly with the accuracy that you're going to need when stalking. Instead, you need a short, powerful rod that won't crack into obstacles, that can place a bait with pinpoint accuracy and that has the power to hustle a fish from danger. A centre-pin reel is the experts' choice, because it puts you in instant, direct contact with the fish and the fight will be electrifying. A fixed-spool reel, however, is almost as good. It's when we get to your line and your hook that the game gets critical. These two items are going to bear the brunt of the battle, and using 15-pound line isn't excessive. Check it over and over for any signs of abrasion or weakness, especially after you've landed a fish and had to pull it through branches or lilies.

I'm dubious about using braid for the main line in situations like these, because it does part unexpectedly if it brushes against

a rock or even the edge of a mussel shell. But a camouflaged braid hook length can often merge into the bottom silt perfectly. Take no chances with your hook or hook knot. Holding a big fish in a confined space creates enormous strain and a hook that is too weak will simply open at the bend.

Watching for a Bite

Bite indication can either be the line slithering across the surface or perhaps you'll be close enough to see the bait engulfed. Generally, however, you'll be using a float, but be careful because fish will be aware of any float that is too large for the job, especially in shallow or clear water. If the fish shows signs of caution, change to a transparent-bodied float. If the fish is still shying away, move to a natural float – a quill discarded by a swan or a goose is perfect. Another option is a twig that floats nicely and casts a little further than that feather. Try lying your float or quill on the surface rather than having it cocked – in shallow water, the carp may come across the stem of the cocked float and be frightened away.

A Time for New Ideas

Stalking carp among the margins in a rich, natural lake is the perfect opportunity to experiment with a whole menu of baits found in the wild. Lobworms are effective as they wriggle vigorously and catch the carps' attention, although they can have the disadvantage of burrowing under leaves and into the silt. Sometimes a couple of dead lobworms prove more effective. Wasp grubs,

caterpillars, a bunch of brandlings, slugs, a dead frog, if you come across one, and even woodlice can all prove successful. Try a dead moth in the surface film or a daddy-long-legs. A large, dead moth tethered to the bottom can also prove attractive. Alternatively, you might choose the maggot approach - if you lay out a big bed of maggots and wait for carp to move over it, you can get them feeding manically. The bottom will fizz up as the carp dig into it searching for the grubs. A bunch of maggots on a size eight hook should prove the answer. In all probability hair-rigging a bait won't be necessary here because the carp feel secure in an area where they never expect to see an angler.

 ▲ ▶ Cover

Carp love cover. It doesn't matter if we are talking fallen branches or lily beds. Of course, they'll roam in open water, especially to reach one place of sanctuary or another, but it's when they feel sheltered that they are at their most secure and are most willing to feed.

Bait Fishing in Action

In the bait-fishing world, new, wonder baits are always appearing, perhaps flourishing for a few years and then usually disappearing. In part, this is due to commercialism: companies are constantly looking to make a quick buck and the new bait that promises instant success is always going to win a gullible audience. The skill in choosing your bait lies in seeing through the hype and recognizing exactly what fish want at any given moment in their lives.

▶ *The fertile river*
Turn over any rock or stone in a fertile river and you will find clusters of natural food underneath. The caddis grub in particular is an excellent bait.

Positive and Negative

There are certain rules. Look at what fish are eating naturally. If they're consuming something with gusto and in real quantities, the chances are that they will mop it up if it's on a hook, too. So, if it's large enough to go on as bait and you can get your hands on it, by all means use it. I can think of loads of examples where I've been successful once I'd cottoned on to what the fish were eating naturally: fish

▶ *Ring the changes*
Too often, anglers use luncheon meat cut into perfectly regular shapes. The fish get suspicious of these, though, so it's best to tear off some meat, leaving it jagged so that pieces fall off in the stream.

▶ *Cubed meat*
If you are going to use cubed meat, then vary how many pieces you use. If the water is coloured, three or four pieces won't go amiss. As the water clears, two is probably about right.

eating the weed that was growing on the pilings of a bridge out in Spain; fish eating caddis grubs found in profusion under the stones in a Czech river; some North American small-mouthed bass that were thoroughly addicted to stonefly larva; Indian mahseer going pop-eyed for freshwater crabs.

If fish have become scared of a particular bait, there's no point in trying to use it. In many parts of the world, the popularity of angling has caused waters to become heavily pressured, and if fish have been caught or hooked on a certain bait, the chances are they won't be eating it again. If you want to hoodwink them a second time, you'll just have to move on to something different or more sophisticated.

Getting It Right

This is where making your baits more appealing and more unusual becomes a real skill. Take a bait as humble as luncheon meat. Most people will use a piece about the size of a stock cube. The fish soon come to realize that these uniformly-sized pieces of meat spell danger. The thinking angler will use a tiny piece of meat – just a shard, just enough to cover a small hook. If that doesn't work and the water is high and clouded, he'll use a huge piece of meat, perhaps half a tin, and he won't cut that piece with a knife so that it's all neat and uniform like everybody else's. He'll pull it apart with his fingers so that it's ragged, with bits falling off, making it much more attractive and much less suspicious.

A further skill is to get fish used to the baits that you will be using. Pre-baiting is an

art. You don't want to pre-bait so much that you'll fill the fish up and find them totally unresponsive when it comes to casting out, but equally you don't want to pre-bait so stintingly that you never turn the fish on to what you're offering. In short, you've got to try to assess how many fish are out there and how hungry they are, and then give them enough of your bait samples to get them excited, to switch them on and to keep them looking for more.

Ploughman's Bait

Let's look at the main categories of bait and see how the skilful angler will take them, adapt them and improve them so that he's one step ahead of all the rest. Perhaps the most common baits for many years have been those you find in your kitchen. What we like to eat, as a general rule, the fish like to eat.

Probably more fish have been caught on bread over the centuries than on any other bait. Bread can be used in crust, flake or paste forms. The great advantage is that fish both like and recognize the taste and smell of bread. Bread is also easily seen, both in coloured water and at night. You can use bread big or small, floating or sinking, and have confidence in it. If the fish are spooked, change the form in which you use it. If you've been using paste, change to flake. If you've been using flake, try some crust. If you've been using white bread, change to brown. Perhaps you could try flavouring your bread with smears of cheese. Virtually all fish adore cheese, either on its own or made into a paste with bread. Today, in most countries, it is sadly overlooked. This is a great shame as there's a huge variety out there - soft cheese, hard cheese, cream cheese, processed cheese – and it has great smell, great texture, is easy to see, and you're always going to be able to offer a suspicious fish something new. Like meat, you can use a tiny piece or a huge piece. Apart from out-and-out predators, there's barely a fish that swims in freshwater that doesn't like cheese.

▲ **Glorious**

This is the time that you need to be out on the summer stillwater, just as the sun is appearing over the woods on the far bank. This next hour of the day will probably see the most frantic feeding of all.

▲ The guzzler

This shot of a carp shovelling in sweetcorn was taken in a large European lake. I have no doubt that the slight clouding of the water also encouraged the fish to feed hard.

▶ Careful presentation

These floating dog biscuits have had a groove filed along their undersides. This fits the hook shank neatly, and then the biscuit is superglued into position. Now you know the biscuit won't come off for at least an hour or so in the water.

▶ ▶ Breakdown

Think carefully about how your bait and the free offerings around it behave in the water. Pellets, for example, may gradually break down, especially in warm water, leaving piles of powdery food that fish love to eat.

The Magic of Sweetcorn

One of the most popular baits worldwide over the past 30 or 40 years – especially for cyprinids – has been sweetcorn. The little yellow grains drive fish of scores of species absolutely crazy. They are visible, give off a great smell and their taste appears to be addictive. There's a lot you can do with sweetcorn: you can use grains singly or even chop them in half, or you can pack 10 grains on a big hook. You can use the juice to flavour ground bait or, if the fish become wary of the original yellow, you can colour it black or red or orange.

Particle Baits

Perhaps the greatest appeal of sweetcorn is that it is a particle bait, a form of bait made up of numerous small items. Again, cyprinids adore particle baits. Baits such as maggot, hemp seed, nuts and pulses all preoccupy a fish, dominate its thinking processes and often drive it into a feeding frenzy. There are several problems with particle baits, however. Firstly, the fish become so preoccupied with them that often they won't look at larger hook baits used over a bed of these particles. You've therefore got to use the particle on the hook, and presentation can be difficult. Also, especially in summer, fry and fingerlings can be a problem with particle baits such as maggots, not to mention eels that sneak out as the dusk falls. So, while particles can turn your swim into a foaming pile of bubbles, they can also make a rod for your own back.

This is where slightly larger particle baits score heavily. They're small enough to preoccupy the fish, yet large enough to present comparatively easily. Peanuts (properly

prepared) are as addictive as sweetcorn. Tiger nuts, tares, butter beans, Brazil nuts, broad beans, cashew nuts, kidney beans, soy beans, chickpeas and black-eyed beans also do well. I've had success with diced-up jelly babies and even some types of mints. All these baits work well, probably for comparatively short periods, but they are so numerous that you can keep chopping and changing and coming up with a winning formula. So, it does make sense to visit supermarkets frequently, scouring the shelves looking for those obscure tins and packets that other anglers have probably never even considered.

Natural Baits

Earlier, I discussed weed, caddis grubs and the like, and the skilful bait angler will learn to make increasing use of natural baits. Naturals will always catch fish, simply because they are there in the wild, forming a part of the everyday menu. Worms are obvious, but caddis grubs, shrimps, slugs, wasp grubs and bloodworms are good, too.

You can buy worms commercially or pick them from the surface of any grassland on a warm, moist night. Look after your worms, keep them damp and throw away any dead or dying ones that will infect the healthy. Worms, like many of the best baits, are immensely adaptable. They can be chopped up to form a really enticing ground bait, used in halves, used singly or in bunches to attract any fish species from perch to salmon. Moreover, they're exactly what river fish expect to find after heavy rain. Thousands of worms are washed to their deaths during floods along any river system each year and fish have come to recognize them as a safe, nutritious food.

I'm not sure where I stand any more on the question of using a small dead bait to catch a larger fish. It somehow seems mean to catch a perch and then kill it to catch a pike. Nevertheless, there are endless amounts of sea fish already dead and for sale in fishmongers, and while we tend to think of these primarily as baits for pike and

THE ART OF DRAGGING
A rake, ideally pronged on both sides, a decent length of rope and you are in business. Just throw it out, let it sink and drag it back through the silt. Scents and a host of tiny foodstuffs are released, drawing in tench, perch and bream. You are also clearing the swim of heavy weed growth and helping your presentation.

▶ *Wrigglers*
Thousands of worms are washed to their deaths during floods along rivers each year, and fish have come to recognize them as safe, nutritious food. Caddis grubs are another great natural bait. They inhabit the bottom of the river, living in cases glued to stone and gravel. Prise them out of their cocoons for one of the least suspected of all baits.

▶ *Creepy-crawlies*
Slugs are a good bait for many fish, especially chub. The size of hook depends on the type of slug used. If you can, try to use a slug without any weight at all – they're often heavy enough to counteract a slight current. Look out too for all manner of nymphs, leeches, crickets, grasshoppers, moths, snails, anything of hookable size on the natural menu.

▲ *Dead baits*
Nearly all fish species, not just the obvious predators, are fish eaters at some time or another. Carp and even bream can be picked up on small, dead fish from time to time. Chub and barbel adore them. Minnows like this can easily be caught in a plastic bottle with a hole punctured in the bottom and a bit of bread bait sprinkled inside.

▲ *A beguiling mix*
The contents of a carp fisher's bucket can be intriguing. The boilies are cut in half to release more smell. One ingredient, hemp seed, is oily and terrifically aromatic. Other pulses and beans complete the mix.

▼ *The pop-up*
The boily here is buoyant, so it can carry the weight of the hook and wave just off the bed. This makes it highly visible to a cruising fish and allows it to be sucked into the mouth with minimal effort.

the big predators, small silver sea fish, such as sprats, can be excellent for many members of the cyprinid family. Moreover, in tinned anchovies you've got one of the best, most instant and most overlooked baits in the entire fishing world.

Special Baits

A far cry from the natural is the laboratory-produced special bait, perhaps a boiled bait (a boily as they've become known) or a paste consisting of endless amounts of carefully prepared, chemically-based ingredients. All of them have a great smell and this makes them particularly effective in waters with low visibility. The boily has revolutionized fishing for carp in particular, but also for other members of the cyprinid family. It's a bait that

usually consists of a dried powder added to eggs and flavouring, mixed into a paste, rolled into balls, boiled to give it a hard skin and then used on the hook or as free offerings. Most boilies are based on high-protein mixes with all manner of essences and additives to make them taste, smell and look good. Boilies can be made buoyant to pop up from the bottom so that they hang enticingly above weed or silt. Mini-boilies are also on the market and are perfect for smaller members of the cyprinid family. You can make your own boilies or you can buy them.

Ground Bait

I've already talked about building up your swim and preparing your fish with free samples of your hook bait, and this is often quite sufficient. There are times, however, when you want something a little more noticeable, and that's where a ground bait that explodes in the water, with plenty of visual impact, comes into its own. The oldest and most commonly used form of ground bait is simply breadcrumbs, but in the modern world the new ground baits have all manner of different additives to increase their scent and visual attractiveness. Consistency is important, too: light ground bait can be used for shallow stillwater, whereas heavier ground bait will be needed for quick, deep rivers. Mix your ground bait up, drop it into the water and see how it behaves.

Don't use ground bait – or any bait, come to that – slavishly. Think carefully whether the fish you are hunting really need to be approached in this way. The more individual baits – especially heavy ones like boilies – that you throw in, the more the fish will be aware of your presence and your intentions. The same, too, obviously applies to balls of ground bait going in like mini hand grenades.

The skilful angler needs to think carefully about all this. Some years ago, one of my closest angling friends caught a massive barbel on one single cast. However, he'd prepared for that cast. For the previous two hours he'd thrown in tiny pieces of luncheon meat. He hadn't thrown these in all at once

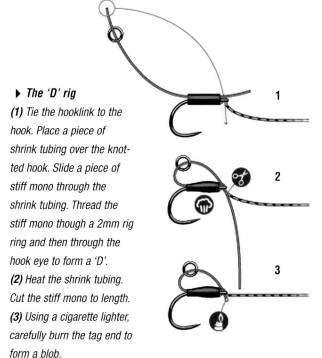

▶ **The 'D' rig**

(1) Tie the hooklink to the hook. Place a piece of shrink tubing over the knotted hook. Slide a piece of stiff mono through the shrink tubing. Thread the stiff mono though a 2mm rig ring and then through the hook eye to form a 'D'.

(2) Heat the shrink tubing. Cut the stiff mono to length.

(3) Using a cigarette lighter, carefully burn the tag end to form a blob.

1

▲ **Stiff rig**

Made of stiff (25-lb) flourocarbon hooklink material, this rig has excellent anti-tangle properties, is virtually invisible underwater and is difficult for a fish to eject.

2

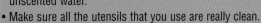

▲ **Combi-rig**

The first few centimetres of coating is stripped from the coated braid hooklink in this rig, creating the combination of a flexible hooklink for good bait presentation and excellent anti-tangle properties.

3

and alarmed the fish beneath, but he'd thrown a piece every five minutes. After two hours, he'd perhaps scattered 40 tiny bits of meat into the swim without alerting the barbel to any danger whatsoever. When his own tiny piece of meat appeared, it was the most natural thing in the world for his big fish to suck it in and be caught.

Opportunistic Baits

Always keep your eyes open for clues along the bankside. Overhanging trees often drop ripe fruit into the water, which can attract and hold fish for long periods of time – mahseer in India, for example, love fallen oranges. Think of baby birds nesting under bridges and on water towers, and how bass, congregate around such places waiting for falling fledglings. If a wind gets up, watch to see if craneflies are blown from the grass into the water, and note which fish species come up to take them. It's the same with grasshoppers falling into a stream. Watch the cattle in the meadow. Eventually they will come to the lake or river to drink and stir up any mud that is there, and in that mud there will be many hiding insects. Fish know this, and they will come towards feeding cattle as though the dinner gong has been struck.

MAKING BOILIES

I don't propose to go through the entire process of making boilies here, because the recipes can be picked up from the packets of the ingredients you will need to buy, but I will pass on a number of useful tips.

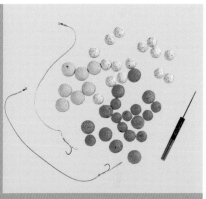

- Before starting to make boilies, always wash your hands carefully in unscented water.
- Make sure all the utensils that you use are really clean.
- If you're going to make boilies on a regular basis then it pays to invest in modern tools such as sausage guns and rolling tables.
- Never smoke when you're making bait.
- Always use boiling water at every stage of the game. Hot water isn't good enough.
- Always follow the instructions on the packets and don't cut corners.
- Ensure that you measure ingredients exactly and don't make haphazard guesses. You'll need proper measuring equipment for this.
- Don't exceed the recommended dosage – you'll kill the bait totally.
- Have everything in front of you before you begin. Baits will go off if you have to rush out for forgotten ingredients.
- Make sure everything you use is fresh – especially the eggs.
- Mix everything thoroughly.
- Tidy everything up and wash everything thoroughly once you've finished.
- Allow baits to cool and then store them carefully.
- Develop a smooth-running routine and you'll soon be turning baits out like a mini factory!

An Introduction To Lure Fishing

In the last 20 years or so, I have fished in approximately 50 countries. Before that, my angling activity was largely confined to the United Kingdom where, certainly until recently, the bulk of predator fishing was done with either live or dead baits of one sort or another. Lure fishing was generally only a last resort. If the live or dead baits had not produced any fish then, towards the end of the day, in desperation, a spinner or a spoon would be put on and cast around here and there with very little expectation of success. Not surprisingly, lure fishing was a long way down the league table of success for many, many years.

▼ Alluring!
This beautiful, lure-caught pike was taken on a cold winter's day and fought hard and deep. Notice how it is being unhooked in a large cradle that will keep it from harm on a hard bank.

Opening Our Eyes

When I began to travel extensively, I was struck strongly by the difference in approach to lure fishing in other countries. Anglers in North America, Scandinavia and Central and Eastern Europe showed an imagination in their lure fishing that was almost impossible to find anywhere in the UK. Americans, Canadians, Swedes, Czechs and Germans took their lure fishing seriously, and it really showed. They had the tackle for the job, they had the knowledge, the enthusiasm and the techniques. Today, the UK is fast catching up with this technique. The internet has vastly improved the ease with which anglers can buy the best lures from anywhere in the world, and information has been equally fast to spread. Moreover, attitudes have changed:

20 years ago, lure fishing was considered lightweight work by most serious British predator anglers. Today, that is not the case. The number of specialist lure anglers has rocketed and their results have laughed the prejudices of the bait men out of court.

A Lesson from the Czechs

Of all the lure fishermen that I have fished alongside, perhaps those from the Czech Republic have impressed me the most, and this is largely down to their determination. They will try and try again to find the right lure for any particular day and never stop trying. For example, they know that dark lures probably show up much better against a bright background on a particularly sunny day. On a day when there is no sun, predators will probably see the water as a veil of darkness, and this is when a bright, striking lure can come into its own. On overcast days, especially, lure fishing is all about trying all the colours and types that you have in your box until you get a take. If predators are not feeding hard, one particular colour or size or movement might just have a better triggering effect than another.

Lure Visibility

Think about where your lure is working. If you are retrieving close to a dam wall, perhaps strewn with algae, a green lure is not going to be seen. Change it to a red one and you stand a far better chance of a predator spotting it.

In clear or cloudy water, you've got to appeal to the pike's vision as well as to its other senses. Shiny spoons, spinners and plugs can reflect light over a great distance underwater, especially when the sun is high. It's a good idea to use glitter on dull plugs to increase visibility. Make sure silver spoons and spinners are well polished to increase the flash factor.

In murky water, too, flashy and fluorescent colours can often do the job. Experiment with bigger or more violently active lures so that the fish can physically feel their presence. Try

plugs with sound chambers, because a rattling ball-bearing can frequently attract a predator. In murky water, slow down the rate of your retrieve to give the predator more time to home in on what you're using. Keep working, keep changing, and always keep experimenting and on even the hardest day you will eventually find the key to success.

▲ *Savage*
Pike are the predators supreme – just look at that mouth, those teeth, those focused eyes.

RADIAL CASTING

Perch are often found near snags, but groups of fish will often patrol open water. This is where radial casting comes in. 'Working your way round the clock' means that all of the water is being systematically searched.

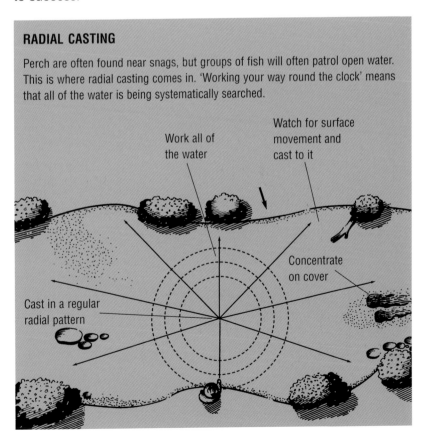

Work all of the water

Watch for surface movement and cast to it

Concentrate on cover

Cast in a regular radial pattern

Reading Features and Structure

When fishing, for predators in particular, the two key words are features and structure. Obviously, predators do move around their waters as conditions alter, and to feed and spawn, but most species establish semi-permanent homes at the very least. Take a brand new gravel pit, for example – no features whatsoever in there, but throw in a sunken boat and within no time you'll find 90 per cent of the pike population sheltering around it. Any changes at all in the bottom topography – either natural or man-made – immediately act like magnets and offer real security in otherwise featureless landscapes.

A Reason To Be There

As we know already, predators spend a great deal of time doing nothing – either waiting for prey to come close to them or waiting for food to be digested. It's important, therefore, that they have a base that pleases them, and the best bases are generally picked off by the biggest fish. A great example is the sub-surface plateaus just off the coast in the Baltic Sea. These provide protection against tides and currents and they are also in the middle of migration routes for herring and

1 OUT IN OPEN WATER
On a large water like this you will find larger predators and prey fish way out from the banks searching over large areas for food.

2 LIGHTLY REEDED
Many fish will come in to light reeds like this to feed, especially at dawn.

3 THICKLY REEDED
In the heart of the reed bed are many small prey fish, even baby predators. They are all escaping from the bigger fish in open water.

1 UNDER THE BRANCHES
A thick jungle above encourages fish to feed in subdued light and increased security. Many insects fall into the water.

2 THE GRASSY BANK
A grassy bank like this also attracts fish. Many terrestrial insects fall into the water, providing a magnet.

3 THE MAIN CURRENT
Many fish, will be stationed in the main current, where the drift of the river brings food towards them.

mackerel. If you want a 60-pound Baltic pike, aim for these places.

So, what are features? All manner of weed and reed beds take pride of place, along with fallen trees and man-made structures such as bridges, boat jetties, discarded shopping trolleys and sunken boats. Look carefully at even the most barren of waters, and features will gradually begin to emerge.

Bottom Contours

Structure simply means a change in the bottom features of the water, either in the depths or in the material that makes up the bottom. Structure also takes in any bankside features such as points, plateaus, reefs, channels and islands. Fish aren't evenly dotted around a water, and in any lake or river probably 90 per cent of the water will be

▶ *Off the freshwater reef*
This pike fell to a rubber lure jigged over a long length of submerged rocks. The area held many fish, including some good ones like this specimen.

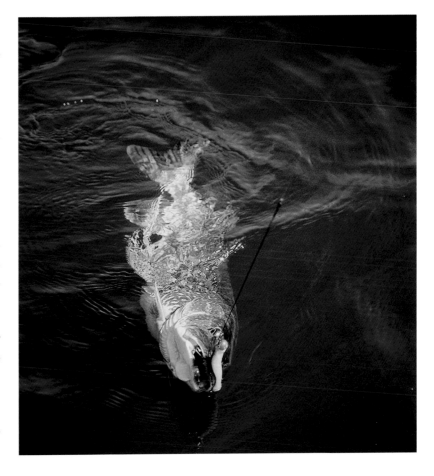

1 THE POINT
Exposed spits of land like this one are always a good place to start. Fish move around them, feeding in the shallows.

2 DRIFTING IN
Look as well into coves and bays. The water warms up here, and carp, especially, drift in to feed.

3 HOT DAYS
On hot days, fish will often be found far out from the banks in the deepest water, especially if the surface is wind-chopped.

▼ *Sticklebacks in hiding*
These sticklebacks have taken up residence in a weedy area, and are preyed upon here by smaller pike and perch. Such areas are best fished using tiny plugs and flies.

completely devoid of fish. Fish will almost always be centred around features or structure, so it makes huge sense to set about finding the 10 per cent of the water that's full of fish before actually setting up a rod.

You can locate features and structure using electronic aids such as fish finders and sonic depth finders. All of the modern ones will give you exact readouts of depths, bottom make-up and any obstructions that could hold fish. They'll also pinpoint the actual fish themselves. On smaller waters, polarized glasses, binoculars and, ideally, a boat will probably serve your purposes. Don't overlook plumbing depths with the simplest of all methods – rod, line and float.

1 DEAD TREES
Bass in particular love dead, fallen branches. When the rains come and the dam fills up, these are sure places to find them.

2 COVES
You will often find predators – bass, pike and perch – in small bays where they can ambush prey and also lie up after hunting.

3 THE ROCKY SHORE
Bass especially frequent margins, particularly those in which there are big stones to hide them.

◀ *An absolute haven*

This old tyre was thrown into a stream and settled near the bridge from which it was deposited. After a year it had become a haven for minnows, gudgeon, bullhead and crayfish.

▼ ▶ *Wood!*

Wherever you find trees and bushes, you're going to find fish as well. But if you're moving into territory like this, you'll need the gear to back you up. Whatever your normal line strength is, double it in conditions like this. Even for a bass of three or four pounds, 20-pound breaking strain is not excessive in such desperate conditions.

Working With Plugs

Plugs have been on the angling scene for generations. Traditionally they are fashioned out of wood or hard plastic, and their aim is to mimic a small-prey fish. A plug has an in-built swimming action, but the vital skill with this method is for the angler to impart life into the plug on its retrieve. The aim of every plug fisherman is to fool a predatory fish into thinking that what is only a semi-realistic imitation is, in fact, the real thing. A mechanical, unimaginative, monotonous retrieve is unlikely to produce results, especially in waters where fish have seen it all before.

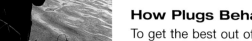

▲ *Precision*

Neil chooses to lure fish with a short rod – seven-feet – and a small multiplier coupled with braid line. The whole outfit is light, quick to use and devastatingly accurate.

How Plugs Behave

To get the best out of plug fishing, you need to know how a plug behaves under the water. Find some clear, shallow water with a hard bottom where you can wade, and then study the action of the plug you intend to use. How fast does the plug sink? If it's a buoyant plug, how quickly does it rise back towards the surface? How does the plug respond to a jerk-type retrieve? Try casting the plug as far as you can – does it tangle in flight? Do you need to feather the spool to prevent this?

Choosing the Right Plug

The choice of plug on any particular water on any particular day is also crucial. Many

experts in the North American bass world talk about finding the right match or pattern. By this, they mean clicking with the right style of fishing at a particular period. For example, it would be madness to choose a surface-fishing plug in the middle of winter when the water is close to freezing and the pike are down deep. Equally, if the pike are lying in shallow, sun-warmed bays you wouldn't choose a great big, heavy trolling spoon or a deep-diving plug that works best at 40 feet. Of course, this is all basic stuff and mostly common sense, but the more experienced you become and the more you think about plug choice, the more you'll tweak the options and reap the fruits of your success.

▼ *Fiery orange*

In very murky water an orange plug like this works particularly well. Fish can pick the fiery orange up at great distance.

▼ *Working the cracks*

It helps considerably if you have an exact knowledge of the topography of your water. Working a plug in the nooks and crannies is a great way to find the fish.

◀ *What a stunner*

A great pike lies beaten, victim of a well-worked lure. Lure fishing – the purest form of predator fishing..

Fishing the Right Location

As in all fishing situations, you'll also need to think very carefully about where you are going to fish your plug. As we've seen before, predators aren't evenly scattered throughout the water, and you need to pinpoint exact locations. You need to be mobile so that you can work large expanses of water, and it pays to wear thigh boots or chest waders so that, if you can safely do so, you can wade out to tackle water that is impossible to approach from the bank. If you've got a boat, a canoe or a float tube, so much the better. The really successful plug angler will pop his plug where other pluggers fail to reach!

This, of course, is where accuracy counts. If you're aiming to work a plug alongside the fringes of a fallen tree, it's no good casting too far so that you get hung up, or too short so that you miss the killing zone. Work hard at your accuracy and be angry with yourself when you get it wrong. Don't tolerate slackness in your approach or your performance. Sweat blood over your plug fishing and success will come your way.

▼ *Black beauty*

Black, like orange, works well in misty conditions. This shot was taken in Mongolia, when the river was in flood. Only black or orange had any impact.

▼ *Biting bottom*

A quick crank of the reel encourages plugs to dive hard, and they often hit the bottom. On a softer bottom this sends up puffs of silt, often attractive to a waiting predator.

▲ ▶ ▶ ▼ *Lures in action*
These shots were taken on an autumnal day, when one has to work hard to interest any fish. Constantly changing the size, colour and action of the plugs was the only way to arouse some occasional interest.

◀ Irish beauty
The picture says it all here. A tempestuous Irish day on a big water with plenty of rain in the air. This nicely shaped pike fell for a big jerk bait worked on a short, stiff rod in rapid, erratic bursts.

Fishing Hard

"KN" was my Indian guide for a couple of years, and he is one of the best plug fishermen I have ever met. He worked incredibly hard at his plug fishing and left nothing to chance. He always replaced factory-fitted hooks with much stronger ones of his own, and those hooks were sharpened to perfection. He'd test every knot, and the reel's clutch would always be precisely correct for the fishing situation.

KN would scout the area to be fished with military precision. He'd spend 20 minutes investigating a pool, mapping out the approaches and looking carefully for any signs of feeding fish. He'd direct my approach completely, leaving nothing to chance. He'd go through exactly where I was going to cast, how many times I was going to cast to each place and how I was going to retrieve the plug. The plug would be replaced several times, even when fishing one single pool. Sometimes a deep diver would be put on if the central channel was to be worked. A popper might be tried over the shallows. If a fish followed and turned away, a different pattern or a different colour would be tried.

This latter point is an important one: KN, of course, wore my spare pair of polarizing glasses and he looked intently into the water wherever possible, following the journey of the plug back towards us. He was constantly watching for any following fish and its reaction to the plug.

Fishing with KN was both a totally exhausting and a totally exhilarating experience. Absolutely nothing was left to chance. Every cast was a deeply thought-out operation, and my success-rate with him began to rocket, as a result of his thorough and expert guidance.

TROLLING TECHNIQUES
An angler can troll solo, but there's always a risk of entanglement in heavy winds, or when a fish takes. With two or three people, one can work the engine and control the boat while the others work the rods. Take turns, and develop the mentality that any success is a 'boat' capture rather than an individual one. Constantly experiment with different depths and lures until you find a winning combination.

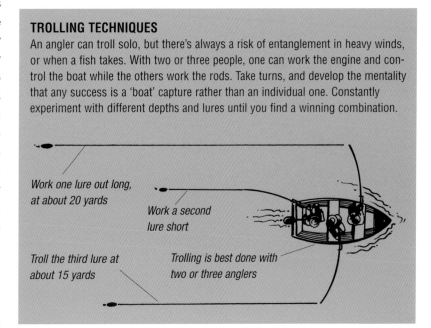

Work one lure out long, at about 20 yards

Work a second lure short

Troll the third lure at about 15 yards

Trolling is best done with two or three anglers

Spoons And Spinners

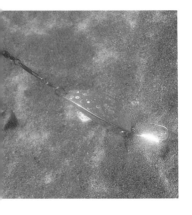

▲ **Silver in the sun**
In clear water, a silver spoon often works particularly well in bright conditions because it attracts the light and throws it back through the water.

▼ **A team effort**
Here, Tim has caught a super pike. Neil rowed and the team used a mix of spoons and spinners.

Everything that I said about hard work and intense concentration referring to plugs applies to spoons and spinners. Once again, the skill is to make a piece of metal appear so realistic that it is engulfed by a predator. To do this regularly isn't always easy. Once again, you've got to consider the size, weight, pattern and colour of the spoon or spinner that you are going to use in any given situation. Once again, you've got to locate the fish with pinpoint accuracy. Once again, you've got to work your lure with imagination in the hot zone. Once again, fish slackly and you will fish unsuccessfully. Over the years, I've been fortunate in watching a great many expert spoon and spinner anglers, and here are some of the skills I've picked up from them.

Sending Out a Message

Sunlight and clear water can spell real problems in many fishing situations, but when using spoons and spinners this isn't always the case. The sun glints off the blade in conditions like this, sending dramatic flashes through the water and attracting the attention of all predators.

It pays to polish spoons and spinners until they shine like new pins and reflect the sunlight even farther under water. In these instances, choose big spoons and spinners – once again to increase the flash factor – and don't work the lures too fast, as a big, jinking spoon worked slowly gives out maximum flash.

Experimentation is what spoons and spinners are all about. While a flashing silver or bronze blade will generally work, there are equally times when a blade coloured black is the only one that fish will accept. You can also try putting a tail on a spinner – wool, tinsel, a strip of bacon rind, a small plastic grub, even a couple of maggots sometimes works. It often helps if a spinner has certain distinctive points of attraction: for example, a slash of red can imitate gills, and a couple of big, black spots can look very much like eyes, or perhaps they just give the fish a definite target to attack.

On any given session, it's a good idea to start with small lures that won't spook the fish, then step up in size until you begin to hit them. If the water is tinged with colour, you will probably end up using some of the biggest lures you have in your box to flash out all the light available and to send a steady pulse through the water. If the water is coloured, don't work your lure too fast because the predators need time to home in on the bait and make a sure hit. When the water is coloured, copper or brass is probably the best choice for the blade. If the water is really murky, then a brightly painted blade is most likely the best – yellow, red or even fluorescent green. If the water is clear, then silver generally works best.

The All-Important Retrieve

If you can see your quarry, think how to work the cast so that the lure is in its line of vision for the maximum possible time. The longer the fish has to watch the lure, the greater the amount of time it has to make up its mind to attack. However, if this approach isn't working, try exactly the opposite. Sometimes, if a predator only sees a lure for a short period of time, it will trigger an immediate, unthinking reaction. Each of these two wildly different approaches can be successful, depending entirely on the mood of the fish.

I mentioned KN watching for any follows. It's just the same with spoons and spinners. If a predator has followed, rejected and turned away, it's very unlikely to accept the same lure a second time round. It's much better, if you've seen a fish that you know is showing some interest, to change the offering. Go bigger or smaller, heavier or lighter. It often pays to rest the fish for 5 or 10 minutes before trying it a second time.

When you are working a spoon, you don't have to retrieve it so that it's constantly on the move. If the bed is comparatively weed- and snag-free, try stopping the retrieve altogether and letting the spoon flutter down and rest on the bottom. You can then twitch it a bit, kicking up silt and sand. Let it lie again. Jerk it back into life. After a minute, continue the retrieve before repeating the process. It seems strange that a predator such as a pike will pick up a piece of inanimate metal, but it's frequently a successful technique. However, watch very carefully for the take: this can be absolutely minute, so strike at any twitch on the line.

◄ ▲ *The lure of the spoon*
Remember that spoons and spinners work for a wide variety of fish species, not just the predators that you would expect. Look, for example, at this beautiful grayling twisting and turning in a clear Scandinavian stream. Even cyprinids sometimes fall for a spoon.

▲ *From the depths*
Spoons and spinners can work well for black bass, especially in the heat of the day when the sun forces them down deep and away from the margins.

Fishing Rubber Lures

Of all forms of lure fishing, rubbers have to be the most exciting, demanding, thought-provoking and skilful way of catching a predator on an artificial bait. They are also extremely efficient. The method has been highly developed throughout the US, Scandinavia and Eastern and Central Europe. Rubber lures come in a bewildering variety of shapes, colours, sizes and actions. Look into the bag of an experienced rubber fisherman and you will find almost every living creature imitated – fish, worms, crabs, frogs, crayfish, crickets, sand eels, prawns, lizards, squid and any wiggly grub that you can imagine.

▲ *A Swedish lesson*
This was one of the many lean, mean pikes that the team picked up in the waters of the Baltic.

▼ *The art of imitation*
The rocks around this lake are full of tiny lizards and geckos that sometimes fall into the water and are taken by the black bass.

Success in Scandinavia

The efficiency of rubber baits was brought home to me in a startling way. I was fishing for Baltic pike with my great Danish friend, Johnny Jensen, and two very talented Swedish guides. For a day and a half, I persevered with traditional plugs while Johnny and the two Swedes harvested fish on rubbers. I was wiped off the water and the message couldn't have been more stark. From that day on, I became a rubber addict, but you've still got to learn how to fish them.

What, then, were the lessons I learnt in those days on the Baltic, and have tried to build on since? The two guides, Pers and Hakken, spent an age on location – that's

where reading features and structure is so vitally important. At that time we were mainly fishing bays, and much of their time was spent studying an echo sounder, looking for plateaus surrounded by deep drop-offs – a favourite area for hunting pike. Failing that, they would search out the thickest of reed beds. Once they had the right location, boy, did they know how to exploit it. Casting was 100 per cent. They knew exactly where to put those rubbers. I wasn't fishing nearly as tight to features as they were and, as a result, failed to catch nearly as many fish.

Working the Lure

There's no doubt accuracy of cast put them ahead of me, but they also had far more experience of how to work the lures once in the water. Watching Pers, I realized that what he was doing was very similar to fly fishing in that he spent every second analyzing the movement of his rubber, just as a nymph master is constantly aware of what the fly is doing as it nears a trout. Pers would watch, hawk-eyed, as the lure fell through the water, waiting for any twitch of the line that would signal the take on the drop. He would then leave the rubber on the bottom, totally alert to any sign that the motionless lure had been picked up. His retrieve would be immaculate – sometimes a twitch, sometimes just a stammer of the rod tip, then a bit of a spurt so that the rubber would rise and then flutter down again in an irresistible fashion.

Just after my Baltic trip, I visited Spain, where I once again saw the importance of working the rubber intelligently. My Spanish friend, Rafa, was fishing for bass. Over and over, he made good, long casts, keeping the line tight and causing the lure to sink in an arc towards him. The lure's tail would have been working all the way to the bottom. He let it rest there for a while to allow the bass to move in and investigate. The odd twitch of the rod tip made the bass curious, then a short upward stroke kicked the rubber fish into life. Rafa worked it in a sink-and-draw fashion, keeping in constant contact. He was feeling the line all the time with his left hand, waiting for a touch too slight to see.

A Limitless Range

One of the great boons of rubber fishing is the variety of lures. If one model, size, colour, action or whatever isn't working, it's easy to switch and try something new. With rubber lures, the idea is to appeal to the senses, so you're looking for a rubber that has the right colour, shape and feel, perhaps with a smell, and certainly appealing movement. In clear water, be careful about jig choice and experimentation. Colour is an interesting issue: what are the considerations? Perhaps you're looking to match the colour of the jig with the food type it is trying to represent. Maybe

something visible in cloudy water. Shape is all-important, as is size. Perhaps you want to imitate a known, desirable food item. There may be times when you want to introduce something to threaten or anger the fish so it will attack with hostility.

Know Your Rubbers

Just as a fly fisherman knows how the flies in his box act in the water, so a rubber lure fisherman must know how his lures work in different conditions. Take a thermometer with you – rubbers behave differently when the water temperature changes and some go rigid and hardly work at all. Others achieve near meltdown when the water gets warmer. To test your rubbers, use the humble, domestic bath. Try every temperature, test your lures and note the results.

Still at the bath side, classify your rubbers, from violent action to subdued motions. Pull each lure through the water to see how it responds. Try all sorts of hooking arrangements and hook sizes; changes will totally affect the way any rubber moves. Vary the weight of the lead head or go for a weighted hook. See how the rubber works hooked up and in a current – your shower-head will come in handy here. The more you know about the action of your rubbers, the more successfully you'll be able to fish them.

▼ *Success at last*

It was a hot day and the glaring sun had sent the bass down deep. This small fish imitation, worked a good 20 feet under the boat, finally did the business for Raffa.

◀ *Intense focus*

Raffa in action is quite a sight as he watches the line with hawk-like concentration. Any movement, any pause, even a suspicion will make him arc the rod up into an instant strike.

Fishing Mini Lures

Lure fishing isn't all about using creations that are big and heavy. In fact, some lures can be little over half an inch in length and weigh no more than a heavy dry fly. The world of mini lures is a thrilling one – fishing in miniature is very tactile, very hands-on, with very little room for error.

▼*On fly gear too!*
Don't forget that the biggest trout in the river grow large by feeding on mice, frogs and anything else that falls into the water. Sometimes a mini lure can be fished efficiently on a fly rod.

Pinpoint Casting

Casting a mini lure – say a spinner or a plug of 1 inch in length and weighing a fraction of an ounce – is an art form in itself. Your rod might only be 6 or 7 feet in length. You will have an accompanying fixed-spool reel or a tiny multiplier that is light enough not to upset the balance. You'll probably be using braid or comparatively light nylon. The art of using mini lures is to flick your lure a short distance into a very tight area between weed beds, under overhanging branches, into a gap in the lilies or a hair's breadth from the reed margin. Accuracy has to be pinpoint. The underhand cast allows you to flick a lure into an opening between overhanging branches that would be impossible to reach from either side. It's a skill that has to be learnt. If you are right handed, try a back cast for placing a lure between branches with an opening on the left-hand side. Again, you're flicking your tiny lure into an area which no one else has considered. The fish know this: that's why they're lying there.

Try the forehand cast for flicking a lure under trees that show an opening on the right. You'll find that pinpoint accuracy is much more easily achieved with an underhand flick in this way than with a cast over your shoulder. All these casts sound difficult and complex but they're not. If you're worried, practise with a stone or a small lead weight tied on the end of your line. This way, should you get hung up, you can easily get your tackle free and you won't lose an expensive lure or risk waterfowl getting tangled up and injured. There are no exact rules – each mini-lure situation demands its own approach and you will probably devise ones for yourself that I've never even imagined.

A Versatile Approach

Mini lures, whether they are spinners, plugs or poppers, can be used for all manner of fish, in all manner of situations. For example, take sea trout in a very low, clear river in high summer. You'll probably find them sheltering under bridges or under branches. They'll be seeking shade and respite from the sun and you'd think they wouldn't feed until night falls, but you could be wrong. Dig out that 6-foot rod matched with 8-pound line and put on a tiny silver Mepps spinner. Flick it with pinpoint accuracy above the shoal and it will land like a feather on the surface. Twitch it back so it glints and hesitates and rises and falls in front of the fish; chances are that soon enough one will make a mistake. Try a mini popper for a European chub or asp, or a black bass anywhere in the world. Rainbow trout will go for them, too, as will steelhead.

Mini Rubbers

Perhaps the art of mini lure fishing is never bettered than when using small rubber imitations for black bass. Bass can be the most critical of creatures, and to fool them with a rubber imitation is one of the most skilful of fishing forms. Your rubber will be an imitation nymph perhaps, or a small fish, or a tiny crayfish. Maybe it's a baby lizard or a newt, but the aim will be to fish it as naturally as possible. Hopefully, you will be fishing shallow, clear water and you'll be able to watch the bass's reaction to your lure. If you can see the fish and their reaction to what you are offering, you're halfway to success.

Generally, though, you will be fishing deeper, especially in bright, hot conditions when the bass won't emerge far from the bottom rocks. Once you lose sight of the fish and your lure, it's your line that tells you everything – when your lure hits bottom, how it's working and when a fish is showing interest. A bass can take your mini rubber at any stage during the cast. It might well intercept it as it's sinking through the water layers to the bottom. It might take it static on the bed or when it's twitched, even once it's been properly retrieved. Hold the line carefully throughout the cast from the moment it hits the water so you can feel if the bass are showing any reaction. Takes can be as gentle as a puff of wind on the back of your hand.

It's a good idea to let your lure lie a good while on the bottom and often bass will gather round it to investigate, looking for all the

world like an aquatic parliament of owls. The odd twitch of the rod tip will be transmitted down the line and make your mini rubber skip a little bit. The bass will become curious. A sharp upwards stroke of the rod kicks the rubber into life and the bass might well move closer. Lift it from the bottom. Let it flutter back. Twitch it. Let it lie still. Chances are, eventually one of your actions will make one bass lunge in and make a terrible mistake!

This is what mini lure fishing is all about: tight, accurate casting; fishing areas that most anglers fear; working tiny lures in imaginative ways and making them look as irresistible as possible.

▼ ▲ *Trying everything*
An interesting shot, this. It's a difficult day because it's calm and bright and the guys are fishing for pike with big streamer flies and the tiniest lures imaginable. In the end, a good fish fell for a crayfish imitation that was only about an inch long.

Trolling

At its simplest level, trolling is the act of pulling lures behind a moving boat in order to attract predatory fish. It's a great technique for lake trout, pike, muskies, perch, Nile perch, tiger fish and even, at times, zander. However, because the fishing is comparatively monotonous and the normal skills of casting and bite detection don't really come into play, trolling is frequently depicted as being unskilful. To an extent I agree with this. However, there is a world of difference between an average troller and a good one. Some trolling anglers are just much more successful than others, so there has to be some element of skill involved.

▲ **African monsters**
Old friends, Jim and Linda Tyree, took this amazing leash of Nile perch several years ago. The fish did die, but they were not wasted: they were fed to the entire village.

▼ **The mists of the west**
This big Irish lough is just the sort of water for which trolling was designed.

Getting the Boat Right

First, your boat must be stable enough to deal with foul weather conditions. It must accommodate two anglers, often with lots of gear. An engine is virtually essential, and it must be able to troll at very low speeds. Reverse gear is also vital, both to retrace steps over snags to free lures and also to chase fish should this prove necessary. Electric motors are particularly useful in still, shallow, bright conditions. Whether petrol or electric, engines should be very reliable, as they can, in certain situations, save your life. Never, ever forget to take oars; there will be times when the engine refuses to fire. Don't forget the rowlocks and do ensure that they fit the boat before setting out on your fishing trip. Importantly, never, and I mean never, forget either the baling bucket or the lifejacket.

Boat rod rests are essential. Screw them very tightly to the boat's sides - the pressure exerted on them when a fish is hooked or a snag is encountered can be enormous. If the water is too deep and dark to be able to see to the bottom, an echo sounder of some sort is a great bonus. Without one, you will be fishing blind over large areas of water – never the shortest cut to success.

Trolling Tackle

For most general work, the best trolling rods are between 9 and 11 feet long, with test curves of between 2 and 3.5 pounds. You might want to go shorter and heavier at times, but for big pike and lake trout, for example, this type of rod is ideal. A rod longer than 11 feet is an encumbrance in a boat.

The experienced troller will nearly always use a multiplier reel. Depending on the size of the fish being pursued, the depth of the water, the amount of snags and the size of lure being trolled, pick a line to withstand all the stresses and strains thrown at it.

Choose your lures carefully. Decide at what level you want to work them and choose top water, middle water or deep working plugs, spinners and spoons.

The Trolling Technique

At the start of the troll, let plenty of line out so that the lure is working between 50 and 70 yards behind the boat. There are certain species – musky and pike, for example – that will take lures much closer than this, but big trout are very wary if the water is clear.

Vary the trolling speed from very slow, to slow, to quicker, sometimes even to short, fast bursts. Only rarely will you take a dead-straight line. You are more likely to adopt a zigzag course along the preferred depths. Critical moments come when the boat changes direction and the lure rises and falls enticingly in the water, often inducing a take.

Don't troll blindly. Look at what your echo sounder tells you. Troll round islands. Try to find man-made structures such as water towers, dams and boat jetties. Look at the bankside for clues. If the bank is precipitous, then its water shelves are likely steep. If the bank is low-lying and level, the water is likely to be shallow. Look for shoals of small prey fish close to the surface – the predators you are pursuing will likely be close by. There will be commercial fish cages on many trolling waters. Work as close to these as you can, always obeying signposts and minding the ropes and chains that tether these cages to the bottom.

Be prepared to do things differently. For example, if you want to get very deep – over 20 yards – then you will probably need a down-rigger. However, depth is not always an issue; most predatory fish come closer to the surface when they are feeding hard.

On many waters for many species, the best trolling conditions are rough ones, but I can think of many days when flat calm and bright conditions have served very well. If you suspect that fish are wary of the engine, don't hesitate to troll on the oar or on the electric motor. There are many occasions when it is imperative to troll with the same finesse you would use to flick a dry fly or a nymph.

▲ *Working the dam wall*
Now we're in Scotland on one of the big hydro-electric lochs in the extreme north-west. Once again, location is paramount and the guys are investigating very deep water – well over 100 feet – near the dam.

THE DOWNRIGGER

A downrigger allows you to troll a lure very deeply indeed, way past its normal working depth. You will also play the fish freely, for when it takes, the line reel is snapped away from the downrigger's cable. Operate the downrigger from the stern of the boat, and lower the rig down with the winch provided. A word of caution: don't use a downrigger if you're fishing solo. If the trolling weight snags and you're in a heavy wind, a small boat can be put severely at risk. The downrigger is especially useful on glacial waters, where depths frequently exceed 200 to 300 feet.

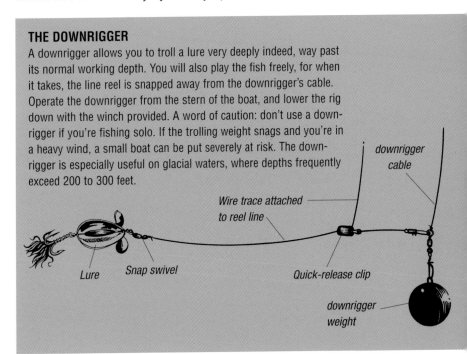

downrigger cable

Wire trace attached to reel line

Lure   Snap swivel

Quick-release clip

downrigger weight

Lures In Action

One of the essential, core skills of fishing is the ability to watch, understand, then imitate nature. Think of a trout so obsessed by mayfly during the early summer that it won't look at any other hatching insects. Predators can, at times, be the same. They will be aware of movements in nature that, for some reason, during certain periods or times of year, will bring them bountiful food. Their survival depends on being switched on to these occurrences. Your skill as an angler is learning to recognize these moments and plugging into them (no pun intended) as a lure angler.

▼ ▲ *Taking the mickey!*
Ian holds a super taimen – an ancient salmon form – that fell to a mouse pattern (below) fished over the shallows. The take was volcanic.

The Magnificent Taimen

For many years, I have been making an almost annual trek to Mongolia in the heart of Asia. The quarry there is an extraordinary salmonid, one of the oldest forms of salmon known: the taimen. These are big fish and can easily grow to over 50 pounds, and they can be caught during the daytime on lures of all sorts and on large streamer flies. It's hard work. Frequently, you have to walk or ride miles to the best pools and runs, and you arrive back at camp, as dusk falls and the wolves begin to howl, quite exhausted.

Salmon on Mouse Lures

The Mongolians watch us return from the day's fishing, shrug their shoulders and look at us pityingly, as though we're quite crazy. They know something that we don't. As the night falls and the temperature drops, the small rodents, of which we see nothing during the day, emerge from their nooks and crannies on the plains. These are mice, marmots and even a lemming-type creature. It's now that they move and begin to feed, and that movement very often takes them into the water. As the darkness intensifies, more and more of these small, furry creatures begin to cross the river because, as we know, the grass is always greener on the other side!

The taimen, being at the head of the food chain, know exactly when and where this movement of mice is most likely to happen and they make sure that they are in a position to profit. The night that my Mongolian host brought this phenomenon to my attention was moonlit. He picked up his child's small teddy bear and hurled it out into the river, where it floated for just 2 yards before being engulfed in a swirl. The teddy bear was soon rejected but a squirrel shot by a hunter the previous day was then lobbed in, taken and never seen again. Naturally enough, not being totally blind to what was happening around me, I learned my lesson.

Today, one of the most exciting ways of taking a big taimen on a lure is to wait for the dark, for the cold to intensify, for the moon to rise and to hurl out a large mouse pattern and bring it scudding back across the tail of a pool. Create a big wake. Make it splash. Invest that furry creation with as much life as you can muster.

Fishing for Pike with Mouse Patterns

The same goes for more traditional predators, the pike especially. It's tempting to think that pike eat nothing but fish, and while fish generally make up the majority of a pike's menu, this isn't always the case, as we'll see in more depth shortly. Pike, in any water, are very aware of what is happening on the surface, as well as beneath it. On many waters I know, spring-time ducklings can begin to take precedence over fish as targeted food items. Perhaps because of this, the best time in my experience to target pike with mouse patterns is in the spring and early summer, if fishing is permitted then.

The way you work a mouse lure depends to some degree on the mood of the pike. My understanding suggests that if they are voracious, working the lure quickly will frequently provoke a response. If the pike are

▶ ▲ *Nearly tempted*

This was a situation where the mouse didn't quite pay off. The pike saw it, came out of the weed and approached it close on two or three occasions, but it wasn't quite convinced. However, the mouse had woken the pike up and shortly afterwards, it fell to a lure that was worked down deeper.

▲ **Predator becomes prey**

Jim was playing the small pike (right) when it was seized and consumed by its great grandmother (left).

▼ **Along the reed bed**

Lures, like this selection, are particularly effective when fished close to cover rather than through barren water.

not hungry, then a much slower retrieval generally works best. I have no doubt the pike will sometimes saunter up to a mouse pattern and take it out of mere curiosity.

Fishing for Baltic Pike

Where do you think the biggest of these predators exist in the world? Canada? Siberia? The great American stillwaters? All of these places do hold big pike, but probably the largest pike in the world are found in the Baltic Sea.

Baltic pike can be targeted several times per year. In spring, for example, they come close in to the reedy bays to spawn. For most of the year, however, throughout the summer particularly, they lie 2 or 3 miles out to sea, sheltering around submerged plateaus and islands waiting to waylay the enormous nomadic herring shoals that patrol these sea lanes. Comparatively few local fishermen target the pike at this time, but those that do either fish live herring or lures of herring size and silvery herring colour.

Gentle Handling

Another major reason that Baltic pike are so huge is because the Baltic itself is vast, fishing pressure is limited and angling pressure does not have a large or damaging effect. Pike are,

despite their size and menacing appearance, one of the most susceptible of all fish to anglers' mishandling. If there is one skill of which we are eternally proud in lure fishing, it should be our ability to land, hook and return a pike with no damage done to it whatsoever.

As often as possible, think single hooks rather than trebles. Do even those singles need barbs? Never go lure fishing for pike without long-nosed forceps and strong pliers. If you're at all apprehensive, wear stout gloves to prevent any grazes and loss of blood. An unhooking mat is a great idea, and if you can avoid netting a fish and simply unhook it in the margins, so much the better. This is the one and only reason you'll find very little mention of dead baiting for pike in this book: too many dead baits are taken down deep and too many pike die as a result.

Exclusive Pike – Exclusively

All of which brings me to quite the most extraordinary pike water I have ever fished in the United Kingdom. The lake is around 80 acres in extent and offers phenomenally good pike fishing, for one obvious and immediate reason – it's private. Strictly Private. The fact that only one other angler, James, and I are ever allowed a day or two every year has protected the pike stocks, which remain as strong as they were when I first happened upon the water some 12 years ago. Both of us only use single-hooked lures, and I think in all our time there only one small pike has come to grief because of our attentions. The message is obvious for the lure angler wanting to catch big pike – invest time and effort in finding a lightly fished water, fish it as carefully as you possibly can and only reveal the where-abouts of the place to those who will show equal respect.

I mention this water for another startling reason. In all the years that James and I have fished the place, we have never seen a single, solitary fish there that isn't a pike. No silver fish. No cyprinids. Absolutely nothing that you would expect the pike to be feeding upon. We have frequently gone out in a boat

◀ **Joy in Africa**
Once again, a village celebrates as a big Nile perch is taken on a lure. Naturally, in most of the world, we practise catch and release, but there are times when the livelihood of the people is the paramount consideration.

in the brightest of conditions at times when the lake is crystal clear. We've looked and looked and not seen a single fish but pike. We've put bait out over exposed, sandy areas here, there and everywhere and gone back and back to see if it's been taken. The bait has simply rotted into the bottom silts.

So, if we're correct, this is an interesting conundrum for the lure angler. Of course, we have had success on lures imitating small silver fish, but nowhere near as much action as on lures designed to look like pike. On the hardest days, only pike-like lures will catch fish. On the easiest days, pike-like lures out-fish silver fish representations by three or four to one. Also, in the summer months especially, we've had almost equal success with surface-fished lures, especially those mouse patterns. The message is an obvious one: the pike here, for one reason or another, are feeding almost exclusively on their own species and on anything terrestrial that falls into the water. Mimic what the pike are looking for and your successes rocket.

A Crucial Quality

James, my companion on the water, shows one of the most important characteristics a successful angler will possess in abundance. I'm not talking about his hunting instincts, his ability to read nature, identify

with it and use it to his fishing advantage. I'm talking about his valour: the derring-do way he approaches his fishing. James has mounted some notable expeditions around the world, but none more admirable than his trip into Lake Tanganyika. The logistics of the journey were dauntingly tough. His jeep ride in took days, and then he lived rough with the locals. They recognized him as a fellow hunter, took him to heart and showed him the best places to fish on the lake, where his lures worked their magic.

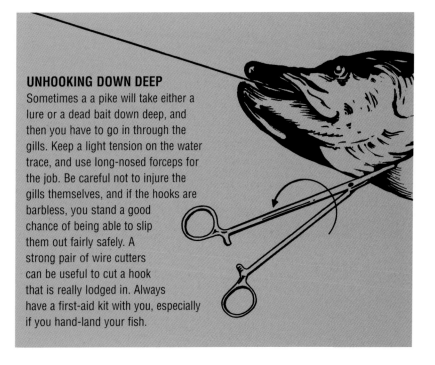

UNHOOKING DOWN DEEP
Sometimes a a pike will take either a lure or a dead bait down deep, and then you have to go in through the gills. Keep a light tension on the water trace, and use long-nosed forceps for the job. Be careful not to injure the gills themselves, and if the hooks are barbless, you stand a good chance of being able to slip them out fairly safely. A strong pair of wire cutters can be useful to cut a hook that is really lodged in. Always have a first-aid kit with you, especially if you hand-land your fish.

Lure Fishing In India

Many opportunities are lost in India because anglers and guides alike frequently insist on fishing bait when plugs and spinners would be far more exciting and, probably, more immediate. The best places to try lures – as in most rivers – are those areas of quicker, white water. Fish don't have long to make a decision, and if something edible-looking flashes across their field of vision they are likely to make an instantaneous move.

▲ **Totally trashed**

Lure fishing in India is not to be taken lightly. This plug was seized by a big mahseer and totally trashed in seconds. They can destroy any lure simply by the power of their lips, and if a plug should get down to the throat teeth, it will be mincemeat.

▲ **Enormous strength**

Here we see a selection of Indian home-made lures. They may not have the variety and sophistication of the lures bought in the West, but they work and, if you look carefully, you can see that they all have one thing in common: enormous strength. The hooks, swivels and split rings are all old, but they are tried and tested and far tougher than you'd imagine.

▶ **A real challenge**

English angler, Dan Goff, loves the challenge that lure fishing presents. It's all action, jumping from rock to rock, working the river and fishing miles of whitewater rapids. Basha, his guide, won't leave his side.

▲ *Stay focused*

Dan is like a coiled spring, focusing intently on the water in front of him. A piece of river like this demands really diligent searching. Flick your lure above rocks, behind rocks, by the side of rocks. Work the gullies. Work the shallow tails of pools. Let a lure just hang in the flow for 30 seconds and allow the current to impart movement. Cast in the same area two, even three times: the first cast might make the fish aware, the second cast will put it on alert and the third cast could prove the crucial one. See how Dan has positioned himself carefully with a 100 per cent secure foothold, which is vital as takes can slam you like a train.

▲ *A critical moment*

The lure is coming close and Dan lowers his rod tip so that he can work it almost to his feet. He's looking intently into the water, looking for his lure and watching for any following fish. If he sees a fish closing in, he might well increase the retrieve speed to force an immediate reaction.

▲ *Accuracy is crucial*

Really effective working off rocks such as this calls for super-accurate casting, so the rod needs to be between 7 and 9 feet in length. This back cast is meant to skip into whitewater and then follow the channel between the rock on the left and the cliff on the right.

▲ *Feathering the cast*

With perfect control, Dan feathers the cast as the lure reaches its entry point.

▲ *Stay alert!*

Dan immediately clicks over the bale arm as the lure hits the water and begins his retrieve. Takes can be instantaneous in waters like this, so he needs to be alert from the very first crank of the reel.

▲ Following the retrieve

Once again, Dan is following the retrieve all the way to his rod tip. A big fish might easily be hanging behind that big rock.

▲ Fish on!

Now it's all drama. Basha has joined him, and together they are trying to slow down a fish that's already charged 100 yards downriver.

◀ Following closely

The pair have followed the fish right down to the next pool, where it is hanging behind a rock. Now is the time to exert maximum pressure and get the fish moving upstream again. Another major run at this stage could spell disaster.

▲ A glorious outcome

The outcome is successful, and the fish is edging towards 40 pounds. The battle has drawn spectators from the hills – everybody likes to see a big fish and share in the glory.

▲ Working his way

Dan continues to work his way downriver,
searching some bigger, deeper pools.
Once again, his casts are accurate and tight,
close into rocks.

▶ ▲ The quarry

This time a dramatic Indian carp is the catch.

▶ Tricky footing

This is a river of many contrasts. On the following day, Dan moves several miles upstream to
where the river is a true gorge. Rocks the size of
houses litter the banks, and the river divides into
channels, often only a rod's length across.

▶ A delicious prize

That's the beauty of lure fishing – you just never
quite know what you're going to catch – in this
case a murrell, a fish much prized by the Indians
for the table.

Chapter Four
Sea Fishing

The seas and oceans of the world offer an endless list of angling possibilities, and demand an equally endless list of skills in order to conquer the challenges involved. Beach casting. Rock casting. Wreck fishing. Uptide fishing. Saltwater fly fishing. Lure fishing. Big game fishing. Float fishing. Enough excitement and complexity here to last a lifetime.

Sea Fishing

It doesn't matter whether you are fishing for striped bass off a New York coast, sea bass close to London, bonefish in the Bahamas or skate off Iceland, you have to understand the fish's environment if you're going to succeed. It's easy to think of the sea as a vast, unreadable environment that is impossible to understand or get to grips with, but this is not the case.

Fathomable Features

Skilful sea anglers do not catch fish by accident. They catch them regularly and by design, and they can do so because they know exactly how to read the many features saltwater possesses. Take an experienced sea angler of any discipline to any ocean in the world and he will immediately point out features everywhere. This watercraft is essential and, because of the size of saltwater venues, it is even more important here than in freshwater. In an average-sized lake you can lob in a bait, ignoring all fish-holding features, and the odds are a fish will chance on it sometime in the day. Not so in the sea, where you could be miles from a feeding fish.

Depth and bottom contours play a vital role, especially where shallows drop off precipitously into the deeps. Shoreline irregularities such as inlets, coves, bays and points all attract fish. The make-up of the seabed is vital, as different species are attracted to different geological areas. Rocks, broken ground, sand, shingle and mud all play their part, as do cliffs, estuaries, creeks, marshes, inflowing freshwater streams, reefs and sandbars. Weed beds are home to many fish, as are underwater caves. Man-made structures, too, play a huge role. Fish will always congregate around piers, wrecks, sea defences, harbours, offshore rigs and even anchored boats.

Time and Tide

Sea water is nearly always moving, and it is important to understand the influence of the wind, currents, and the strength and height of the constantly differing tides.

Sea Bass

Like freshwater fish, sea fish exhibit wildly differing characteristics. Take two of my favourite species – the bass and the mullet. I can walk five minutes from my house to the shingle spit that runs four miles to the west and even further to the east. At the right time of the year, when the weather and the tides are perfect, I'll see the bass at work. They'll be chasing sand eels and any number of species of small fish. They'll even come into the brackish estuaries to hunt sticklebacks. They'll chase small flatfish and sometimes send up puffs of silt where they're digging for them. You'll see them sometimes in shallow water with their tails waving as they dig for crabs hiding between the stones. These are fish with a big spirit, a big mouth and a big appetite, and providing you can locate them, hooking up isn't that difficult.

Grey Mullet

Now let's take the mullet, pretty much the same size and not at all dissimilar to look at. However, these creek mullet behave in a totally different fashion. It's dawn, in June, with an incoming tide. You sit on the marsh head watching the water push across the muds, and soon, when it's only a hands-breadth deep, you will see the mullet appearing. They'll be there in huge shoals following the very furthest fringes of the tide. Some of them are big fish – 4, 5 or even 6 pounds – and they're hungry. Again, you see them on their heads as they feed, their tails and their backs wavering, perhaps catching the first rays of the rising sun. These mullet should be easy to catch, you think. After all, they're even feeding right there, almost under your rod tip.

You couldn't be more wrong. Back in the 1970s, in the course of three or four years I managed to hook just four – after scores, if not hundreds, of attempts. Why? Because they are feeding on tiny organisms that live in the surface film of the muds. The mullet are simply hoovering up microscopic food particles, and your lugworm, rag worm, bread flake or sweetcorn look to them about as edible and as appetizing as a rock. Now, some thirty years later, I'm just learning to catch them on fly tackle and the tiniest imaginable black and brown goldhead nymphs tied on size 20 hooks – sometimes.

Size 20 hooks! Next month, I'm fishing with a mate off the north coast of Scotland for giant skate. Up there we'll be using hooks 100, perhaps 200 times the size, and in that one thought lies the wonder of sea fishing. It is simply a sport of never-ending skills to be learned.

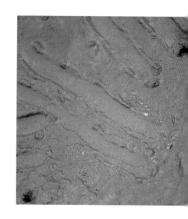

▲ *Watch for the signs*
The sea isn't always a massive, deep, unreadable place. Certainly around the coastline, where the water can be shallow and clear, you can learn a lot. On the flats (left photograph) the water is clear enough to see the bonefish feed. You can also see the marks left by mullet (above photograph) as they browse on the mud-flats when the tide is in.

▼ ◀ *Looking for bass*
Sea bass, like freshwater bass, are all about structure. Look for them around rocks, large weed beds, gulleys, drop-offs, breakwaters, boat moorings – anywhere that food is likely to collect.

Beach Casting In Action

This is the rough, tough side of angling skills. Fishing off the shore over rough ground in strong winds and in big tides is physically gruelling, and is demanding for both the angler and his tackle. You could not think of a scenario more removed from the angler fishing a dry fly or flicking out a tiny lure for a black bass. Fishing from beaches like this can call for long walks in atrocious conditions. Beach casting rods are built to be tough, and reels are almost invariably multipliers that work harder for a living than any other reel on the planet.

A Range of Skills

Fishing like this is virtually always about bait, and that bait is frequently hard come by. The chances are that the crabs will have been individually grubbed up from underneath their rocks and that the lugworm will have been dug in backbreaking circumstances from the muds.

It is likely that the targets will be cod, codling, haddock, flatfish, pollack, bass or any one of a dozen species that in the heavily netted waters of the northern hemisphere are probably scarcer than they have ever been. The big catches that fell to rod and line from the shore years ago are now largely a thing of the past. To catch anything these days over many marks takes a huge amount of skill.

This was brought home to me when I accompanied Hardy Greys' product manager and expert, Tony Anderson, and their Commercial Director, Ian McCormack, out for a day just north of the English company's factory on the northeast coast as it approaches Scotland. As we walked from the cars with a mountain of gear over perilously slippery rocks, I soon realized that this was a tough man's sport, but equally one demanding a high level of skill. Its 'macho' nature can blind one to the delicacy of it all.

Okay, Tony's rod, reel, line and terminal gear are immensely powerful, but that doesn't mean all these devices aren't used with great skill and consideration. While the bait might look a hideous concoction of peeler crab and worm, it's still threaded onto the hook and tied there with enormous manual dexterity.

Where and How

Of course, fish aren't scattered around the sea like currants in a bun, but have exactly the same territorial requirements as the

▼ *Splendid isolation*

A shore fisherman like Tony often finds himself in more rugged, isolated places than any angler is ever likely to experience. Take care. Don't take risks with cliffs or slippery rocks. You don't want to be caught injured and on your own, in a dangerous situation with the tide beginning to turn.

mostaristocratic brown trout. Tony knows exactly the sorts of places that his quarry might live in, and if it means him wading out to some distant and difficult rocks to punch a 100-yard cast out into the teeth of a gale then Tony will do it.

You might well think that a fish in such a wild environment, faced with such a big bait, on such heavy tackle will inevitably give a bone-crushing bite that is impossible to miss. This is not always the case. Watching Tony and Ian stand on their rocks, their rods constantly to hand, fingers on the line, made me realize that this touch legering style of theirs is every bit as sensitive as anything I might employ on a small, clear river. They can feel what sort of ground their bait is fishing over and the very moment a 3-pound codling breathes on their bait at a distance of 80 yards. This is high skill, often displayed in conditions that want to kill you.

You might also think that when a 5- or a 10-pound fish is hooked on gear as gutsy as this, the fight will be a foregone conclusion. Again, not so. At about 1pm, Tony felt a quivering on his line and then, at distance, a gentle take. He struck hard – and his rod just walloped over. The strength of the tide was enormous, and trying to control the fish in the current proved virtually impossible. The area was strewn with rocks, gullies and forests of tough weed. Again and again, the fish found sanctuary, but Tony was able to guide it out. Just when success looked probable, the fish found an unyielding snag and it was gone. Tony shrugged – 5 pounds, 10 pounds perhaps, but a monster in conditions like this.

▲ *The delicatessen*
One of Tony's secrets is to match the best baits with the season. His baits are always fresh and mounted with great care, to keep them secure during the cast and to withstand the pounding the sea gives them.

▼ *On the rocks*
Tony is constantly looking for places where the shoreline and the tides work together to produce fabulous fish-holding areas.

Fishing The Tropics – The Bonefish Flats

Not all bonefish flats, lodges, boats, guides or seasons are equal. Time and money are both important factors, and you don't want to waste either, so spend as long as it takes on research and you won't regret it. The timing can be very important: the flats are very susceptible to bad weather conditions, so choose periods that are traditionally quiet. Location, too, is vital: in general, the quieter and less pressurized the flat, the less spooky and more easily caught the bonefish will be. My advice would be to go with a reputable outfitter or, failing that, on the trusted recommendation of someone you know well. A suspiciously cheap trip without any testimonials to back it up can be a big disappointment.

Complete Preparation

Any bonefish trip is a big investment in time, money and energy, so give yourself the best chance of success and don't skimp or cut corners. From top to toe, get your clothing right. Proper flats shoes will help enormously by giving you really secure footing and protection from nasties. Lightweight, UV-protective clothing is a great breakthrough and will keep you safe and cool through hours out on the flats, and always wear a hat with a large brim both for protection and to cut down surface glare. Choose your polarizing glasses carefully and always take a spare pair – they're as essential to your fishing as sunblock is to your skin care.

Take the same concern over your gear. You should consider taking two or three

▼ **Smell the roses**
The bonefish flats, dotted throughout various parts of the world, are truly some of the most scenic places from which to fish.

movements of the fish better than you, a visitor, will ever do, no matter how experienced you are as a flats fisherman. The combination of wind, tides, depths, food supplies and bottom make-up are all crucial and quite baffling unless you know the area like the back of your hand. Flats can be enormous, and without local knowledge like this bonefish can be as hard to locate as needles in haystacks.

A guide, too, will be able to read the flats in different weather conditions and at different stages of the tide. He will be able to keep you on your toes and take you to new areas, constantly keeping the adrenalin flowing. Vitally, he'll see fish when all you're aware of is an endless expanse of water. Of course, with experience, your bonefishing techniques will improve.

◀ ▲ ▼ *Stalkers*
Fishing the flats successfully is all about hunting the prey. These are huge expanses of water, and you've got to move large distances quietly and carefully, always scanning the water for glimpses of fish.

outfits to deal with different weather conditions. You might prefer to fish very light, but this can be difficult if the wind has risen. When you're bonefishing, reels are definitely not just line reservoirs: half way through a 100-yard run, you'll know exactly why an ultra reliable clutch is so important. For that same reason, check and recheck all your knots from the drum of the reel to the fly on the point. If there's a weakness anywhere in your tackle, then a bonefish will expose it. At the end of the day, rinse rods, reels, boots – everything - down with a good spraying of cold, fresh water.

Before you set off, especially if the gear you have bought is new to you, take time out to familiarize yourself with it fully. Learn to cast quickly, accurately and precisely over long, medium and short distances. Practise casting to the left, then to the right and even, sometimes, behind you, quickly, easily and above all safely. Any hesitancy with your gear when you're out there on the flats will cost you time, and that means missed fish.

Get Experienced Help

When you're out there, aim to get a guide and, like everything else we're saying here, choose the best you can. The main reason for this is that, as a local, he'll know the

Learning to See

Remember that a hunter of any type of game, finned or furred, is scanning a large area, looking for a telltale sign. For example, if you're eyes are flickering through a forest, you're just looking for a flash of white, perhaps, and not the whole deer. It's the same with bonefish. You want a general overall impression of the flat in front of you and,

thereafter, you're looking for a positive hint. This can be the flash of a silver side as it tilts and catches the sunlight, or it can very probably just be a moving shadow, which is often more obvious than the fish itself. In shallow water, look for the tips of dorsals or tail fins breaking the surface. Look, too, for mudding fish creating clouds of sediment as they feed in shallow water. Get used to the phenomenon known as nervous water. This looks as if the surface is somehow vibrating, shaking, definitely on the move in a strange way. In windy weather, study the pattern of the ripple very closely. Anywhere that ripple is broken or transformed in some way can indicate a shoal of fish swimming just subsurface. You probably won't see the fish themselves, but the disturbance of the ripple pattern is a giveaway.

The Bonefishing Technique

When you're actually fishing and you see a bonefish and you're going to cast to it, don't take your eyes off the fish for a second, whatever you do. Keep it constantly in your vision or the chances are you will lose it altogether. Speed and accuracy are the two watchwords when you are fishing, but don't push yourself past your limits. It's a lot better to remain calm and in control than to try to speed up and bodge what you're doing. The odd sigh of exasperation from a guide is to be expected, but remember you're the one ultimately in control.

A fish is on. If you are on a boat, do make sure that the decks are free of obstructions and any line at your feet can hiss out unimpeded. If it doesn't, you're broken. When you're retrieving, forget the old English figure of eight technique and instead strip back

▲ **In the crystal seas**

This is what it's all about – drama in a waterscape that is stunningly beautiful. Stalking fish on foot like this is the ultimate thrill.

◄ **Going afloat**

A shallow-bottomed skiff can be a real bonus. It can get you over deeper troughs that are impossible to wade. You also have more mobility to track fast-moving fish.

with your rod tip pointed almost to the water's surface itself. Quick strip. Slow strip. Pause. You can make your fly do anything you want if you concentrate on every second. If you don't get back to the lodge totally exhausted at the end of the session then you just haven't been trying hard enough!

Stay Safe and Enjoy

If you're in the water on the flats – and most of us actually prefer walking to our fish than being boat-bound – take care. Stingrays can hide beneath layers of mud and silt, and stepping on one can be a serious business. As a result, it pays not to actually lift and place your feet, but rather to drag your feet forwards, always keeping them in contact with the bed. This way you will touch a ray instead of actually stepping vertically on top of it. If you see a couple of rays scoot away from you in alarm, you'll know this has been a really good bit of advice.

Above all, enjoy every moment out there on the flats. Don't be sucked into the size and numbers game. Set your own objectives and keep them realistic. The flats are simply the most marvellous places on the planet, and if you're sensible you will try to get the very best out of your guide: ask him about

the birdlife, the turtles and why the fish are where they are. A good guide will really respond to an interested customer. You'll get far better value for your money than if you're quiet, broody, don't show interest or are unappreciative of the efforts he's making.

Remember, a quick photograph and that bone goes back. The first run has a serious effect on them, and a healthy stock of fish is essential for flats-fishing in the future, and for the livelihoods of all those associated with this most tantalizing branch of the sport.

▲ *Not alone*
It's not just your quarry that you'll find yourself enjoying the shallow seas alongside. There will be all manner of sharks, rays, skates and turtles, along with exotic shells and weed forms. Most of these aren't dangerous, but keep your eyes firmly peeled.

◄ *Evening success*
You'd never quite call a day on the flats hard work, but it can be gruelling. Perhaps the nicest time is when the sun is just beginning to sink and lose its glare, and the fish are beginning to feed particularly well.

Big Game Adventure

When it comes down to the skill factor, I confess that I'm personally unsure about a lot of big game fishing. I have been out over blue water on charter boats and enjoyed the experience to a limited degree, but too often, it seems to me, the results are dependent on the skills of the skipper and crew, the time of year, the quality of water you're fishing over and, to some degree, the amount of money you are willing to throw at the whole experience. On very many occasions, it seems that other people are doing all the work and the angler is really reaping the benefit of other people's skills rather than his own talents.

▲ **The sporting artist**
Whether fishing for dorado, sailfish, salmon or even pike, Shirley is at home on any water in the world. Waters also feature prominently in her internationally acclaimed paintings.

▼ **An all-action game**
Once the sailfish are hooked, it's all hands on deck. If you can keep the action on the surface, it's a dynamite experience.

A Personal Account

However, Shirley Deterding is a long-term friend of mine who has massive experience of fishing on all continents, and if she says that a particular fishing style has merit then I'm willing to listen to her. She certainly came back from Guatemala full of what she'd been enjoying and very definite that it had a lot to offer the serious fly fisher looking to try something different. She was at pains to express the skill of her boat crew, but that does not mean to say that she, herself, was a passive observer. This is one of those occasions when I can't really do better than quote Shirley herself.

"Obviously, I was hugely dependent on my boys for getting me to the right places at the right times of day. They were also the ones with the eagle eye, looking out for the sailfish and pulling in the teasers like crazy when the big fish showed. These were really two important elements that I would have struggled with on my own, so I'm not claiming sole credit for the big fish that I caught.

"However, I don't feel that I was simply a useless woman having absolutely no impact whatsoever. Firstly, you have to possess decent casting skills on a rocking boat in heavy seas when you're chucking out a heavy fly. It's all too easy to get a fly in the rigging or, worse, in somebody's ear. You must also be accurate. It's no good just

dumping a fly in the general area of a sailfish. You've got to put it exactly where you're expecting a hit.

"Your retrieve also has got to be spot on. Remember you're fishing in clear water for big fish that possess great eyesight, so they're not easily fooled. You have to pull the fly back in a really lifelike fashion and make them believe they're hitting a small, injured fish.

"And then, if you do get a hit, you've still got to set the hook yourself. It's all too easy to mess up on this. The trick is to delay the strike and not panic because of your excitement. Try, if you can, to count to three or four and direct the strike away from where the fish is running. That's important. Otherwise you simply whip the fly out of the fish's mouth.

"So, you've got a big fish on and it's running hard. The next skill is keeping a fish from sounding during the fight. If a fish goes down deep it becomes impossibly hard, both for the sailfish itself and for the angler. You're putting both of you under impossible stresses unless you succeed in keeping the fish on the top where you can fight it with a reasonable amount of efficiency. It's imperative that you get the fish in as fast as you can before it tires itself unduly in these warm seas. Furthermore, if the fight lasts too long, you run the risk of sharks coming in for the kill.

"Quick release of the fish is vital, and most boats don't encourage you to take fish from the water for weighing or for photographing. If it's a special fish – your first or your biggest or whatever – a quick photograph on board is permissible, but 95 per cent of fish go back without ever leaving the water, and this is where the skill of your crew comes in. They're remarkably good at leaning over and flicking the fly out with long forceps or a stick especially designed for the job. Crews pride themselves on their ability to put fish back with the minimum of fuss and maximum regard for their welfare. It's an essential part of the whole scene of sailfish.

"So would I do it again? You bet I would. It's exciting, the fish are beautiful and the role of the angler just can't be underestimated."

▲ *Getting close*
As the fish near the boat, the adrenaline really begins to pump. One mistake now on a short, tight line and the game's over and done with.

▼ *Never to be forgotten*
Just a quick photograph, a permanent reminder of a magnificent day with a fly rod in hand.

The Florida Experience

I recently photographed a product-testing session for Hardy Greys, the UK tackle company. They were trying out some new saltwater rods and reels, so we decided to go over to Florida and trust ourselves to one of the top guides out there, Dave Gibson. Dave proved a wonderfully entertaining companion for a week, able to point out all the wildlife around us, and to take us to the best bars at night. But it was his fishing abilities that struck me forcefully, reminding me just how many skills a top guide at sea needs to master.

▼ Howard's delight
The reefs give up exceptionally hard-fighting fish in an amazing range of species.

Safety First

On the simplest level we have to admire his boatmanship. His boat is truly the tool of his trade, essential for whisking his clients at high speeds over vast distances. To do this successfully and safely, Dave has to maintain his boat in tiptop condition and know all the potential hazards over many square miles. Travelling fast, often over low water, is not an exercise to be undertaken lightly.

Nonetheless, the heart of the matter is actually finding fish. Okay, Dave uses a GPS, but this is no substitute for intimate knowledge of the area and only really serves to help locate the boat in those last few, vital yards. What Dave has built up over the years is a vast and intimate knowledge of the bottom make-up over his huge territory. He knows where the coral heads are and all manner of structure, both natural and man made. He must consider the time and size of the tides, the direction and strength of the winds and the constant changing of currents that I would never even have guessed at. He also has to keep a constant eye on the weather, because out here storms can come

◀ Silver kings
Tarpon are truly the silver kings, not just off the Florida coast but through the warm waters of the world. Scintillating to look at, they are fascinating in their habits and when hooked, fight as fast and hard as any fish on the planet.

out of nowhere and a lightning storm, in particular, can be deadly dangerous.

Fishing Considerations

Once fish have been found, Dave has to consider the best way to approach them. He doesn't want to blunder over a coral head and cause the fish to panic, or spook a group of tarpon by getting too close. He thinks about the depth of the water and its clarity. He considers the brightness of the sun and its angle. He's aware of the water's drift and how strongly and how fast the wind and tide will push him. Moreover, he has complete control over his boat, either with the engine or by poling.

These considerations are particularly crucial when Dave is with fly anglers, who have to put lines out anything up to 30 yards or more. He knows, too, that the wind must be taken even more into account if a fly is to be placed with total accuracy in front of fish feeding deep in the mangroves.

If Dave is out with bait fishermen, he will advise on the best bait fish or prawn to use and how to mount it. Moreover, he's a true master with a drop net. Once the bait is ready, Dave knows whether to fish it static or in the drift.

Looking After the Client

Dave knows the importance of assessing the fishing. If it's poor at a certain mark, will it get better or should he cut his losses, fire up the engines and move, sometimes miles away? He's also fantastic at reading the mood of the anglers with him and how best to maintain their confidence and enthusiasm. When Dave does move on, he constantly scans the horizon, aware of what other boats are doing and where they are heading.

When a client hooks into a vast, leaping, dervish of a silver king, Dave knows how best to conduct the fight and to manoeuvre the boat to help his angler, as well as having an uncanny ability to predict any possible crises. Once the fish is defeated, Dave knows how and where it's best to release the fish, taking into consideration its welfare, as well as the desire for his clients to get that all-important trophy shot.

All guiding, anywhere in the world, is difficult and demanding but nowhere else have a I met a guide who has to take on board such a vast number of considerations in fishing situations that are constantly changing. Dave would pick us up early, sometimes on the point of light breaking. He would work with us all day, covering huge amounts of water in his quest for fish. He'd advise us, criticize us, even model clothes for us. We'd often stay out until the stars began to appear, and it was no wonder to us that he often fell asleep over his supper.

▲ ◀ *A great guide*
Dave Gibson is a genius at finding fish like this coral-dweller, using prawn and other bait. Don't think it's just the big fish that fight hard: even five-pounders can bend a fly rod in two.

▼ *As the sun sinks*
As the light fades, tarpon in particular move and feed hard. Many locals will only consider going out when the shadows lengthen.

Bass On The Fly

For freshwater bass fishing, you are unlikely to need anything stronger than your general trout fishing kit. This isn't always the case on the sea. While 6-, 7- and 8-weight rods can work admirably well in calm conditions, most of the time the sea isn't like a millpond, so be prepared to invest in 9- or even 10-weight gear. You also need to be aware that when you are sea fishing there's always a chance of hooking into something much bigger than you might be expecting. For example, a good pollack hooked off the rocks can destroy light gear. If you're in a boat, there's sometimes even the chance, albeit remote, of hooking into a small or medium-sized tope.

▼ *Rods and reels*

A collection of different weight rods and reels can be vital if you are fishing at different depths around different features in rapidly changing weather conditions. Always hose your kit down with fresh water after it has done saltwater work.

Reel and Lines

It's as well to have at least two different sized reels – one to take 6- or 7-weight lines and a larger one for boats and heavier water. Floating lines are sometimes all you will need, but there are going to be occasions when you have to get a fly down, so a selection of lines, from intermediate to fast sink, is important. It's a wise idea, therefore, to look for a reel that offers the possibility of a number of cheap spools. It's important to have gear that's sufficient for the job – you don't want to sell yourself short and find yourself struggling on the sea. When fishing from a boat, especially, depth can be critical, so if you're not contacting bass in one zone, then change lines continually until you find where the fish are swimming and feeding. A lazy angler is rarely a successful one when it comes to saltwater bass fishing.

Choosing the Right Pattern

There are endless fly patterns available today that will land you a sea bass. In essence, bass in the wild are looking to feed on sand eels, elvers, tiny fish – anything that is silvery and ripples sinuously. Translucent silvers and greens are, therefore, always a good starting point. Each area tends to have its own favourites, so it's wise to listen to local advice. However, you can't go far wrong with clousers, deceivers, bait fish and squid patterns. Alternatively, if you think the bass are feeding deep, over rocks, on crabs, why not try a crab pattern on the end. Sea-bass fishing on the fly is still in its early infancy, and it is this pioneering aspect that makes it so attractive to so many anglers.

Some Basic Tips

The warning about sun cream and sun block is even more applicable at sea, where the salt exacerbates the burning process. Polarizing glasses and a peaked cap or a hat

with a brim are important. If the water isn't warm enough to go bare-legged, breathable chest waders are a must if you're shore fishing. So, too, is a line tray: without this, loose line will simply catch in the rip and soon be all over the place. Pay special attention to clothing: a nice day on shore can easily become wet and freezing cold once you're afloat. Don't take chances and make your day a misery. Look after your catch, too. If you're going to take the odd bass to eat (and why not?), gut it and clean it on the beach, on the boat or, at the very least, as soon as you get home. Don't leave this job and jeopardize wasting a fish. The bounty of the sea is increasingly precious to all of us, and a meal of fresh sea bass that you yourself have caught just hours before is a privilege that mustn't be wasted.

Salt and Corrosion

Salt, of course, is a big problem, and the last thing you want is your beloved rods, reels and accessories destroyed by corrosion. It makes absolute sense to buy gear that is anodized and saltwater resistant. Check this out carefully before making a purchase. The

◀ Choosing the fly
Sea bass come in close to the shore to hunt the small fish and crabs that are hiding there. Flies should look, therefore, like small, vulnerable, tasty food items fluttering helplessly in the tide.

second great bit of simple advice is to wash everything thoroughly in cold, clean water after a saltwater outing, and that includes estuary fishing. Note, too, that salt doesn't just work its malevolence on rods and reels, but can also rust hooks, forceps, zips and even the studs and eyes of wading boots.

Your waders are expensive, so look after them. Don't allow them to fester, crumpled in

▼ In the surf
To get the better of sea bass, you have to be in there with them putting the fly where it counts. First-class waterproof clothing, a buoyancy aid, good balance and a bit of nerve are important ingredients.

▲ *Low water clues*

At low tide, get out and look for clues to sea bass location. Rocks, gullies and weed beds are all great starters.

▼ *A hint from the skies*

The sky can give you hints to bass location. If you see gulls swooping down upon small fish on the surface, there's a good chance that there are bass underneath.

a corner. If they remain damp, the salt will work on them and cracks will begin to appear. Rinse them and then hang them upside down to allow air to circulate, and to allow them to dry off naturally and keep their shape.

It's also vital to pay close attention to the state of your line, especially if you've been casting over rocks or abrasive sand. Wipe it down carefully after use to prolong its life.

Finally, even though you've rinsed your rods and reels, it's not a bad idea to dry them down with a soft cloth. Take special care with reel seats, and from time to time use a little light oil on them.

Shore Technique

Shore fishing for bass is probably the easiest and cheapest way to get into this exciting sport. A rod, lines, flies and waders are all you need.

Weather and Tide

The best conditions for fly fishing for bass from the shore are relatively calm ones. You don't want a big wind, as this makes fly fishing physically difficult and, more importantly, it will stir up the sand and make the water cloudy, so calm, clear water is ideal. If you can get out early or stay out late, then you'll probably hit the bass in prime feeding mood.

In many places, bassing off the shore doesn't depend too much on the state of the tide. Even in low water, for example, when fish get caught up estuaries, they will tend to mill around but are still willing to pick up food and take the fly.

Finding Features

Bass love to forage amongst big rocks and, generally, the rougher the ground the better. So look for beaches that are mostly rock and boulder with comparatively little sand or gravel. Fissured rocks, large boulders, crevices, weed and all similar features are really attractive to the bass.

Search for areas that will hold passing food items. Walk the beach at low water, making a note of pools still full of water at the lowest of the tide. Note the position of weed beds and big boulders – these are good places to concentrate on once you start fishing. Also, look out for deep gullies amongst rocks, because bass use these as highways from one feeding area to the next. Don't worry too much about depth - bass will be happy in water anywhere between 1 and 12 feet deep.

Cast and Retrieve

You don't have to strain massively to cast huge distances. Very often you will pick up bass just a few yards out in the surf. It's better to cast short distances and approach gently rather than splash around and scare the fish. You don't really need to work the fly much at all in a strong tide because the sea will do it for you. If, however, there's little flow – say you're up a low water estuary – then it pays to give the fly some good tweaks and keep it on the move, simulating a fleeing fish.

Boat Technique

A lot of fly-caught bass can be taken from the shore, but there's no doubt that a boat gives more options and allows you to cover far more potential bass-holding features.

Locating Bass

The sea is a big place, and finding the bass is the first issue. Just like our black freshwater bass in Spain, you should be looking for features. These can be reefs, wrecks, gullies, drop-offs, weed beds, rocks, submerged islands – anything that harbours the sand eels and small fish that the bass like to feed upon. Also, it goes without saying, look for the gulls. Wherever you see gulls diving, you can be sure that small fish are being pushed to the surface and bass are going to be the most likely culprit, so get yourself there fast.

Inshore Waters

There are two distinct types of sport included under this title. Firstly, let's look at fly fishing for bass in the shallower, calmer estuaries. In the estuary, you will have bright, clear water and frequently a very smooth surface. Most of the fish you are pursuing are school bass in the 1- to 2-pound bracket, and they're often visible. For this sort of work,

▼ *Bass coastline*
You'll find bass wherever there are features, because wherever there are features there is food upon which they thrive. The groynes, sea defences and rocky outcrops harbour endless crabs and tiny fish, while the freshwater stream brings all manner of food items from the village just inland.

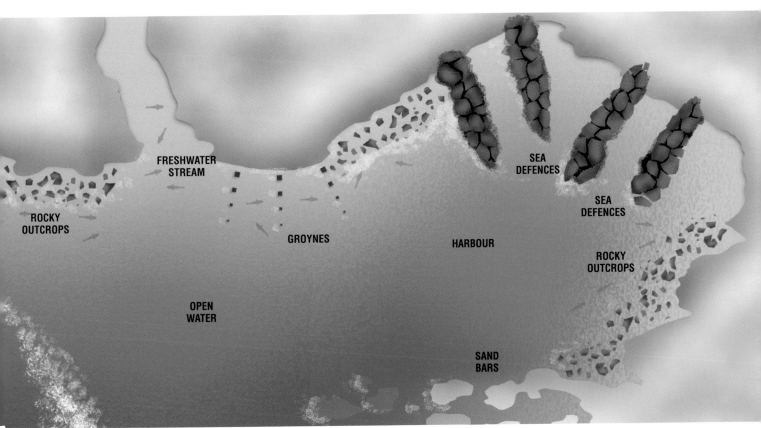

ROCKY OUTCROPS

FRESHWATER STREAM

GROYNES

OPEN WATER

SEA DEFENCES

SEA DEFENCES

HARBOUR

ROCKY OUTCROPS

SAND BARS

▲ ▼ From the shore
When fishing for bass, spinning can be as effective as fly fishing, and you do cover ground a lot faster. Whichever method you use, be mindful of the fish you are taking. Be aware of size limits, and remember that bass take five years to mature, so just occasionally, try to limit yourself to only one for the pot.

you can make do very happily with a 5- or 6-weight, 9-foot rod – the Hardy Angel TE is has won loads of supporters for this kind of task. You're fishing a floating line here and using comparatively small flies – say, tied on an 8 or even a 10. In fact, this is just like still-water fishing for trout and the same gear will suffice. Leaders don't need to be heavier than 8 or 10 pounds, but they should be fluorocarbon. As for flies, the smallest possible clousers are hard to beat.

Open Ocean

Away from the estuary or the shoreline, it's a

completely different ball game. Now, you are fishing over deep water, probably in a swell, possibly catching the wind, and you need to get down deep. You might need 9- or even 10-weight rods and reels. A fast-sink line is probably necessary – a full line probably gets down deeper and more quickly than a shooting head. The tides and the saline content both make it more difficult to sink a fly deep. You are aiming to fish your fly 10 or even 15 feet down, possibly for much bigger fish. A fluorocarbon leader of 10 or 12 pounds is a must. You're probably going to be fishing bigger flies – streamers, for example, on a 2/0 or even a 3/0. Dark olive and white are good colours, and anything made of Arctic fox fur really flows in the water. Look for pearly, translucent patterns as the current vogue for dressing flies in the colours of small pollack.

The Double Haul

If you're serious about taking up one of the most glamorous and quickly developing styles of fly fishing in Europe, then you've really got to set about mastering the double haul technique. A lot of times you'll be on a pitching boat, in screaming winds, casting big, heavy flies long distances, and this is demanding and potentially dangerous work.

Without the ability to double haul, you are both limiting your fishing and potentially endangering yourself.

Working the Fly

Fishing these big flies down deep calls for slightly specialized techniques. You shouldn't always be ripping the fly back to the boat but rather letting it work in the tide. Either cast the fly into the rip or let the current simply pull the line off the reel. Once you think you've achieved the required depth, let the fly rise and fall with the flow of the water. Twitch the fly back, stop. Twitch again. Sometimes give solid pulls of a couple of feet or more and then stop again. In short, you are trying to make the fly dart and flutter like something small and alive.

Don't neglect your poppers, even here on the sea. They can be deadly in shallower, clearer water and at those times when you can actually see the bass hammering into prey on the surface. It's often a good idea to fish your popper on a dropper with a streamer underneath it. Bass frequently chase the popper only to turn away at the very last moment. That's when they will often pick up on the streamer or clouser, even one that's just working enticingly in the current. Again, for excitement, you just can't beat the dramatic, visual take.

The Right Boat

The perfect boat for sea bass fishing probably hasn't been built yet, but there are still several things to consider when choosing your boat. It needs to be stable, because a lot of the time you'll be standing up, casting in the swell. You need the side of the boat to reach well up to your thighs. A rail at shin level is neither safe nor comfortable, and you'll find yourself knocking into it a lot of the time.

Decks shouldn't be too smooth, and if they have a slightly adhesive surface, so much the better. Equally, think carefully about your footwear and look for the sole that gives the best grip. You should be looking for a deck that is as open-plan as possible, without cabins or aerials or anything to hamper the flow of line. In fact, a line tray is a good idea in itself.

A boat with a shallow draught is also preferable, because many times you'll be hunting bass close-in along the estuaries where there is only a foot or two of water. Of course, think safety and seaworthiness - reliable engines, lifejackets, up-to-the-minute weather forecasts… take absolutely no risks.

▼ *The right fly*
Howard and Juan discuss the right fly for a Spanish sea bass. Notice the use of breathable waders and wading jackets – staying dry all day long will considerably enhance your fishing experience.

▲ ▼ *Lugworms*

Lugs like this are one of the favourite baits for most sea fish species around Europe. Digging them at low tide, however, can be back-breaking work.

Sea Fishing in Action

Any good sea angler who takes his sport seriously will want to dig his own bait. However, it's a job that demands experience, technique and physical resilience. I should know. For a year after college, I dug worms for a living. That was 30 years ago, but my hands still bear some of the scars inflicted and the small of my back has never been quite the same.

Earning Every Penny

A typical day would see me and my fellow bait diggers meet up three or four hours before the winter dawn broke. We would then walk over the marsh head and out across the mud, sometimes for three or four miles, to arrive at the worm beds just as light was breaking. We'd then have to find our patch, drain it and dig methodically and quickly, an eye always on the tides and for any sign of creeping mist. We'd dig for three or four hours, until we'd found between a 1,000 and 1,500 worms, and then we'd head back for home.

The walk back was always the hardest, thanks to an overwhelming tiredness and the sheer weight of the worms in the bucket swinging against the shoulder blades. At some point in the early afternoon, once the worms has been counted, washed and packed, I'd start thinking about… yes, doing a bit of fishing before supper and going off early to bed.

Understanding the Feeding Fish

Bait fishermen will know all about rag worm, lugworm, prawn, soft crab and bait fish of endless varieties, and which fish are feeding on what at any particular time, but the fly fisherman must also know what his fish are up to and what his flies are meant to imitate. Out in the Bahamas, our guide, Magnus, would get up well before the rest of the group each and every morning, just as the sun was beginning to rise. We'd wake up to find him invariably at his vice, tying flies for the coming day. The previous day, he'd have been seen peering into pools, looking through weed, lifting stones and rocks, searching for any clues, any pointers as to what the bonefish were eating. His flies were mini masterpieces, imitating crabs or shrimps with breathtaking accuracy. To have complete and utter confidence in whatever you are offering the fish – be it a couple of prime, succulent worms on a hook or a fly tied to perfection - is a bonus beyond words.

The World of the Sea Trout

It's that piece of the world between the land and the open sea that fascinates me most of all. Here, the tide ebbs and flows, sometimes there's water, at other times exposed mud and sand. This is a marvellously exciting, shifting world. You'll find seals, sea otters and more species of birds than you can begin to count. The weather is also massively unpredictable: sometimes you think the mist will never break, then there are fissures of blue above and within minutes the sun is beating down and you need to remove your jacket.

There are several species of fish to target in this world of constant change, but one of the best is surely the sea trout. Sea trout, we know, are browns that have decided in their own swashbuckling way to go to sea and will only really return to freshwater in order to

spawn. However, many sea trout won't go that far from their native river, and they love the estuaries, creeks and inshore gullies and sandbanks.

There have been times in my life when I have been obsessed with these fish in these places. As a kid, I used to bait or lure fish, but over the last 10 years, it has been fly only which, in truth, hasn't changed the rate of my success. What's important is knowledge of the environment and the habits of the fish.

In some places, your best chance lies with the flood tide, in others with the ebb. Sometimes, it's the sea pools at the lowest water that you need to target. You may need to tramp miles and follow runnels of water through an endless wasteland of mud until you reach the long, still, mysterious pool that is your goal. If you're lucky, the sea trout

▲ *A yard of silver*
Sea trout come into rivers to feed and especially to breed. They tend to lie doggo during the day but as the sun sinks and the night sets in, they move upriver, often foraging as they go.

▼ *Hebridean scene*
Sea fishing in the northern hemisphere often gets better, the more remote you become. Certainly, the north of Scotland can provide tremendous sport around islands and rocky outcrops.

▲ *Fun in the estuaries*
John Wolstenholme holds a
stunning sea trout taken
from a southern hemisphere
estuary. Richard is playing a
decent flat fish that snapped
at a shrimp fly retrieved in
low water (right).

▼ *The grey ghosts*
Mullet are found almost
worldwide and are fascinat-
ing to catch. Generally,
you've got to pursue them
with the tiniest baits to
replicate what they feed
on in nature.

sometimes give themselves away by chasing prey or splashing after an off-course terrestrial cranefly. On other occasions, there will be no visual action whatsoever, and you will retrieve your fly in hope rather than expectation. However, that won't stop you retrieving your fly with all the skill you can muster. You know how a crab works as it scuttles from stone to stone, and that's how you want to make your fly behave. Your eye is constantly on the water, looking for signs of movement. It's also on your watch face, because you know you don't dare play games with the incoming tide.

Sea Trout in the Arctic

The toughest sea fisherman I ever encountered was a man called Geiri who took us to the north coast of Iceland for sea trout. When we failed to catch one in the rivers, he told us he'd walk us out to sea – and he did. As the tide ebbed, we waded the estuary in water nearly up to our armpits. We then walked the north shore of the creek for an hour whilst the sun went down and the stars came out. The night, he told us, was the best time. We stopped when we came to a point where a big, deep, fast channel swirled close-in to the shoreline. We waded 20 yards out so we could fish the channel effectively and there began to cast.

The wind was biting. The stars glittered. Although it was after midnight, there was still enough light above the Arctic Circle to see big, big sea trout occasionally thrash themselves out of the water 50 or 100 yards away from us. Just once I had a heavy, electrifying tug, and Geiri got into a fish that ran out virtually all his backing before throwing the fly. Eleven pounds he said, and then cursed. Then, before the tide flowed again, we walked fishless all those miles back home.

The Tricky Mullet

Perhaps the most difficult fish to catch anywhere in the sea is the mullet. Sometimes, it's true, harbour mullet can be easy when they are weaned onto a diet of bread, chips or whatever the public throw at them. The mullet of the open creeks and freshets, however, are a different matter. Like the sea trout, they come and go with the tides and the

seasons but, unlike the sea trout, they are notoriously picky when it comes to food items. Often, they will simply scrape the algae from the surface of the muds and refuse anything offered bigger than a pin-head. What makes it more difficult still, is that they are hugely spooky. With those big eyes of theirs, it seems they can see you coming 100 yards away in clear water. Murky water doesn't fare much better, as they can feel your boots on the soft mud or crunching over stones and shells. You can't even net them – believe me, I've tried. They'll hit the net, retreat, and then come again and clear it like an Olympic high jumper! If you're lucky enough to hook a mullet – they will occasionally sip in a tiny goldhead fly twitched agonizingly close to their snout – you're into a fish as fast as a bonefish, but with considerably more resilience.

Boat-fishing for Sailfish

Then there is boat fishing, perhaps with fly gear, for sailfish. I once went out of Oban, on the west coast of Scotland, and though I had

two bites, I missed them both. You'd think with fish this size they'd be easy to hit, but they're not. A guy with me had just one bite, which he hit, and that was skill indeed, but I'm not sure about the rest. It was all heave-ho for the next hour until the fish loomed from the dark water. The guy's pumping technique was tight and disciplined, and he'd made sure that his gear was sound, so the least we have to grant him is extreme competence.

▲ On the rocks
Some sea fishermen love the rocks, and are quite willing to scale dizzying cliffs to get there. Other fishermen know the surf beaches intimately and they'll lure, bait or fly fish there knowing exactly when and where to find the fish. These are skills that come from considerable experience and lessons handed down by fellow anglers.

◀ Happy days
Our angler is justifiably delighted with this fabulous capture from the Caribbean. The fact that it was fly-caught only increases his pleasure.

Index

Page numbers in *italic* refer to illustrations.

CONVERSION GUIDE

To Convert	Multiply by
Inches to Centimetres	2.540
Feet to Metres	0.3048
Yards to Metres	0.9144
Miles to Kilometres	1.60934
Ounces to Grams	28.3495
Pounds to Grams	453.592
Celsius to Farenheit	1.8 and add 32